# THE SONGS OF THE MOTHERS

# THE

# *S*ONGS

## OF THE

# *M*OTHERS

## MESSAGES OF PROMISE
## FOR THE FUTURE CHURCH

JOE MORRIS DOSS

 CHURCH

Church Publishing Incorporated, New York

Library of Congress Cataloging-in-Publication Data

Doss, Joe Morris.
    The songs of the mothers : messages of promise for the future church / Joe Morris Doss.
       p. cm.
    Includes bibliographical references.
    ISBN 0898693802 (pbk.)
1. Church renewal. 2. Ecumenical movement. 3. Christianity and culture. 4. Bible.
O.T. Samuel, 1st, II, 1-10—Criticism, interpretation, etc. 5. Magnificat. I. Title.

    BV600.3 .D67 2002
    262'.001'7—dc21

                                  200207407

Church Publishing Incorporated
445 Fifth Avenue
New York NY 10016

www.churchpublishing.org

5 4 3 2 1

# To My Chaplains

Urban Tigner (Terry) Holmes
Robert Marsh Cooper
William Stuart Pregnall
Roland Cox

# A Note on the Dedication

Few could hope for the caliber of the mentors I enjoyed as a young man. The list of those at whose feet I was fortunate enough to sit reads like a "Who's Who" list of that generation. There is Steve Bayne, who was not only my teacher in ascetical theology and canon law, but with whom I worked for two years as the consultant during the inception and initial efforts of the Board of Examining Chaplains. Boone Porter not only taught me liturgical theology, he also became one of my most valued friends and colleagues, especially on the Council of Associated Parishes for Liturgy and Mission. A youthful Bob Wright and I bonded during our first year in seminary together—him as a teacher and me as a student. And my gratitude for all he has continued to offer me is great. Sam Wylie was so much more than merely my seminary dean: whether it was in Europe, a café in New York, or the parish in New Orleans, Sam was teaching and guiding me as a protégé. Almus Thorpe and Dick Rising were the staff and I was the consultant for the creation and early formulations of the Board of Theological Education. Dick Norris and Jim Carpenter were especially important to me as professors of theology and Dick was my thesis professor. David Richards has been pastor to me and my family members during great moments of need throughout my priesthood and episcopacy and we all love him.

Thank you, friends.

# CONTENTS

# A NOTE OF GRATITUDE

May I offer my sincere thanks to all of those who contributed so much to this work. Katherine Zervigon read as I wrote page by page and gave me such helpful advice that her name could well be placed on the cover. Clay Morris read the initial manuscript and offered advice I was happy to accept. Jonathan Williams, almost immediately after graduation from Sewanee with all available honors the English Department offered, edited the work before I submitted it to the publisher. Joan Castagnone of Church Publishing was delightful to work with and enormously helpful as the editor. The support of my wife and two children, together with their critique and advice, is deeply appreciated.

# FOREWORD

## A NOTE ON THE TITLE

The heartbeat of this work lies in the comparison of the songs of Hannah and Mary. I have long wondered why I have never seen a comparative study of these two expressions of the early Yahwistic ideals that ultimately became the Christian gospel. The importance of each stands alone as a statement, beautiful and fundamental, of the faith. Together they offer a key for insight into the connection between the Jewish and Christian faiths, and they sharply lay out the way the early church understood the person and the mission of Jesus. Taken together the church is granted a poetic window into the way Jesus must have developed his personal vision for his mission and for the mission of the church. Sunday after Sunday, indeed day after day, Mary's Song is recited in churches and homes all over the world and throughout the ages, yet the words seem too easily accepted for the sake of piety and love of Our Lady without taking seriously enough their challenge for Christian mission and without appreciation for what they tell us about Jesus. Most Christians would not recognize Hannah's Song, so little is attention paid to it.

In this work the comparison of the songs is found in the context of the discussion of justice. However, their themes and their attitudes run through the discussion of all of the issues touched on here. The vision of community should be seen implicitly throughout the songs; the grasp of authority for what we have come to term mission and ministry should be recognized in them. The section on the early church's theology of baptism, the radical nature of mission, and the doctrine of God, and in particular God's suffering of the process of creation, could have been drawn out of them. However, it is my hope that the reference to the two songs in the title and the comparison of them in the section on justice will set the table so that the wonder of the songs will be evoked throughout the book.

The primary way in which the title applies throughout the work is seen in the purposes for which it is offered. *The Songs of the Mothers* seeks to place the church today in the context of the sweep of the whole story of the Judeo-Christian experience. One might say that the question is being asked about how the church of the future will look back and view our moment in history? The thesis offered here is that we are engaged in one of history's watershed reformations, and that we have been since the critical study of Scripture took hold and began to make its impact toward the turn of the twentieth century. The question then becomes one of discerning what we are to do in our own time within this great movement, how we are to take charge and shape the reformation to come inasmuch as we are capable, given both the new opportunities and the limitations of a long and complex process. The agenda for this generation is defined in terms of certain issues that have to be faced in order to move forward into the church of the future. The bulk of this work is an examination of those issues.

May the reader be warned that the words used to describe each of the issues identified will be rather extensively redefined and will hardly be grasped by reference to the ordinary usage today. For example, justice as used herein is not simply a matter of a legal system or of the normal understanding of social justice, but a complex question regarding the way the church is to form the link between the kingdom and the world in concrete terms, the question of embracing the way things are with gratitude as a gift of God and the question of changing them according to the vision of God's kingdom.

The reform in which we find ourselves calls us to go back to our beginnings, both the Jewish beginnings in the first covenant and the Christian beginnings in the early church. Given the aims of this work, the two songs of the mothers, Hannah and Mary, open our hearts and our minds to the way forward into the future church by singing the fundamental messages of promise that nourished the children of God from inception.

# I.
# A CALL TO
# REFORMATION

The Christian church is in a period of major reform. Our reform is comparable in scale and importance to no less than the Protestant Reformations of the sixteenth century. This reform will not be complete until the church is genuinely ecumenical, and the church will not become genuinely ecumenical until it is genuinely reformed.

Like all major reformations, ours is driven by two inexorable and simultaneous forces, external and internal. The external pressure comes from a radically changing world, the transitional movement from one cultural era to the next. As the body of Christ the church must always humble itself to enter incarnationally into the existing human situation. The internal pressure for reform comes from the rediscovery of our origins. Biblical scholarship has given us a fresh picture of the early Christian community that composed the Scriptures of the New Covenant. When any institution becomes newly aware of its origins it will find itself questioning its present life and practices in light of those origins. Today, the church finds itself questioning everything all over again. It is necessary to refer to the early church of our origins for our model rather than the reformations that followed.

Our first task is to discern our role in this reformation in order to carry it out. The purpose of this book is to identify the primary issues of the reformation, at least for the work of this generation, and address them. Positively stated, our agenda can be identified in terms of (1) Justice, (2) Ministry, and (3) Community.

# REFORMATION

The tidal wave gathers slowly and imperceptibly far out at sea, the result of unsuspected forces. The time comes when the watchful may make it out. Then it becomes inexorable, the wave growing relentlessly into a wall on the move, taking all at sea with it, and rushing to smash the settled and secured. Rivers will run backward, and some will change their courses forever. Valleys will be filled and hills will be laid low. Flames will beacon solitary in the middle of an unending lake. The Christian church is unable to turn and flee the great wave of reform that is striking home. The institutions and workings of an age are about to be overrun by forces so powerful that the familiar landscape will no longer be discernible.

The church is always reforming itself. However, there seem to come certain moments in the life of the church when the pressures for reform become so pervasive, massive, and radical that the changes they bring about are defining, as though the church is beginning again. The Christian church is facing a period of just such sweeping reform. In fact, we were engaged in this reformation throughout the twentieth century, but it is only now that we sense how we are being overtaken, how the forces of reform that have been building internally and externally cannot be denied. Our reform is comparable in scale and importance to any that have gone before. This is perhaps the Ecumenical Reformation, a significant and necessary step toward the drive to unity for which our Lord prayed. Not once but four times—that his followers "may be one" as he and the one to whom he prayed are one, "completely one" (Jn 17:11,21,22,23).

The church certainly will never be satisfied until it is united. However, the church will not become ecumenically united until it is genuinely reformed and ready to assume its role in a new era of human history.

No nook or cranny of the church is being left unevaluated and unaffected. In the lifetime of today's leadership, the church has been dominated by a continual focus on issues of change. The plethora of movements, the questioning, and the areas in which vastly important changes have been called for is overwhelming: ecumenism, liturgy, authority, sexuality, biblical criticism…the list goes on and on. One is challenged to think of any area of the church's life where the reform is not reaching, questioning, demanding. Try to think of a single controversial and divisive issue that the church has managed to sidestep. Consider what the generation of the last half of the twentieth century faced and consider what is now on the agenda. There are those who have considered the list of issues that have arisen, one after another in what sometimes seems to be an unending sequence, as some sort of a liberal agenda, as "changes" to reject or to endure. But it is not just about changes; it is about reform. Many consider this focus on issues of change a distraction from the main business of the church, but this is not going to go away. Reformation is at the heart of God's will for the church at this time.

In most important respects, the Christian church will always be the same fundamental institution with the same general call to mission. In this day, as in each era, our primary effort as a Christian community will be to build strong congregations in which the reign of God can be truly experienced and where people are offered the good news. Parishes are called to heal, to bless, to reconcile, and to praise God in thanksgiving. All congregations, in all ages, have in common the steady life of converting, confessing, worshiping, serving, and transforming. Clergy are called at all times to the essential jobs of leadership and caring that have been performed by their predecessors through the centuries. However, we are gradually beginning to recognize that we will not be able to rely on the given nature of institutions, structures, and systems so many previous generations have assumed would be adequate. Nor will we be able to look to many tested and proven models as we seek new institutions and structures. The church faces such an array of new issues and challenges that the shifts and adaptations it must make go beyond the matter of mere change. People are gradually beginning to recognize the massive nature of the undertaking and to understand that it is about universal reformation. Increasingly, people on opposite sides of the issues that divide us, and up and down the spectrum that measures the range between liberal and conservative, are couching their positions in the context of the need for church reform.

Those of us debating these issues have gone beyond thinking that we could make some difficult adjustments, overcome a few outdated ways of governance, incorporate scientific and psychological insights, update opportunities in technology and communication, and fundamentally carry on as before on our way to converting the world. As exciting and widely appreciated as it was, Vatican II has come to feel like a halting first step, which had come grinding to full stop—the extent of Roman Catholic effort at reform for years to come. Meanwhile the Roman Catholic Church seems determined to hang on to the model developed by the Gregorian Reformation, the medieval church, rather than the early church. The issues of the Protestant Reformation have played themselves out, but instead of marking new paths and finding joy in the diversity of traditions that have developed and should prove lasting, the mainline denominations seem unable to adapt to the new discoveries about the life of the early church, hanging on instead to the models founded in the Protestant Reformation. The mainline American denominations find their energy sapped by right-wing fundamentalist sects that are taking the Protestant center stage. Mainline Protestants must take the right-wing fundamentalists seriously because the media and politicians do and because of their relatively significant numbers in some sections of the United States, but the church itself will receive little contribution from those who isolate themselves from its broader life and history. The church, ecumenical and denominational, has gradually come to recognize the fact that we are in the middle of a major and long-range reform.

## CHANGE AND HOPE

The call to reformation cannot be music to every ear. Change is difficult for anyone at any time, and under any circumstances. Nevertheless, the necessity of facing into our reformation is simply a matter of facing reality. Reality is our friend—always to be embraced rather than resented and resisted. I cannot help but think of one of the first writers whose work signaled the need for the coming reform, Gregory of Tours. His most famous work, *History of the Franks*, was composed in the sixth century, toward the end of the first hundred years of Frankish rule in Gaul. Even though he was the scion of a wealthy family, an outstanding bishop of the church, and educated as well as his society could allow, Gregory was unable to write in the classical Latin style. Yet in using the bastardized Latin he had available, he was able to draw on the vernacular of the people and to portray life in the sixth century, as raw and brutal as it was, with a vividness and immediacy that scholars like Erich Auerbach doubt would have been available any other way.[1] In one passage, Gregory has his mother appear to him in a dream, asking him to write. When he complains about his frustration in being unable to write in the classical style, he receives the answer: *Et nescis, quia nobiscum propter intelligentiam populorum magis, sicut tu loqui potens es, habetur praeclarum?* "Do you not know that we hold the way you are able to write in higher esteem, because the people can understand it?"[2] Gregory explained that as a bishop of the church that proclaims the incarnational faith, he felt compelled to tell the people's story in their own daily language. His analogy was apt; he claimed to write in the tradition of the disciples, who had deliberately chosen to proclaim the gospel in the Bible by using the *koine*, or market Greek of the common people, rather than the classical form used only by the well educated. Most scholars agree that Gregory's writings made a definitive contribution to the gradual development of the language we enjoy today as French. Indeed, it is not clear that we would have the same modern language without his work.

Like Gregory, we must recognize that when we lose something we hold precious due to cultural change, something of great value might develop out of our loss. To remember such lessons in the history of our faith enables us to face our own challenge with trust. The proper Christian attitude toward the future is hope, and for the Christian this leads to profound confidence in the face of any realities—from lions in the Roman arena to the need for reform at the turn of the millennium.

If we are being called to a special vocation of reform, our task is not ultimately to solve problems we wish would go away. Rather, God is calling us forward. There will be times indeed when we will look at the situation and feel that we are being compelled to adapt, not because we want to or because of some grand strategy, but because we have to cope with concrete problems such as economics. The problems are all too visible and pressing for any involved Christian to miss. The statistics of the church's decline cannot be ignored. The extent and depth of the controversies raging within the church cannot be discounted. Everyone must share the anguish of those who sincerely believe that the many and far-reaching changes taking place within the church threaten, and perhaps betray, fundamental tenets of its faith. Whole classes, sexes, and races of faithful Christians continue to experience oppression and exclusion. The church's theology is misunderstood, ignored, and misused. The church's life is trivialized. No one is happy or satisfied with the present state of affairs. Life grows steadily more complex and more difficult at every level of church life and for practically every institution within it—whether it be a congregation, a seminary, a publisher, a monastic community, an institute, or a grand cathedral. The future is uncertain in every regard. The root problem goes to the very core of the church's identity and purpose.

However, this particular crisis or, more appropriately, this call for a reformation is not to been viewed negatively by the church. At the foundation, it is God calling us into a new day, shaping and forming us for a new era.

The forces causing the great reformations are always twofold and simultaneous: (1) the pressures caused by changes so vast in the world that they spawn what we think of as "a new age" in history and (2) the desire of significant portions of the church for reform reflective of theological insights that are increasingly widely held. These forces can be called respectively the external and the internal forces for reform.

# THE EXTERNAL FORCES FOR REFORM

> At the present time the church is like a ship exposed to every wind and battling through a sort of Bay of Biscay. One reason for this situation has nothing to do with the ship—it is caused by the condition of the sea. The church exists in and for the world and as such lies open to the influence of the unprecedented changes which the world is experiencing.
> —Leo Joseph Cardinal Suenens (1904–1996), one of the great contributors to Vatican II

There have been three watershed reformations in the two millennia of church history: the Constantinian the Gregorian Reformation, and the Protestant Reformation. Like the earlier great reforms in history, reform in our time is driven from the outside by forces of radical cultural upheaval. The Constantinian Reformation is more often referred to as a "settlement," yet it certainly was a tremendous re-forming of the entire life of the church. It helped shape a church that was no longer a persecuted and marginalized minority, but that had become an established religion—playing a powerful role in the culture of the Roman Empire and exercising enormous influence on the development of civilization through the centuries. It responded to, and helped shape, a world taking leave of classical antiquity, and which finally survived the collapse of the Roman Empire. The Gregorian Reformation responded to, and helped shape, the new feudalistic culture of the West. The Protestant

Reformation and the Roman Catholic Counter-Reformation responded to, and helped shape, the Renaissance. The present Ecumenical Reformation seeks to be responsive to a new era in history that is now evolving. The church will respond to it and help shape it.

The church finds itself caught up in one of those rare transforming periods when the page of history is being turned: the Hellenic world of the Roman Empire gave way to medieval feudalism and then medieval feudalism to the Renaissance. The world is changing definitively, however incomprehensibly. The page is turning. We do not yet know what the next page will present, but we know that it will offer a very different sight.

Some Christian observers look into this unknown future and offer highly positive predictions. Other prophetic voices echo Cassandra. While one does not have to strain to hear either the positive or the negative sides, the fact that we are in the midst of a picture-changing cultural transformation seems to be a reality accepted by all points of view.

## CASSANDRA

At a diocesan conference in 1992, Alan Jones, dean of Grace Cathedral in San Francisco, spoke of entering once again into dark ages, "a roller coaster of change and upheaval on which we are lost." He was quite articulate in describing an era in which transcendent values and much of our academic and cultural heritage would be practically lost to us, an age in which technological and economic benefits would overwhelm and swallow the human quest for truth, beauty, and the good. He predicted increased tribalism and isolation. "Talk of what good may come of all this leaves me slightly depressed, feeling guilty about what won't happen and puzzled about what goes wrong." Even so, he foresaw some merit in this future. We would let go of what we had been falsely proud of and we would be forced to realize our total dependence on God. He expressed confidence that the future will be God's, though it will be a tough one for us.

The dean may have taken as an example the effects of what is often termed "globalization." Many are predicting that globalization will become the *zeitgeist* for the epoch following the Cold War. Thomas Friedman wrote *The Lexus and the Olive Tree* to explain globalization. He suggests that the defining economists of the Cold War system were Karl Marx and John Maynard Keynes. In comparison, he considers

Joseph Schumpeter, a former Austrian Minister of Finance and Harvard Business School professor, and Andy Grove, a former Intel CEO, to be the defining economists of these early years of globalization. Marx and Keynes each wanted to temper and manage capitalism. Schumpeter and Grove prefer to unleash all of its forces. Rampant free market capitalism is identified as the essence of globalization.[3] In *Capitalism, Socialism, and Democracy*,[4] Schumpeter defines capitalism as a process of "creative destruction": the constant destruction of what is, in order to create and make room for what will become new and more efficient products and services. Grove agrees, taking one of Schumpeter's key phrases as the title for his book, *Only the Paranoid Survive*.[5] It describes his view of the present state of work in Silicon Valley, California. According to each of these current observers, paranoia is the business model for globalized capitalism. Only those who are constantly looking over their shoulder to spot who is out to get them by creating a better and more efficient new product, only those who can stay one step ahead of the competition out to destroy them by taking their place, only those who can use technological breakthroughs to destroy their own products and services with better industry-transforming innovations of their own making, "only the paranoid" can survive. Governments and unions and any other agencies that try to protect that which is, or to set any priority other than creative destruction, get in the way. Workers, as well as industries, as well as national economies, are expendable.

James Surowiecki, the business columnist for *Slate* magazine, reviewed these books and concluded:

> Innovation replaces tradition. The present—or perhaps the future—replaces the past. Nothing matters so much as what will come next, and what will come next can only arrive if what is here now gets overturned. While this makes the system a terrific place for innovation, it makes it a difficult place to live, since most people prefer some measure of security about the future to a life lived in almost constant uncertainty....We are not forced to re-create our relationships with those closest to us on a regular basis. And yet that's precisely what Schumpeter and Grove after him, suggest is necessary to prosper [today].[6]

While Friedman and entrepreneurs wax enthusiastic about the radically new future of globalization, many others view their predictions with fear and anxiety. If the operative slogans for the coming age are "creative destruction" and "only the paranoid can survive," the future we face sounds quite dark indeed.

One of my favorite images for how badly things might turn out on a new page of history comes from Henry Bruel, one of the formidable American preachers of the post-World War II era. During a talk at a 1987 Associated Parishes Council meeting, he imagined the experience of the nineteenth-century trek across the vast plains and mountains of the American West. Decisions had to be made about what possessions would be left behind. People would realize how certain things left behind were not just useful objects, but that they represented something concrete and meaningful about one's life, perhaps the life of a family, perhaps even generations of a family. Gifts and legacies would have been especially meaningful, perhaps passed down by loved ones and standing as a sign of the family beliefs, values, and traditions. Families had to leave so much behind. Then, even after the chosen valuables were packed and the journey begun, there would invariably come the moment when some of the precious goods had to be abandoned. We know many of these valuables had to be dumped out of the back of covered wagons headed down a westward trail. There lay grandmother's armoire, the bridal chest, the ancient china tea set, the portrait, the hand-carved tools, the musical instrument. Along would come the next group of travelers, riding past the strewn evidence of the heritage of the people who preceded them. They, in their turn, would find themselves tearfully tossing aside the excess baggage of their cultural and spiritual heritage in order to survive and travel on. This, said the preacher, is what we are presently doing in order to move on and survive on the next page in the book of history.

## PROGRESS

The dangers and evils of globalization have been well documented. But there are some observers who see a positive side of globalization and welcome change. Some Anglicans believe their communion may represent the ecumenical church to come. The decision of the Evangelical Lutheran Church in America (ELCA) and the Episcopal Church to enter into intercommunion with one another, with the intention of gradually uniting, is widely viewed with enthusiasm. In fact, it may have a healthy reforming influence on the two denominations, particularly as churches that maintain a hierarchical tradition and yet rely on democratic modes of governance. An optimist may go so far as to predict that the influence of intercommunions on the ecumenical church may eventually exert a major and felicitous influence on worldwide secular events.

There are those predicting that we are only now entering into the American age. Perhaps the predominance enjoyed by North America in the latter half of the twentieth century was only the preparatory phase. Certainly now that the Berlin Wall and all it symbolized have been torn down, America finds itself having to accept the responsibilities as well as the privileges that have belonged to different nations and empires during defined spans of history when they were looked to as leaders among nations. The ascendancy of the United States is unique in that it has no equal or seriously challenging rival, while simultaneously there remains a strong coalition of supporting allies that coalesced during the grand crises of World War II and the Cold War. There is neither need of nor hope for a "balance of power" policy. The United States, fortified with its alliances, is the sole prevalent superpower. Though the current complexities of international politics restrains even a sole superpower from acting at whim, the rest of the world is subordinate.

The cultural preeminence of the United States may exert a cultural influence that the ecumenical church will not be able to resist. Friedman suggests one positive aspect of globalization may be that American values, principles, and ideas of governance we have come to cherish most will be accepted gradually by others, even peoples and institutions that have rejected or ignored them in the past. This would be especially good news for the prospects of new democratic governments and increased respect for human rights.

For example, the fundamental premise for modern governments, the sovereignty of the nation-state, is already being challenged by regard for such basic human rights as articulated in the American Declaration of Independence. Since the rise of the international community of nation-states it has been accepted that no nation or group of nations should interfere in the internal affairs of a sovereign and recognized member. It has been assumed that the stability and security of the world depended on this principle. A nation or members of the international community could enter into the internal affairs of a sister nation-state only if certain well-defined criteria of self-interest were met, involving such matters as threats to its own security and sovereignty. At present it seems that this universally accepted principle of international law is being reassessed. Perhaps as much as one-half of the world seems to have moved its thinking to a point at which the internal violation of fundamental human rights is viewed as sufficient grounds for international interference and policing. The Pinnochet case and others that quickly followed it signaled a clarion summons to international law. One may predict that the protection of human rights will eventually be accepted as a principle that is granted priority over national sovereignty.

In such a world, the ecumenical church will no longer be able to resist the movement toward the Anglo-American values regarding democratic procedures and processes. The influence will be so pervasive that churches, from the Vatican to sectarian congregations, will have to find models for how to live with democratic modes of governance. No doubt there will continue to be a healthy tension between democratic procedures and the traditional authority of magisterium within churches. Nevertheless it will be necessary for the church to adapt to democratic principles of openness, accountability, and respect for individual rights.

We may anticipate casting aside the precious baggage of our heritage and entering into dark ages. Or we may look forward to a more refreshing and enlightened time. Or we may assume the future will hold about the same balance of improvements and new problems as most new periods in human history. The point is that most of us sense that the page of history is turning. We are beginning to accept this as commonplace knowledge. What future generations will view on that page is not what we are given to look upon. The force of a changing culture places enormous external pressure upon the church to change as well.

## THE VOCATION OF REFORM

Whenever the page of history turns, the church must acculturate, for ours is an incarnational faith. The church is driven to reform by external forces because it is finding, once again, that it must be capable of pervasive and fundamental adaptation if it is to offer its uniquely incarnational faith in the next phase of human history. We can no more ignore this call than the church could have ignored the developments of feudalism and the Renaissance. Just so, the church today is finding that it cannot hide from the issues of cultural transformation, a transformation which already seems to be getting away from the church, a culture which seems all too ready to ignore any transcending word. Our prayer should be for God to guide us to influence the change so that the world will be, in Richard Niebuhr's great phrase, more "transparent to the Kingdom."

Perhaps the idea of such a reformation seems only to confuse things further at a time when the church's membership is already off-balance, fretting about the future and concerned whether the church as it is known will survive. Lord Macaulay's famous words come to mind: "Reform, reform, don't talk to me of reform. We have enough problems already." It is certainly true that change causes conflict and conflict, never wanted, is even less welcome during a time of uncertainty. In a congregation for which survival seems to be the first and driving issue, as it is in so many, there will be the strongest of motivations to avoid conflict. Therefore it can hardly be supposed that change, much less a change as radical as a reformation, will be easily embraced.

Perhaps it will be suspected that this is all exaggeration and that full reformation is unnecessary. There are those who believe that today's call is only to "renewal" and to a more serious personal faith by individuals. There are those who are ready to depend on a "revival," that is, on a return to certain values held more precious by previous generations and thus to a revitalization of the church which had seemed wed to them.

We would do well to consider how Christians have felt at similar times in history. Picture living somewhere along the Mediterranean Sea when Rome and the civilized world as they knew it was being over-run by ruthless Germanic tribes. We would not have enjoyed the benefits of historical knowledge with its lessons of survival, since there was so little written history prior to the Greek and Roman civilizations. Of course, we would not have learned the lessons of the last two thousand years of history in which Christianity has been able to adapt to the rise and fall of so many kingdoms, governments, cultures, and ways of life. The only civilization about which we could have known anything significant, the culture that had dominated the period of written history, the only civilized world we could possibly conjure up in our imaginations, and certainly the only one we could imagine supporting Christianity, was the Hellenistic Roman culture. If someone had asked us to picture the medieval feudalism that would develop through that long period subsequently called the Dark Ages we would have found the suggestion incomprehensible. The very threat of such "dark ages," dangerous, isolating, and in every way difficult, would have caused us to grow faint-hearted indeed. Little would we have been aware that we were on the cusp of a reformation in which the church would grow, absorb the "barbarian tribes," and emerge in a new civilization that would be known as Christendom, enjoying what would be remembered as "the age of faith." Certainly, the generations of Christians who lived through the process of these developments could not have understood their role in this larger historical movement, and, certainly, they would have longed for "the way things were."

We may draw the same sort of picture for Christians who lived through the turmoil of new possibilities and demands that led to the Renaissance. It took centuries for the Protestant Reformation to surface as a recognizable and defining movement. Many people seem to forget the scores of events and important precursors preparing the way for Luther to nail his famous theses to the door of the medieval church. That door was already opening. Anglicans know how well prepared the church in England was for its sixteenth-century break from Rome, beginning at least by the fourteenth century with reformers like Wycliffe. If the church has been engaged in a reform now for over a hundred years, history teaches us not to marvel over the fact that we are just now beginning to realize it.

# THE INTERNAL FORCES
# FOR REFORM

The reform is the church's own choice and doing. It is driven internally by forces just as demanding as those imposed externally by cultural change. It comes primarily from new information and understandings about our origins. Out of the church's birth experience come our most important and essential lessons. When we rediscover these lessons we must reform ourselves. It is to the early church that we are turning. We can identify three things that we are in the process of recovering from the early foundations of the church about its self-understanding:

- the mission of the church as God's grand causes of creation and kingdom;
- the identity and purpose of the church as initially grasped in baptismal theology;

- the understanding of the Divine Trinity revealed in the incarnation as going out to and being moved by the human community, God who suffers creation and kingdom.

These three theological understandings compel us to reform the day-to-day life of the church from top to bottom. Perhaps the recovery of these three insights will form the basis for a new and broadly accepted theology of the church.

The engine driving the internal forces for reform has been biblical scholarship. Biblical scholarship has compelled us to look beyond the particular traditions that distinguish us from one another, all the way back to the early church where we rediscover our genuine and shared origins. I think of the courage and faithfulness of those nineteenth-century biblical scholars who decided to study Scripture with the same critical eye they used on any other document, and I find I am deeply moved. These people had confidence that the task they accepted would ultimately pay off as the Bible was experienced as more authoritative and more effective. They knew that criticism of their work would be dire indeed, that they would be attacked personally and accused of faithlessness. They realized also that their confidence in Scripture could not be verified in their lifetime. It can truly be said that they offered themselves sacrificially in their labors. As a result most Christians find the Scriptures more powerful and reliable because the Bible has been subjected to critical scrutiny and the finest scholarship available. We have learned far more about the Scriptures than we could have in any other way. However, in the enormous effort of critical study we have learned about more than Scripture. There was an unexpected benefit, one of enormous importance.

Through the study of the Bible during this period, knowledge grew exponentially about the community that wrote and compiled it, that is, about the early church. This in turn has provided a vast body of information about the foundational practices and attitudes of the church, information that had not been previously available. It has caused us to question what we do and why we do it in the light of what they did—that is, in the light of our origins.

We have learned that what we do and why we do it is grounded in far more recent times even than the early church. The truth is that the great branches of the church have seen the origins of their particular and specific traditions, their driving and distinguishing characteristics, in certain eras of reform that came later in the church's history. The Eastern

Orthodox churches look to the fourth century, which spelled out the new life of the church after Constantine established it. The Roman Catholic Church looks to the medieval period, emerging from the Gregorian Reformation. The Protestant churches see the sixteenth century as their defining age. The Anglican Church—validly or not—claims all three defining periods in the conceit of comprehensiveness. Each tradition is challenged to look beyond its special moment in history and examine itself in the light of the whole church's origins. This period of the early church, often referred to as the patristic age, stretches from the apostolic age to the sub-apostolic age and through the first three centuries.

Whenever a group or institution rediscovers its origins, everything about its contemporary life and practice is automatically thrown into question. The reason behind the beginning of things has a special kind of importance. This is markedly so for the church, for we claim a communal unity, a very real "connectedness," with those who have gone before. We have always maintained a fierce loyalty to the church as it was founded. Consequently, as our knowledge about the founding community increases, we cannot help but examine our current perspective and practices.

Those who have recently received theological training know of the rising importance of the early church leaders and theologians in seminary education. It is no longer enough to be an expert in a particular field for seminary teaching. One must be prepared to judge and interpret what one reads in each discipline through the lens of patristic scholarship.

By examination of the early church and the origins of our whole tradition we are able to understand accretions and variations to practices that have since developed over centuries of use, evaluating them anew. Using the standards of Scripture, tradition, and reason (reason is always founded in experience), some of what has been added to the tradition will be found wanting. However, our tendency will be to discern what is valuable within these accretions and variations and, instead of putting them altogether aside, we will be more likely to re-form them. That is to say, we are most likely to understand and appreciate the response each generation of the church made to the tradition as it was received and then passed on—even those behind practices and notions we might find problematic for today. Therefore we will take the tradition and try to recover the valuable aspects that have been lost or obscured while culling away that which is considered inappropriate for the church's present life and needs. Examination of our origins may also be expected to spark formulations of new and original theological notions of how ministry should be practiced and how the church should be governed in our time, as long as they are consonant with Scripture, the constitutive tradition, and reason.

Clearly we do not want to copy everything the early church did to express its life. In understanding the conception and the evolution of the institutional arrangements we are not engaged simply in archeological diggings. Rather, we're seeking to emerge with a re-formed and newly self-aware church. For example, one can predict that we will forgo the early practice of baptizing adults nude (in North America at least). In the same vein, what we have learned about the baptismal theology and practices of the early church compels us to offer baptism as part of the Sunday Eucharist with the participation of the whole worshiping community, but that was not exactly what the early church did. We live in a very different time and we are—and we will be—a very different culture, calling for different expressions of our community life. Nevertheless, it is true that our reformation is radically conservative in that we exhibit a tendency to return to the very first ways of seeing and doing things. It is also conservative in that we will not completely abandon the lasting traditions of the intervening history. Very few long-standing traditions are ever finally discarded outright; they get "re-formulated." That is what we are up to.

Is this costly to the church? Of course. Do we have fewer members because of our audacity in facing the issues of change that have arisen? Of course. Do we have less money? Of course. Are we more troubled? Of course. Personally, I can think of only one reason why we have already begun engaging in reform against what the world would consider our best interest as an institution: we have been called by God.

The task for our generation is to discern our role in the reformation in which we find ourselves and carry it out. We need to identify the most profound and foundational issues of reform to which we are called. Consider how the medieval church needed to work, gradually and painstakingly, toward a resolution of the dichotomy that had been defined between faith and reason. It was the synthesis wrought by Thomas Aquinas that was largely viewed as a reconciliation of faith and reason, and this satisfied the medieval world that he had constructed a comprehensive theology on which the church could stand united.

We need to go deeper than any call for specific changes that have formed the agenda to date, however crucial and immediate one may consider each of them. The foundational issues transcend our debate over the particular questions of controversy as they appear on today's left to right spectrum of liberal to conservative positions. This is not to belittle the importance of those positions and of those certain bones of contention, for ultimately it is our deeper foundational issues that underlie the decisions the church will make to resolve these differences. We may ask, what are the keys to resolving our differences?

# ORIGINS IN THE EARLY CHURCH VS. ORIGINS IN A REFORMATION

In actual exercise the modern church has looked not so much to the early church for its foundations as to the reformations that proved formative for its various traditions. Each of the three great reforms provided the defining moment for the life and practice of one of the three great branches of the Christian church. The Orthodox churches look to the Eastern tradition as shaped out of the fourth-century struggle of the Constantinian Reformation; the Roman Catholic Church looks to the medieval tradition that emerged from the Gregorian Reformation, especially reinforced by what is termed the Counter-Reformation; the Protestant denominations look to the traditions coming out of the Protestant Reformation of the Renaissance. The Anglican Communion, with its claim to comprehensiveness, is largely made up of parties that identify with one of these reformation traditions. I believe that each of the three branches of the church has its roots more in the particular reformation that defines its distinctive tradition than in the life of the early church.

We may say that, out of the historical struggle of each of the major reformations, each one of the great branches of the church continues to find the identity that distinguishes it from other Christian branches. The problem for each of these major branches today is that they are being pushed to go behind their defining moment and special tradition to the originating tradition shared by all. Consequently, when each of the branches of the church is called to return to origins that are shared by all parts of the church it often receives this call as a demand to yield traditions so precious in its history that it was willing to struggle and even fight on behalf of those traditions and against the earlier shared tradition. At best, the actual origins of the whole church get shunted back into a secondary role. As has already been noted, the way we perceive our origins, whether individual or institutional, carries special power for us. Clearly the origins to which we actually look have more power than those we hold in theory. The call to turn to the early church to rediscover our shared tradition over against the limited and particularizing "reformation tradition," therefore, is often highly conflictive within each branch.

Often, "traditionalists"—as those adhering more to their particular brand of a reformation tradition than to the broader tradition of the early church like to call themselves—will oppose change by charging that it is merely a capitulation to modern thinking and current trends, when in fact the issue at controversy might be rooted in early church theology and practice. Change is being pressed because many in the church today are rediscovering the vision of the early church and yearn to live it out. It is not because they see the ideal church in that early community; anyone who reads Scripture is privy to all the enormous flaws in the various churches. It is because in the new knowledge about the early church Christians are being informed once again about the baptismal theology of the apostolic age, about the urgency and the absolute sense of importance concerning the cosmic mission which drove the audacious effort and sacrifices of the baptized, about the new grasp of community as communion, and about the fresh understanding of God's own internal struggle on behalf of creation and the kingdom. It is possible to define the struggle for reform within each of the great branches of the church today as one between the shared tradition of the early church and the tradition of the reformation that distinguishes it from the other great branches. This is an inevitable component in the birth pangs of the Ecumenical Reformation.

# REFORM OF THE REFORMS

We can approach this discussion from an entirely different perspective, one that is neutral. Starting with the understanding that all reforms need reforming by later generations, and that, like all of the church's history, our Ecumenical Reformation is in continuity with those preceding it, one approach is to consider the issues addressed by those movements. Do any of their solutions to the troubles they faced remain as challenges for us? Are the churches clinging to any of those solutions and therefore resisting the call to reform modeled on the life of the early church? I suggest that each of the previous reformations left us with one of the key issues for reform in our day.

Our reformation can be understood as "a great reform of the great reforms." Each of these movements stands out among the notable efforts in human history, and within the life of the church. They were wildly successful in accomplishing what was needed at the time. There is no excuse for judging what they did in terms of the needs of our own day. Nevertheless, the heritage they have left us needs to be reformed, for they established traditions, attitudes, and practices that we can no longer accommodate. Consequently, we can recognize the basic issues for our day by identifying the issue each previous reform has left for us to reform. It is axiomatic that all reforms will eventually require reforming. If history is understood, then this will not be cause for condescension toward our forebears; it will instead require humility on our part as we go about our own efforts. We must be aware that whatever we may accomplish for the church will not establish the perfect church. Having dared to reform the work of those who came before, we begin in the knowledge that our reform will need to be reformed by those who someday will struggle with a changing world and a troubled church.

It is time to examine the great reforms and discover which of their vestigial characteristics create problems for us today. For example, it is clear that the cisterns of medieval Christianity have dried up and can no longer quench our gospel thirst satisfactorily, despite a determination on the part of many within the Catholic tradition to hang on to scholastic concepts for the philosophical foundation of theology. The reality is that we simply do not think that way any longer, and we do not see the cosmos in the same way that the medieval scholastics saw it. When we try to apply a dead worldview to life in the church we reduce the faith to the strictly limited sphere of "the religious," separating the life we lead in the church from the life we lead in our daily round. It distances God from the world. It denies the intimate relationship between the ordinary and the extraordinary that is the distinctive insight of our incarnational faith, and for the sacramental churches the foundation of sacramental theology. The results are disastrous: mass apathy and groundless piety. At the same time, the issues, though not the insights, of the Protestant Reformation have played themselves out and are increasingly irrelevant, except for the considerable virtue of historical understanding. This is not to say that the diverse expressions of Christian community uncovered by Protestant denominationalism are not of value to the Christian future. In much the same way Episcopalians have been rapidly losing interest in high church/low church controversies while continuing to rejoice in Anglican comprehensiveness. We must move beyond old ways of defining the church in terms of Protestant and Catholic, and in the almost exclusive theological language of election-salvation.

## THE CONSTANTINIAN REFORMATION

The first great reform was the Constantinian Reformation. In A.D. 314 it was a crime to be a Christian; by A.D.373 it was a crime not to be. On one day Christian leaders were highly worried about orders for persecution coming from inside the palace; on the next day they were themselves on the inside of the palace and being protected by the palace guards as they lounged with the elite. At one moment the countenance of the emperor was feared; in a short time the emperor's face was used in church art to depict the face of Jesus. The Christian church became established. The complications of causes and effects in this picture boggle the imagination, but it is clear that issues of church and state, of church and secular society, and of church and religion were raised, and have never been resolved satisfactorily. Soon the church was learning to co-opt and to serve the empire. The empire certainly learned how to use, as well as serve, the church.

This new relationship, synergistic and adversarial, was to be rather short-lived for most of Latin Europe. No sooner was the church the established "religion" than the empire that established it began to stagger and reel, rather quickly yielding up its order and cultural heritage. In many ways it can be said that it was primarily the church, and especially the papacy, that held Western civilization together through its dark ages. In the Greek culture of Europe, Caesaropapism gradually led to a church that embraced its patriotic role for each given people and its subservient role within each given political system.

The long historical pattern of interrelationships that ensued between church and society varied greatly according to the times and the cultures. It is becoming clear that the Constantinian Reformation is finally and utterly unraveling. The church is only now truly becoming "disestablished." This is a primary paradigm shift, one to which our reformation must be sensitive.

What relationship should the church have to the world and to the powers of the world? The question weighs heavily today and demands a definitive interpretation, one that will motivate the church and attract the people of the world who yearn for the justice, the community, and the care of the God who is love.

Positively stated, the issue the Constantinian Reformation presents to us for our reformation is justice. Justice as here employed does not refer to the limited nature of a legal system. In my mind the term "justice" is relatively comprehensive and takes unto itself peace and social harmony, as when we talk about economic and social justice, as well as of the goal of law. The role of the church is to act as the connecting link between the world in which we live and the heavenly kingdom of God that we labor to see established. In a very real sense this can be described as a task of holding us faithful to our ideals while living in a world in which these ideals must be compromised and politically applied. However, this role of linking world and kingdom is not a simple matter of holding up ideals over the compromises, frailties, and sinful failures of this world for the establishment of justice. It is the goal of Christians to become at home in the world; it is simultaneously necessary for Christians to realize that we are in exile and to yearn for the kingdom until it is founded. In what sense can we serve justice in such a situation? Would God have us act as a power within the world to influence it, or as a religiously detached prophetic instrument? We really have not sorted out these questions to anyone's satisfaction, though our best minds in each generation have tried. Perhaps it is true, as it is growing more popular to declare, that we cannot understand our role as long as we labor under the Constantinian burden of establishment. Under any circumstances, operating from the position of establishment has been a factor in how we have tried to exercise this role; that position is changing rapidly, and we must re-form our entire approach to serving as the link between the world and the kingdom.

One of the consequences of the Constantinian Reformation was a slight but significant shift in the popular sense of the church's mission. Before being recognized by the Roman emperor, the church of the early fourth century had been paying attention to a different set of matters. Its fundamental posture remained evangelical. The church had already survived separation from its roots in Judaism, the death of its founding leaders, and the necessity of institutionalization. But the common culture within which the church found itself, Hellenic and secure within the *Pax Romana,* was ready to hear what it had to say. The church found that it had a powerful message for a religiously hungry world, good news about the two most pressing religious issues of the day: a system of morality and human mortality. The church itself modeled what was preached, however imperfectly, because it lived with an urgency of mission in anticipation of the return of Christ and in welcoming the kingdom of the new age even in its own. However, the church grew while dealing with the formulation—through the resolution of controversies and conflict—of the great theological concepts that best explained the true faith to most of them most of the time. It was of course couched in terms of the common Hellenic culture while remaining faithful to the Jewish tradition. The church developed a biblical canon to go along with its sacramental ministry for the protection of the transmission of that faith. It faced periodic persecutions and threats of persecution, and thus it was not only for the intrinsic value that the church focused on the formation of community with a high commitment among its members as well as to the faith, and to the difference between the life of a Christian within these communities and the society they had begun to term "secular." One of the primary components of community and commitment was the high standards it held for initiation—especially in the lengthy and indepth system of formation termed the catechumenate. ·

Given all these factors, almost every baptized member could be assumed to be a sincere and serious "believer" and a theologian to the extent that they could articulate the faith to an unbeliever. Clergy needed no extra or special training for ordination. As the entire society of a great empire in the Roman West and in the Byzantine East became Christian practically overnight it was natural that the great and pressing need shifted from evangelization within Hellenic society and the development of communities for which the member was willing to die, to the need to provide the masses of new membership with genuine understanding and faith, and to hold them to it with discipline. That is where most of the energy for mission went, including the composition of the great liturgical texts, the creation of monastic movements, the sacrifice of missionaries, and the resolutions of the great councils. The key to the mission of the church was orthodoxy. This right belief was to build a church that exercised its belief for the influence of good for the society in which it was now religion itself. In order to do so it would need to be as powerful as possible.

Very soon the empire itself began to collapse in the West. The potential converts became what the civilized Mediterranean world of antiquity called barbarians. These new targets of evangelization did not share the common Hellenic culture. For example, they demanded a more objective, and precisely defined rendering of the faith, a sort of scientific, or perhaps "fundamentalist," approach to religious questions. As the church adjusted to the Constantinian Settlement of the established church, even as it coped with converting the new pagans that overran vast parts of Europe, even as it moved north and began the initial developments of feudal society, even when conversion was again key to the church's mission, the focus was conversion to right belief. The desire was to establish the church in each society for influence on behalf of good, and eventually it became the desire to become Christendom.

## THE CHURCH WITH ROOTS IN THE CONSTANTINIAN REFORMATION

We have observed that each of the three great reforms provided the defining moment for the life and practice of one of the great branches of the Christian church and that each of these branches of the church has its roots more deeply in the particular reformation that defines its distinctive tradition than in the life of the early church. Consequently, when we identify an issue for reform today that arose out of the "originating reformation" of one of our "churches" we will discover how that particular branch has special trouble in addressing that issue.

The Eastern Orthodox churches most clearly identify themselves with the Constantinian Reformation. They know that event as the defining and shaping moment for their tradition. Consequently, we may suppose that the Eastern Orthodox churches will have the most difficult time in reforming themselves over the issue of justice. For example, when some within the Western church suggest that the question of the ordination of women is, among other matters, an issue of justice, the reply from the Eastern Orthodox Church seems to be puzzlement and reference to the patristic tradition as it became defined during the Constantinian Reformation in the fourth century. It does seem to be the case that the Eastern Orthodox churches tend in practice to be somewhat more focused on the kingdom of God in heaven than on God's promise to establish the kingdom on earth. With a tradition that prides itself on transcending history, is it not true that the Eastern churches have been more firmly wed to the actual historical situations in which the church has found itself at each stage of history, and more captured by the historical powers that be—as in its tradition of Caesaropapism?

## THE GREGORIAN REFORMATION

The second great reformation is usually given the name of the pope who came to represent its spirit, who most clearly saw its necessity, and who initiated many of its institutions: Gregory VII. His problem was relatively clear. As feudalism became the established way of life, economically, politically, militarily, and socially, it threatened to engulf the church. For one thing, the all-powerful landlords saw no reason why they should not govern the church within their sphere of authority. They saw no reason to allow a bishop or a remote system of ecclesiastical government to rule where they had absolute control over everything else. The landlord might very well have built the local church or monastery and then hired the clergy and endowed the monks or nuns to minister to the religious and social needs of the people in fealty to him, and to pray for him and his family unto perpetuity. Inevitably conflicts would arise in such a case and the landlord would expect the hirelings to exercise their sworn loyalty to him over against the hierarchy of the church.

Gregory's most important reform was to rescue the church from the newly powerful secular landlords and rulers by separating the "laity" from the clergy and raising the status of the clergy. The results were immediately effective. "The church" was quickly and easily reduced in the popular mind to "ordained ministers." The clergy now constituted a "professional" class, managed and controlled by the hierarchy, primarily the papacy—protector of the tradition, the property, and the integrity of the church. The church was successful in struggles against the secular powers and in incorporation of the masses (even the conquering invaders) by convincing them that the sacraments were the transcendent channels of grace necessary for salvation, and thus by turning its mission into the operation of a vast sacramental machine entirely controlled by the clergy. This reform carved the basis for medieval Christianity and Christendom.

This system was wildly successful and finally accomplished the great mission of establishing right belief and personal faith for the masses. The period of the medieval church was deemed the age of faith. However, the reform that shaped medieval Christianity created grave difficulties for our own time, leaving us with unresolved questions about authority and ministry, especially clericalism. Not many people today are comfortable with the way ministry and the authority for ministry and governance are being handled, or how the theorizing about these issues is proceeding. The challenges of dealing with the problems of abusive hierarchical authority, clericalism, and a sacramental system designed to support each can be stated positively—the church is seeking to redefine our baptism as the source of the ministry and governance of the church.

Notice how the mission of the church shifted from belief and faith to "religion." In the era deemed "the age of faith" and in a society deemed "Christendom," the focus of the church's effort and energy turned to the development of a grand system for the practice of belief and faith. It was founded on a complicated sacramental system through which the church delivered the effects of religion to the masses. The emphasis was on the transcendent, and on having life on earth conform to real life in heaven. The church began to picture society in the heavenly realm, with its ranks, rewards, punishments, and clashes between absolute good and evil, and to define that picture as doctrine. Life on earth was viewed as only partially real, merely a passageway for the saved into the heavens. Instead of the pagan pyramids and ziggurats, exalted, skyward-pointing cathedrals were constructed. Though the cruciform shape touched the ground the point was the same: the church was the purveyor of a system in which certain sacred places, sacred occasions, sacred objects, sacred rites and rituals, and sacred persons brought the people into touch with the transcendent. The primary mission of the church was to serve as the religious institution in society.

## THE CHURCH WITH ROOTS IN THE GREGORIAN REFORMATION

If we ask which of the great bodies of the church is most identified with the Gregorian Reformation, finding its identity primarily in the medieval institution and traditions produced by this reform, we would have to conclude it is the Roman Catholic Church. Concomitantly, it is the Roman Catholic Church that faces the greatest difficulty with the recovery of our original theology of baptism and mission, with their implications for ministry and authority. It would not be illegitimate to say that today's contention within the Roman Catholic Church is largely a matter of how, when, and where it would be appropriate to separate from the medieval church. It is my belief that the most important as well as the most difficult step of reform for the Roman Catholic Church will be to free itself from the dogmatic limitations of scholastic philosophy. The other members of the catholic family of churches, namely the Orthodox, Anglican, and Lutheran churches, share the difficulties with the issue left by the Gregorian Reformation in direct proportion to the extent that their Catholicity is defined by scholastic philosophical concepts and medieval piety instead of by a renewed understanding of sacramental theology founded in the early church's concepts and piety.

The catholic family of Christians invariably wants to remain loyal to the fundamental theology of ordained ministry that the Gregorian Reformation established, complete with its reliance upon apostolic succession. Catholic Christians are aware of the failure of the Protestant Reformation to solve the problems of ministry that it identified, both ordained and lay. It certainly failed to empower the baptized *laos* as ministers. Soon the Protestant population was turning to a common refrain: "The Presbyter is but the Priest writ large." Most of all, Catholic and sacramentally sensitive Christians refuse to throw the sacramental baby out with the devalued bowl of baptismal water. We would prefer to restore the full implications of what the baptismal waters signify about ministry. We would prefer to find a deeper appreciation, not a lesser, for the sacramental nature of reality. This desire seems to include an increasing number of Protestant theologians as they learn far more from the early church than their reforming forebears of the Renaissance had available to them. Nevertheless, the need to reform holy orders, to recapture the full ministry of the *laos*, and to settle the many struggles and confusion regarding authority, is terribly necessary for today's church.

## THE PROTESTANT REFORMATION

The third reform for our discussion is the Protestant Reformation and the radical individualism that was so central to it, an individualism that came with the Renaissance but which has remained with us and grown increasingly radical. Along with the newly discovered individualism of the Renaissance came a narrow of Protestant Christian mission to evangelism, based on a certain narrowing understanding of election-salvation. When the religious system of Catholic Christendom had become corrupt in actual practice, deep-seated reform had to take place. It did so in the Protestant Reformation and in the Counter-Reformation. In each case the election-salvation of *individual* souls became the overwhelmingly important and most energized business of the church. All else became peripheral; indeed any other activity, such as the prophetic, had to be justified case by case, and any terminology other than election-salvation had to be explained. Other traditions, including principal scriptural traditions like that of the Wisdom literature, were ignored or deprecated.

We can all be grateful for the Renaissance concern for that which is human. This concern led to an appropriately high regard for the individual. We are grateful that the Protestant Reformation led the whole church into recognition of the place of the individual in God's heart. Most of the virtues of Western culture—political, social, scientific, artistic, academic, techno-economic, all particulars, however delineated, are captured in the insight that in God's eye each individual is a cosmos unto him or her self and that the protection of each individual's rights and opportunities is of the highest importance. Developing one's authentic selfhood and being faithful to that particularly differentiated self, rather than giving in to conformity and the pressures of society, is a human task that the church has learned to support wholeheartedly.

However, our individualism has gone too far and led us astray. Our appreciation of the corporate nature of reality has been all but lost. We no longer have any real sense of the whole. Any grasp of the interconnectedness of the parts constituting the whole is taken as a mental abstraction, something people in our American society seem unprepared to apprehend as concretely real. The results are destructive beyond measure for a Christian worldview and for parish communities. Christianity is reduced to personal and private religion, a system of individual beliefs and ethics; faith is reduced to a feeling; the world is reduced to a series of discrete individual objects, all set before the subjective self separately with no interconnection. There is no room for God in such an object world except as conceptually reduced to one grand individual among others. Positively stated, the issue the Protestant Reformation presents for us is community. In order to develop Christian community we need to recover our human ability to see and appreciate the corporate nature of the church, and, indeed, the communal nature of reality. We need to recover our sense of the whole. This will be hard work but I believe the work will prove worthwhile, for the frustration caused by our inability to create the rich and profound sense of community to which God calls us is enormous.

## THE CHURCH WITH ROOTS IN THE PROTESTANT REFORMATION

The Protestant churches have their distinguishing origins in the Protestant Reformation and in the culture of the Renaissance. Consequently, they sanctioned the radical individualism of that period and became relatively obsessed with the issue of election-salvation that dominated the sixteenth-century reformation. Individual ethics were viewed as the primary criteria for election-salvation. It is the Protestant churches that today demonstrate the greatest difficulty in going beyond the more radical individualism of our own culture. Anglicans, Lutherans, and other denominations that consider themselves both Protestant and Catholic will share this difficulty to the extent that they identify with the evangelical fixation and, especially today, Protestant fundamentalism.

As an Anglican I must stress an Anglican peculiarity relevant to the matters at hand. If Protestant churches are likely to have an intrinsic problem with the issue of individualism arising from the Protestant Reformation, Roman Catholics are likely to have an intrinsic problem with authority and clericalism arising from the Gregorian Reformation, and the Orthodox are going to have an intrinsic problem with social justice, then Anglican claims of comprehensiveness place us in the position of having unique problems with all three of the issues of reform instead of just one. Anglicans can never look down upon the faults of any sister churches, for Anglicans identify with each of them and must claim full ownership of any feature to be criticized. Surely, as Anglicans apply them in various church "parties" these problematic features get exaggerated.

## Transition

This analysis leads us first to seek the recovery of our self-understanding from the early foundations of the church in Christian mission, in baptismal theology, and in the doctrine of God. We will examine the ultimate mission of the church: God's causes of creation and kingdom. We will compare the identity and purpose of the church as initially grasped in baptismal theology with more recent traditions of baptism. We will review the original insights about God as revealed in Jesus, which were seen to contradict pagan understandings of the transcendent; primarily we will focus on the issue of suffering to understand God's relation to us and to Christian mission. Perhaps the recovery of these three insights will form a basis for a new and broadly accepted theology of the church, as the church evolves in its thinking and its unity enough to accept such a theology.

In the light of these three insights, we will explore each of the three theological problems that have been left for reform from previous reformations, the three key issues for our reform:

- community
- ministry
- justice.

These issues are the keys to our reformation, the pivotal issues on which turn the matters that we must resolve in our day and which presently divide us, the foundation on which we will build our institutions and structures for the coming church. They pose real dilemmas for all Christians, from the most conservative to the most liberal. We will find few formulas, but we can define, examine, and shape understandings that will contribute to some resolution.

The terms I employ in naming the issues have to be redefined to some degree, especially to draw the distinction between the secular and Christian understandings of each term. At the same time, the three issues intertwine. Justice, ministry, and community are perfectly interdependent matters, sharing an inseparable reality. We cannot keep them penned up in discrete boundaries, even to examine them theologically. When we examine the Constantinian genesis of an established church—a position from which the church has been unable to define its proper relation to the world and to the kingdom, i.e., to stand squarely for justice—we will also witness how this contributed to the diminishing sense of urgency about the church's mission and ministry.

When we see ordination supplant baptism in importance, we see the church, newly defined as the clergy, try to separate itself from the world in one sense, while, at the same time, seeking new vistas of worldly power. However, the distinctions between each of the three issues are also valid, and I shall try to make them clearer as we go.

## ADDENDUM

Other religions are also undergoing reform for their own reasons and, though they are not incarnational religions, the profound and radical changes taking the world into a new era demand reform of all religious communities. For example, a significant number of governments have become instruments of various strands of Muslim fundamentalism that have held onto extremist doctrines and practices no longer acceptable for mainstream Islam. It would be as if certain Christian sects controlled governments that accepted the moral authority of clergy preaching renewed Crusades to seize control of the Holy Lands that established communities of monks who formed the core of their fighting forces, and that fought with the cultural attitudes of Richard the Lion Hearted and his twelfth-century knights. In the newly established globalism of our day it will not be possible to divide the world into *Dar al Harb*, the house of war ruled by all non-Muslims, and *Dar al Islam*, which is destined to dominate the former. "Orthodox" Islam will lead the reform of the broader community.

The Jewish community has been engaged in obvious reform movements and dealing with fundamentalist controversies in the same time period that the Christian reform has been gathering momentum. There now are large segments of the Jewish religious community that describe themselves as "Reformed." Reformed Judaism has become the most influential of the Jewish grouping in the State of Israel, in the United States, and throughout the Western world. One of the features of each movement has been the effort to seek reconciliation between Jews and Christians, especially those groups within each community that have embraced reform.

✦ ✦ ✦ ✦ ✦

# SUMMATION

The old church is dying and reform is needed. If we are not intentional and proactive about harnessing the forces behind this, internal and external, if we do not take charge and direct our own reform, we will lose control over vast changes and they will overwhelm us. The forces of economy alone will dictate our future unless we cooperate with the realities and take advantage of the opportunities.

The needed reform is well underway, and has been for generations. It is driven by internal forces, based on detailed rediscovery of our origins in the early church, and increasingly it is driven by external forces of world change. Our approach begins with the recognition that all reforms will eventually need to be reformed and examines the previous great reformations. When we understand their issues and the success they enjoyed, we can see how each has left us with an issue begging for remedy in our day. The Constantinian Reformation of the fourth century established the Christian church as the privileged faith of Western culture. But today we still wrestle with questions of how to relate faithfully to the world, especially in terms of the unjust powers that be, while remaining faithful to the kingdom we are to welcome. The Gregorian Reformation of the eleventh century solved the new feudalistic threat of a take-over by the all-powerful landlords, including the emerging state powers, by separating the clergy from the laity and making the latter dependent on the former. This has left us with questions of clericalism and authority. Culturally the Protestant Reformation relied on the individualism of the Renaissance and theologically it was preoccupied with an individualistic interpretation of election-salvation. Since then, individualism has grown so radical that those of us of the Western culture that spawned it can no longer grasp the interconnectedness among the elements of creation, especially people. The responses of the great reformations to their issues and calls to mission were highly effective for their needs in their time, but they remain for us to resolve in terms of the needs of our time.

## NOTES

[1] Erich Auerbach, *Mimesis: The Representation of Reality in Western Literature*, trans. Willard R. Trask (Princeton: Princeton University Press), 94.

[2] Ibid., 93.

[3] Thomas L. Friedman, *The Lexus and the Olive Tree* (New York: Anchor Press, 2000), 11.

[4] Joseph Schumpeter, *Capitalism, Socialism, and Democracy* (New York: HarperCollins, 1984).

[5] Andrew S. Grove, *Only the Paranoid Survive: How to Exploit the Crisis Points that Challenge Every Company* (New York: Bantam Books, 1999).

[6] James Surowiecki, *Rogue Missives*. The Motley Fool website, January 6, 1997.

# II.

# *JUSTICE*

Justice lies at the heart of the role given to Jesus and to the church he gathers: to bring together heaven and earth, creation and kingdom. The work of Christianity, in cooperation with God, is history. The work of Christianity, in cooperation with God, is to transcend the limitations of history. History leads to the kingdom, the actualization of a human society that is perfectly just in all regards, a culture without violence and oppression but enjoying the reign of that peace which passes all understanding. Jesus brings heaven and earth together in the gathering of his community, calling it to his incarnational ministry of service to the world, a sacrificial service of healing, blessing, and reconciliation, a service establishing the justice and peace that welcomes the kingdom of God. This is the fulfillment of the destiny for which the world was created from the foundations.

God's plan for human society is to be discerned in the origins of the Jewish people, especially in the dramatic reversal experienced in the Exodus and in their valiant attempt to form a responsive society in the Promised Land, one that reflected the compassion and righteousness of God's own nature and life. It is fully revealed in the messianic Passover of the cross and resurrection. The seeds had been sown in the wilderness wanderings of faithful Abraham away from the new paganism of the Tigris-Euphrates Valley and into the Promised Land. The divine plan for the human family resounds in the songs of the mothers, especially in the connection to be heard between the songs of Hannah and Mary. In their hymns, psalms, and canticles we hear the message of the prophets and of the Christ together: if there is no justice there is no God, but only idols of the illusory wealth, status, privilege, and power that people think will satisfy their humanity and that lead to the sin of violence.

The justice to be found in this world, and while working to welcome the kingdom to come, is best defined by the church in terms of its paradoxical mission: creation and kingdom. How can we fulfill God's will that the human being love this life as it is given to each person as a gift while simultaneously judging it and working with all of our heart and soul to improve it, and finally to perfect it?

# SONGS OF THE MOTHERS:
## The Tradition Handed Down

There are few moments as exciting in the life of a human being as when a woman discovers that she is pregnant and when the child actually comes into the world. People everywhere and in all times report that such moments are dominated by an intense and overwhelming spirit of gratitude, no small amount of trepidation, and a fresh sense of the wholeness of life. While the imagination flows to very personal and specific family matters, it is likely that the mind also will begin to ponder the grand issues concerning life. If one could, one might burst into song and dance. It would be quite human to give voice to a song rising spontaneously from the deepest seat of the heart, one that is dedicated to the child. This is actually the setting and the scene for what happened when various women in the Bible contemplated the event of motherhood. In most cases the news of their expectancy was reported as a surprise. The songs of the mothers, conceived in laughter and joy and awe, were handed down through the oral tradition and in the various ways the Scriptures were composed.

There are the songs of two mothers which stand out as extraordinarily special. They were sung centuries apart from one another, yet they converge and are inseparable. What they reveal about the nature of God and God's causes, especially taken together, can be submitted as a summary statement. The influence of each has been surpassing. We are now in a time when their news, at the very heart of the good news, has been obscured where not lost—or trivialized in rank sentimentality. The Song of Hannah anticipates and is completed by the Song of Mary.

Hannah was the wife of Elkanah. He had another wife named Peninnah. Hannah was unable to have a child, but Peninnah had several, both sons and daughters. Moreover, she lorded this over Hannah. Scripture says that this went on for years (1 Sam 1:7). Even though Elkanah assured Hannah of his love and gave her twice as much as his other, more productive, wife, Hannah was miserable. During the time each year when the family went up to Shiloh for their thanksgiving sacrifice Hannah would be especially distraught, weeping and refusing to eat. Finally, Hannah bargained with God, vowing that if she were granted a male child she would dedicate him to God. Hannah did become pregnant and gave birth to a son, whom she named Samuel. After the baby was weaned, Samuel was taken to Shiloh and left to serve God under the direction of the priest Eli. Hannah's song is a prayer dedicating her only son in joyful praise of the God whose promises to Israel were sure to be fulfilled, just as God's steadfast faithfulness to a barren woman had been fulfilled.

When Mary reached the appropriate age she was betrothed to Joseph, a respected citizen who could actually claim King David as an ancestor. Suddenly, in the dramatic visitation of the angel Gabriel, Mary found herself chosen to be the mother of Jesus. Gabriel promised that Mary's child would "reign over the house of Jacob for ever; and of his kingdom there will be no end" (Lk 1:33). Straightaway Mary traveled into the hill country of Judea to be with her kinswoman Elizabeth, wife of the priest Zechariah. Elizabeth was six months pregnant. There was more than kinship and the elation of pending motherhood to bind these two women. Luke had opened his gospel with the story of Elizabeth and her pregnancy. She was of the house of Aaron, barren and too old to have children. As with Mary, Luke portrayed an announcement delivered by the angel Gabriel: Elizabeth was to bear a male child who would have a special mission on God's behalf. John, who would come to be called the Baptizer, was to serve as the forerunner to prepare the way for Jesus to exercise his Messianic ministry. When Mary walked into Elizabeth's house and greeted her, the child John leaped in Elizabeth's womb "for joy" (Lk 1:44). Elizabeth blessed Mary and the baby she carried. With that Mary expressed her gratitude in a song of faith that magnified the great and sweeping promises of God according to Israel.

It requires little imagination to picture the way these songs were preserved and handed down, whether written by the mother herself, produced by a developing tradition, or shaped by an individual redactor. My heart thrills to the picture of the mothers of Israel, generations of mothers, in a moment of singing the matriarchal Song of Hannah to their infants. It soon may have become a psalm for liturgical usage in Jewish community observances, but surely the mothers who followed Hannah in the Jewish tradition sang the song to their own precious children nestled at their breasts.

All indications are that Mary, the mother of Jesus, knew the Song of Hannah by heart, the song in which the mother of Samuel gratefully dedicates her newly born son to God that he may do his part in the fulfillment of the fundamental promises of the God of Israel. There can be little doubt that Hannah's song formed an important part of Mary's tradition. In it she must have found the pattern and themes of her own personal response to the news that she was pregnant with Jesus. Perhaps Mary had heard the song at her own mother's breast. Would it not have been natural for Mary to turn to this song to express her hopes and purposes for her baby? We can be sure that his mother's song was highly influential for Jesus, shaping his sense of personal mission. When we hear Mary's Magnificat we can little wonder that his opening proclamation was, "The time has come. The kingdom of God is at hand."

There may be nothing more important to what provides meaning in each of our lives than the songs we hear at our mother's breast, and these songs often reflect the sort of thoughts the mother has at that moment of gratitude when she dedicates the new life of her baby in personal prayer. They tend to be songs that carry certain of the important traditions of one's culture and, directly or not, of one's religious roots. The songs of the two mothers must have been formative. For example, we can consider the influence the Song of Hannah, mother of the first prophet Samuel, must have exerted on each of the prophets who followed as their mothers would have sung it ever so softly and fervently to them. It very well may be that the content of the prophetic imagination was formed by this mother's song. Perhaps Jeremiah listened to this song, as, according to his personal testimony, he was being called and formed as a prophet while still in his mother's womb.

If we have need to speculate about the impact of these two songs, the songs of the mothers Hannah and Mary, we should wonder only about how our own society would have been inspired and changed if these songs had been offered at the breasts of Christian mothers down through the centuries. This section is an attempt to allow these two songs of the mothers to have their full say in the scheme of things. In fact, what they have to say should be definitive for Jews and Christians. For each was offered to elucidate two of the most important turning points in human history. Across the ages the songs of two pregnant women in praise of God, the Song of Hannah and the Song of Mary, connect and proclaim the central desires of the people of God. They lay out the meaning of the prophets and of the incarnation. They declare who Jesus is and circumscribe the identity and purpose of those who would answer his call. In them, the church can rediscover the

promises of God for the future church; thus do the songs of the mothers
rally the People of God to the Ecumenical Reformation.

### The Song of Hannah

My heart exults in the Lord!
My triumph song is lifted by my God.
My mouth is stretched over my enemies,
because I rejoice in my victory.

There is no Holy One like the Lord,
nor any rock to be compared to our God.
Talk no more so very proudly,
let not arrogance come from your mouth;
For the Lord is knowing and weighs all actions.

The bows of the mighty are broken,
but the weak are armored in strength.
Those who were full have hired themselves out for bread,
but those who were hungry now are well fed.
The childless woman has borne sevenfold,
while the mother of many is forlorn.
The Lord destroys and brings to life,
casts down and raises up;
gives wealth or takes it away,
humbles and dignifies.
He raises up the poor from the dust;
and lifts the needy from the ash heap
To give them a seat with noblemen,
bequeathing them a place of honor.
For the pillars of the earth are the Lord's,
and on them he has set the world.

He guards the way of his faithful ones,
but the wicked perish in darkness;
for not by might does one prevail.
The Lord! His adversaries shall be shattered;
against them he will thunder in heaven.

1 Samuel 2:1–10a

### The Song of Mary

My soul magnifies the Lord,
and my spirit rejoices in God my Savior
for he has looked with favor on the lowliness of his servant.
Surely, from this day all generations will call me blessed;
for the Mighty One has done great things for me,
and holy is his name.
His mercy is for those who fear him
from generation to generation.
He has shown strength with his arm;
he has scattered the proud in the imagination of their hearts.
He has brought down the powerful from their thrones,
and lifted up the lowly;
he has filled the hungry with good things,
and sent the rich away empty.
He has come to the help of his servant Israel,
for he has remembered his promise of mercy,
the promise he made to our forebears,
to Abraham and to his children forever.

Luke 1:46–55

The first thing to be observed is how similar the two songs are. The connection between them is commandingly direct in content as well as in structure. It is legitimate to picture Mary composing her own song by breaking into an inspired psalm. It would have been uncontrived: she would have enjoyed such profound familiarity with Hannah's work that to incorporate its structures and keynotes could have occurred quite naturally. It is also legitimate to picture Mary sitting at the family table and referring to Hannah's work while composing. It is just as legitimate to imagine that Luke referred to the first canticle of dedication and wrote a similar song, attributing it to Mary as a most clever literary device to articulate his gospel vision about the role and personhood of Jesus, the Jewish literary device of a mother's song. He would only have done so, to be sure, because he considered his personal vision commensurate with the one held by the mother of Jesus.

Of course, it would be unwise to ignore, or in any way to underestimate, the importance of the many and varied experiences of God's people that took place between the composition of Hannah's and Mary's songs. For what it is worth, Mary's song also has other allusions from various texts familiar to any Jew of the age. Nevertheless, and under any circumstances, it is clear that the two songs of Mary and Hannah are directly related and point to truth that lies at the center of the gospel. There can hardly be any doubt that Hannah's majestic hymn served as a key first to Mary's song and thus to the gospel as understood by Luke.

Each song paints dramatic, Exodus-like pictures of sharp and surprising reversals. They are surprising because, like the Exodus rescue of the Jewish slaves from the Egyptian empire, normal expectations are turned upside down and what is revealed is a new and amazing understanding of fundamentals: the nature of God, the make-up of the universe, the divine plan for a just human society. At the heart of the songs are the compassion, justice, and righteousness of God. This is God's glory. These songs remain astonishing to us today, wherever or however we live in this world—so surprising in the world we know that we too still find them difficult to believe, and discover our hearts leaping in exaltation when we grasp the meaning of God's "victory" that they articulate.

Mary and Hannah sing praise for God's favor of the humble and lowly. Unexpectedly, God has sided with the poor and the weak; unexpectedly, God has overthrown the rich and hushed the proud; unexpectedly, protection and mercy is in store for the faithful who "fear" God, while the wicked will be cut off; unexpectedly, the hungry will be fed while the rich are sent away empty. In other words, Hannah and then Mary concludes, the world will be treated the way God treated Israel in the Exodus experience and as God called it to be his servant community. In other words, Mary is saying, the prophets were right after all: the future shall accord with promises made to the first ancestors and there shall be justice at last.

Luke most intentionally begins his gospel with a pattern of surprising reversals by God. As has been demonstrated in Hannah's song, this is not a new pattern. It calls for a new order of society under God's reign and that new order will be a reversal of the familiar pattern. This pattern of reversals that is established will continue through the cross and resurrection, a pattern of dying and rising that borders on tragedy and on comedy—a divine play transcending ordinary human wisdom and power.

## THE NEW COSMOLOGY AND GOD'S NEW PLAN FOR HUMAN SOCIETY

In order to understand the pattern of human life that leads to and follows the dying and rising of Jesus Christ, in order to appreciate the full significance of the astonishing nature of the connection between the two songs of the mothers, it is necessary to start at the beginning. Mary's song refers to a beginning seen in the promises to Abraham, and as we shall see, she does so appropriately. However, the meaning of the prehistory of the Jewish people in the form of ancestral legends can only be comprehended within the context of the original Passover story of the Exodus experience, that chain of events starting with the release and escape of the chosen people from Egypt and culminating in their settlement in the land of the Canaanites. This is where we must first place our focus.

It was probably during the reign of Rameses II (1290–1224 B.C.), that an insignificant band of Hebrew slaves slipped from bondage in Egypt and experienced what was remembered as a miraculous rescue from Pharaoh's army at the Red Sea. It was a diplomatic and rescue operation directly attributed to their household god. Their leader was a man of improbable vision named Moses, who declared to them that the Hebrew god had called him to this mission and with shocking intimacy had offered the identity of the divine name, handed down to us as Yahweh. Given the common understandings of the ancient world this would have given Moses confidence in a measure of knowledge about God's own essence. This is the first event presented in Scripture that can be called "history." It is in this event that we begin to understand why a certain small and mixed company of people was called into a unique community: the People of God.

Their leap from bondage into freedom broke the credibility of the widespread orthodoxy of their time, an official religion of special privilege and power. That is, it generated a whole new understanding of the nature of God. It recognized the reality of a moral universe, suddenly discovered as dynamic. It established a completely fresh vision of human purpose. It demanded a new understanding of community for the accomplishment of that purpose. It established justice as an integral component of a faithful response to the Jewish god, one unseverable from that god's causes.

Gradually the new vision emerged. Life together in the community that covenants to be the People of God was the gift of a loving God.

That community existed to serve God's creative purposes for the world. It was dedicated to the redemption and restoration of the entire created order, and it was dedicated to the future fulfillment of creation in a state of cosmic harmony they termed *shalom*. An appropriate expression of the community's purpose was found in the perspective that regards history as being moved purposefully by God toward that final goal. The early Yahwistic community oriented itself to God's future by seeking to establish communal structures that reflected the life of a god they had come to know in their experience. The divine life was to be especially expressed in law, worship, the arts, and the various institutions of society. The effort to have the whole society share the life of the gracious god was comprehensive and pervasive. It was their intention that all of the structures for community life were to be drawn inferentially from the ongoing experience of the God who rescued slaves and set them up as the People of God: those structures called for justice and compassion.

That original model continues to live for us, translated by the vision Jesus of Nazareth proclaimed of the kingdom of God and by the church's vision of his role in it. Jesus was gathering the People of God that ultimately is to welcome the kingdom of God. The church is the community of the kingdom to come that Jesus called, and is calling.

The Hebrew and Christian Scriptures form a unique body of historical literature that speaks from the point of view of the victim and not that of the righteous community of persecutors. We can usually accept the dictum that "history is written by the victors." It is true that the story that survives and is passed on is the one related by dominant groups and it is told from their perspective. The story, as it would be offered by the vanquished, the oppressed, and the poor, is usually lost or destroyed by those who take control. The Bible is remarkably distinctive. It tells the story of a nation that traced its origins to a slave rebellion, a nation divided and denounced by its own strongest voices for failing to live up to its vocation, a people taken into exile and scattered into lost tribes, a people that lived for six hundred years under foreign domination and constantly yearned for liberation from bondage until finally it was utterly destroyed by the oppressor and driven from its Promised Land. Then the Christian Bible continues with the story of a people gathered around the person of a man who was executed in the most humiliating and degrading manner, and who, at the time the Scriptures come to a close, are suffering a series of terrible persecutions.

The Bible is a remarkable exception in historical literature and one which, in its very existence, insists that the standards of success in human history be subject finally to God's purposes rather than to the ability to exercise coercive power, to purchase goods and services, and to enjoy special advantages. Certainly, it demonstrates that the Jewish people were not unduly impressed with the standards of "success" as established by the pagan world. But then, how could they be when their fundamental identity was formed as the oppressed, as a people of slaves, whose only glory is a god who chooses slaves and yet is more powerful than the god of the mightiest empire?

The Exodus story is so familiar that we are inclined to miss the world-changing impact it had on those who experienced it. The rescued slaves and their immediate heirs discovered radically new insights in their experience of the event, but because we have been shaped by these very insights, we bring them to our reading of the story as given assumptions about reality. Thus does the story tend to be reduced to one more stirring drama about good guys and bad guys, about oppressed and oppressor, about underdogs and powerhouses. Our challenge is to read the story with the fresh eyes with which the ancient world viewed reality.

Joseph Campbell came to the conclusion that the civilizations that emerged in the ancient world held a remarkably common understanding about purpose and order, with religion at the center of this perspective. We know with some real precision when and where the commonly held mythology and cultic activity enjoyed its beginning: Sumeria, 3200 B.C. Soon each city-state and empire around the world was making the same effort to align its life in accordance with the heavens. These endeavors supposed that there was a heavenly order of things that ruled life on earth. Even the rule of the gods was subject to the heavenly order. Furthermore, it was presumed that human society would prosper if it could conform to that order and match it, if earth could imitate heaven, as it were.

The Sumerians had discovered through long and careful scientific observation that there were certain visible heavenly spheres that moved in established patterns and according to hard and fast laws along the courses followed by the sun and the moon and among the fixed stars. They began to draw conclusions, coming to believe that heavenly life and order was manifested in the stars. They conceptualized the stars as sort of a material projection of what went on in heaven and thus, since heaven ruled earthly affairs, they could reveal to the knowledgeable what was to be on earth. If the stars imitated the heavens, then earthly life could imitate heaven by predicting the stars. They decisively settled "on the almost insane, playful, yet potentially terrible notion that the laws governing the movements of the seven heavenly spheres should in some mystical way be the same as those governing the life and thought of men on earth...an imitation on earth of the cosmic order."[1] This discovery and this idea were the highly conscious creation of something entirely new: the professional priesthood, a profession assigned the task of helping rulers to read the heavenly designs and conform to them. They were given to study the stars and the entrails of creatures, to sacrifice to the gods, and to demand moral conformity. So fixed was their attention and so powerful their conclusions that in many cities and empires the priests were authorized to kill the king if their reading of the stars indicated this was the heavenly course to follow.

This cultural syndrome spread from the point where the Tigris and Euphrates reach the Persian Gulf eastward and westward. It reached the Nile and became Egyptian around 2800 B.C., was adopted in Crete in one direction and the valley of the Indus in the other around 2600 B.C., reached Shang China, circa 1600 B.C., and somehow, between the seventh and fourth centuries B.C. emerged in Peru and Middle America. Almost every civilization had its mounds and ziggurats that pointed to the heavens, architectural symbols of its efforts to connect heaven and earth. The early Sumerian temple tower supplied the model for the Greek Olympus, the Hindu-Buddhist imagery of the world mountain Sumeru, and the Aztec temples of the sun. This worldwide religious system is what we usually think of when we use the word "paganism." It was an attempt not only to be in touch with ultimate reality, but also to understand, please, appease, and manipulate the various gods and creatures of the heavens that ruled the earth. It invariably adopted and adapted sacrificial systems inherent in primitive religion. Perhaps religious sacrifice was primarily an effort to cope with the violence that the gods loosed upon the world and which could at any time threaten civilization from within and without, though it was also used for prediction and control of events.

In the archaic high civilizations everyone played his or her role according to the rules of the celestially inspired divine game, the world-ordering harmony of heavenly spheres. For our purposes it is sufficient to recognize the effort to arrange a social order in accordance with what they assumed was a heavenly order. Campbell points to their "need to bring the parts of a large and socially differentiated settled community, comprising a number of newly developed social classes (priests, kings, merchants, peasants), into an orderly relationship to each other, and simultaneously to suggest the play through all of a higher, all-suffusing, all-informing, energizing principle."[2] Each of the emerging civilizations was to develop a profoundly felt psychological and sociological need to establish an earthly order of coordinated wills. The civilizations of the ancient world developed a rigid pecking order of privilege and power—on earth as they conceived it to be in heaven. This system worked to put everyone in his place, and keep him there. It created the stability as well as the energy required for the development of culture and high achievement. The Egyptian term for this order was *Ma'at*. Egypt was a kingdom capable of supporting the ambitious building programs of its rulers and the luxurious life of its upper classes, while most of its workforce had to accept a standard of life at near subsistence level in order for it to do so.

What worked for Egypt worked for all the ancient empires. All of them used the same basic system and held to the same basic cosmology. Their social systems were constructed on the idea that the gods created some human beings to enjoy a greater measure of wealth, power, social standing or status, and privilege than others. Some had been chosen to rule over earthly societies as the agent of the sponsoring god. Indeed, it was assumed that the gods had created a pyramidal order for human life in which everyone had a natural and divinely appointed place in society, graded in value on a scale beginning with the single ruler at the top and descending with increasing numbers until the vast majority of peasants and then slaves formed the large foundational bottom. The reason the gods had arranged earthly society in this pyramidal form was readily apparent. Later in the medieval and Renaissance periods of Europe, nation-states would urge monarchial theories of the divine right to rule and develop rationalizations about the divine placement of people in social ranks. To this day the royal coat of arms in England states the claim, in the Norman French spoken by Henry VII who placed them there: "By God and My Right." The ancient system was even more powerfully fixed as the natural order of things. Far more. The rigidly fixed order of the hierarchical civilizations as a cosmological reality. There was no more people could do about their stations in life than they could do about the gods. The social order of civilizations was arranged to imitate the heavenly order, that is, it was assumed that the heavens were arranged in a pyramidal social order. That is why the religious architecture of these new civilizations uniformly employed the ziggurat. The architecture formed an image of the heavenly order to be worshiped and imitated by the earthly order, the hierarchical shape of the pyramid.

To the people of the ancient world it was obvious that a particular person was the ruler because the most powerful of the gods of that civilization, the chief god residing in the temple, had chosen to sponsor him in the position which matched that god's own in the celestial sphere. There would be an established mythology of creation in which a god became chief of the heavens, usually by defeating the forces of chaos, perhaps having to exert the coercive power of violence over other challenging gods as well. From time to time the more powerful gods found it necessary to discipline the lesser gods, keeping them in their place. The chief god in heaven was the most powerful god in terms understood by a world ruled by empires: the ability to defeat any takers with greater violence than they could marshal and to rule subjects through compulsion. This established the order of the cosmos, with lesser gods granted their place in the heavens.

The order of the earthly civilization was established and secured derivatively by the warrior god's human representative, usually termed king or queen, through armed power and proper administration of the kingdom. Its central institution, the temple, was patterned after the heavenly prototype in celebration of the origins, that is, of the defeat of chaos in the process of the creation of the universe and the cosmic ordering of things. The head of the temple and ruler of the kingdom derived his or her position from the decree lodged in the original ordering of creation. In many civilizations the ruler was thought to participate in the divinity, to be the human equivalent and manifestation of the sponsoring god. It was not uncommon for the divine attributes to be assigned to the ruler.

The next most powerful god in the heavenly pyramidal order chose the next most important person on the social ladder. This god was worshiped by that person and his followers as their personal god, and was second in social appreciation and religious worship only to the chief god of the temple. So the pattern went on down the scale that ordered human society. Such lesser gods often were given special attributes and spheres of power and responsibility, and thus many people on different levels of society might turn to them in prayerful need, much as today some Christians pray to certain saints who are considered patrons of certain causes. At any rate, the least and weakest god of all, obviously, was the personal god of slaves. Such lowly gods would not be found in the official temples at all, but were relegated to the households of humble worshipers, unnoticed by other people and, it was presumed, by other gods.

The order over which the ruler presided was thus conceived as one grounded in the essential nature of reality. In the case of Egypt, which for a long time was recognized as the most powerful kingdom on earth, the god of the Pharaoh was widely recognized as the highest god in all the heavens. Certainly, the Egyptians made the claim that their god was more powerful than the chief gods of other lesser empires. Few were in position to argue, even while devotedly worshiping the gods who had chosen them.

Moses was given a radically different vision, and had the courage to act on it. Scripture tells us that he was raised with the status and privilege of an Egyptian prince and knew all the rules of the cosmos. Whether or not the burning bush is metaphorical, the new vision this exiled man received about the true ordering of the cosmos and the hegemony of the god of the Hebrew slaves was so radical, so improbable, so unique, so unimaginable, that it can be deemed miraculous that it came to him in any fashion. The motivation to carry this vision out in the face of the empire, and the heavenly sponsorship of the empire, had to have a source Moses accredited as genuinely divine.

Moses heard the call of Yahweh and looked across the wilderness toward Egypt. There was residing in the capital city temple the chief deity, the absolute sovereign, whose rule was administered by the Pharaoh. Moses knew the Pharaoh's power and authority, affirmed by the assignment of divine attributes of his patron god and having an unending stratum of officials dependent on his rule for their position and welfare. Indeed, each of them had a sponsoring god who was dependent on the Pharaoh's sponsoring god, or all would collapse. Essential to social harmony was the obedience and acquiescence of all individuals in a given society, their acceptance of the station in life assigned to them by the gods. The hierarchy of power and authority on earth reflected the hierarchy established and accepted by the gods in heaven. There would be no sympathy to be found in anyone of that society for his demand to let slaves go free.

But God had decided to reveal a new plan for the human family. This was not simply revolutionary in the sense of the American or the French or the Communist Revolutions. This stood heaven and earth on its head. It was a far more revolutionary discovery than when Columbus proved that the earth was round and discovered a "new" world, a more vastly changed vision of the cosmos than twentieth-century pictures of earth from outer space. The god of slaves proved to be more powerful than the god of Pharaoh! It would be several centuries before Israel became monotheistic, that is, before the religious genius of this special community would grasp that the God of Moses was the one God who was real and that there were no other gods. Nevertheless, the God who would choose slaves to manifest sovereignty on earth was immediately acknowledged by them as the Almighty God who rules heaven and earth, the one capable of overcoming the all-powerful gods of the mightiest kingdom on earth.

The contrast of the old gods with the new God was stunning. Here was a God whose power was supreme but whose cause was the welfare of the lowliest human creature. Here was a God who could rule all forces but who could care less about the power or the influence, the pedigree or the standing of those chosen to represent that god's sovereignty, purpose, and divine life to the world. Here was a God whose slightest whim could yield immediate effect but whose compassion demanded justice beyond that which human society countenanced, for in this Exodus event the God of Moses condemned religious and social systems which were founded on special privilege, as well as class systems, for the structuring of human society.

Soon the community this God called into being came to a stunning realization: every individual within the community, without regard for any personal characteristics, achievements, or standing, was loved for who that person was, and loved so profoundly that there could be no comparison with any other person. Furthermore, each individual, however humble or worthy, was to be treated by the community of God with the dignity and respect God personally has for them, with no room for any form of oppression or exploitation. Everyone was to be treated this way because this is the way God treats everyone: graciously. The idea that God treats people not as they deserve or as their worldly accomplishments might seem to merit was a great shock, one that has never been fully absorbed, a revelation that it seems will never be perfectly apprehended. Even so, through the centuries the People of God have continually recognized God's gracious activity in the rescue and redemption of the oppressed of all ages. In that recognition they have been grasped by the meaning of being called to the community of faith.

## THE ROOTS OF GOD'S NEW PLAN FOR HUMAN SOCIETY

It is now time to pause and acknowledge that the ancient picture of the relations between heaven and earth is somewhat more complicated and diverse than is being drawn here, especially in the more rural and isolated areas where civilization was not so highly developed. This is, perhaps, due at least in part to the conservative nature of religion, and of all human efforts, toward progress. Paganism was a religion of civilization, a society that needed subtle, careful, and stable ordering. The religious and social views that had grown out of the older and more primitive societies that were organized in clans and tribes continued, especially in those social forms, to differ rather sharply from the advanced societies of the highly centralized city-states. As we remember that not all of the world was urban and civilized and thus consider the differences in the view of the cosmos held by less civilized peoples, the point must be remembered that the ancient world was not sufficiently complicated to take away from the impact the Exodus had on its commonly held view of reality.

Even so, the probability is that the new vision which came so forcefully to Moses, however new and radical it may have been for one raised in Egypt, was probably not so much new as recovered and reformed. It would have been rooted in the older tribal traditions in contrast to the newer traditions of civilization, and this finally brings us back to the beginning of the story of the Hebrews and the promises mentioned by Mary. In a sense it seems that Moses was called to return conceptually to the distant origins of the ancestral faith held to by the slaves he was sent to rescue, the faith of a wandering Aramean.

The arts of grain agriculture and stockbreeding, which are the basic forms of economy supporting the emergence of non-nomadic civilizations, seem to have made their first appearance in the Near East somewhere between 7500 and 4500 B.C. As we have seen, the religious and social view of the archaic civilizations started in Sumeria in 3200 B.C. In between, the pattern of belief that developed can be loosely described as based on the relationship of the clan to a patron god. The clan, or tribe, related to its deity in an intimate way that created a close bond and this was paramount. The god of the clan or tribe was especially identified with ancestors and the relationship was founded primarily in the experiences of the clan. As opposed to the god of the Pharaoh, who was more oriented to a perpetual dynasty and to the sacred land of Egypt, the tribal god was oriented to the tribal history: the way it contained and civilized internal violence, the victories it won under the leadership of its patron god, the way it faced defeats and therein responded to its call back to the ways of its patron god, its learnings about human interrelationships and how to live together in the clan and its constituent families, its migrations, its new green pastures, its expansion. The tribal and household god was worshiped as the source of peace, prosperity, health, and progeny.

Does this not sound like the relationship between Abraham and the god who required faith while promising vast generations of heirs to come? Does this not describe the sort of understanding we find in Genesis about the relationship between the growing clan of Isaac and Jacob and their special deity? Then, in what strikes me as the best novel ever written, a ruling kinsman offers them a place in civilization to save them from famine. How it happens we do not know, but when we next see this clan they have grown into the twelve tribes that stem from the brothers who went down into Egypt under Joseph's protection and sank into slavery.

Scripture opens in the first two chapters of Genesis with the beautiful and sweeping story of creation, related in two versions, and then proceeds to explain the fall in a grand myth. The next ten chapters describe the start, growth, and spread of human sin. It is interesting to note that this fundamental scriptural understanding of sin is told almost entirely in terms of violence. Sexual violations can be read into the stories, but it requires psychological and mythological sophistication. In fact, little is said about sex or greed or any lesser action than the use of violence to intimidate, harm, or kill. There is inference about what lies beneath the surface and serves as emotional motivation—jealousy, fear, revenge, self-righteousness, racism—but once sin takes off, the action is almost entirely that of violence. It begins with murder, the killing of a brother, continues with clan vengeance as a policing instrument, relates God's own attempt at using violence as a solution to the problems of sin by flooding the world to start all over with the family of one relatively righteous man and the animals of creation—concluding with the covenant of peace between God and humanity—and finally tells the story of the Tower of Babel. This last is a story about the climax of sin's power and pervasive spread in all areas of human life.

There are many nuances to the story about civilization's attempt to build a tower that would reach to the heavens. It shows sin in even the highest and most well intended efforts of advanced civilization. It is not a statement of disapproval of the diversity of races, languages, and cultures. Indeed, there is a previous mention of these differences (Gen 10), with no prejudice implied. Instead, the story of the attempt to build a great tower to the heavens serves to recognize that the many cultures and languages and peoples have become not only the occasion for diversity but for divisions among the peoples of the earth. It laments humanity's inability to genuinely communicate, to enjoy a united community within the fullness of its body, to cooperate in civilized achievement for the common good. People are scattered to live separately as rivaling races, in competing nations, holding to languages and cultures that distinguish us from one another and divide rather than bestow us with cause to celebrate our diversity. We know what divisions and differences lead to: prejudice, conflict, war, empire building, and oppression. The story of the spread of sin ends with a world order based on privilege, status, coercive might, and wealth.

Thus the Bible offers us a picture of reality, a picture of the way things are. At this point, the story begins to turn and the rest of Scripture tells the gradually unfolding story of the redemption of this human predicament. It is a story of the People of God, who struggle to live in this world under the reign of God. It is not a straight and unwavering pathway; there is much backsliding and getting lost. Nevertheless, the development is relatively clear and direct. The story of the Tower of Babel is not to be resolved directly until the Pentecost story reverses the impact of the world's "babbling." There, instead of failing to communicate and causing disunity throughout the world, the sounds of the inspired who have been brought into touch with the transcendent can be understood by everyone from everywhere and the apostles of the resurrected Christ are sent into all the world with the uniting message of God's good news. It is, however, immediately following the story of the tower that the story begins to turn and tell about God's actions to redeem the world.

The next story is Abraham's. That story is the turning point. When the lens of Scripture looks away from the Tower of Babel the next scene on which it focuses shows the family of Abram, as he was known in the pagan city, leaving Ur. Its religious tower, the Temple of the Moon, constructed at the highest point in the city, is fading into the distance.

Ur was a sister city to Sumaria between the Tigris and Euphrates and, of course, had established the religion of the Fertile Crescent. It was this pagan religion that was symbolized by the pyramidal tower reaching toward the sky in the prideful assumption the life of the heavens could be imitated. In an act of faith that is breathtaking, Abraham and his family responded to the call of a new god to reject the religious ways of civilized paganism and seek a more primitive wilderness in which to establish a new clan and a new people. This people would enjoy a special intimacy with the newly encountered god who called him forth and they would be blessed in very special ways. They would be a great nation and "in you all the families of the earth shall be blessed" (Gen 12:3b).

The promise of God to Abraham and his children not only laid the foundation for that of the Exodus; fundamentally, it is the same promise. In each case, there is a promise to form a people with whom God would enter into a special relationship, a people to be God's agent in overturning the common understanding of the way things are and the way the universe works, a people who would eventually establish a revolutionary new cosmology and reveal God's new plan for human society. Abraham even was to do away with the commonly accepted violence of human sacrifice. God called Abraham out to overturn the order of human society based on the luck and the resources and the opportunities and the clout of all sorts that allows some people to "lord it over" others. This revelation was a long way off at the time of Abraham. Only in the light of the Exodus experience could the People of God truly comprehend who they were and what their role was to be in history. Only after experiencing the identity of slaves who get rescued could the children of Abraham make the full connections with the early legends of their beginning, with the movement out of Ur into a comparatively barren land without the benefits of progress and civilization, with the disturbing stories of Isaac and Jacob and a family's wrestling with one another and God, with the betrayal of Joseph, and with his forgiveness, which rescues them by bringing them down into Egypt where they become slaves. Only after the Exodus can there be clarity about the promises to Abraham and his children about which Mary sings.

That is why the scriptural accounts maintain the importance of the connection between the Exodus and their ancestral beginnings. God spoke to Moses and charged him to introduce himself thus: "The LORD [Yahweh], the God of your fathers, the God of Abraham, the God of Isaac, and the God of Jacob, has sent me to you" (Ex 3:15). Again, Moses was instructed to deliver the people of Israel with the declaration to them, "I am the LORD. I appeared to Abraham, to Isaac, and to Jacob....And I will bring you into the land which I swore to give to Abraham, to Isaac, and to Jacob..." (Ex 6:2a, 6:8a). Scholars are in agreement that the Exodus event created the new community that we know as the People of God, but it is likewise clear that God prepared this birthing for hundreds of years. It is no wonder that the generations to follow have been able to discern the parts of a divine plan running through and guiding all of history.

Of the many insights and lasting concepts that have come out of the Abraham story there is one on which we must take the opportunity to elaborate, a historical perspective to which we have made reference several times. An appropriate expression of the Exodus community's purpose was found in the perspective that regards history as being moved purposefully by God toward that final goal. That goal is termed the *eschaton*, a Greek word referring to the end things, and theology concerning with the *eschaton* is termed eschatology. This is a revolutionary and peculiarly Jewish concept. It is widely assumed that it arose out of the attempt to understand the movement of Abraham and his acceptance of a very tough personal road in hopeful anticipation of a future for the generations to come. He would share in their promised blessings in anticipation, for he knew very well that he would be dead long before his children could become a great nation. It would seem that his faith was such that he could trust in the fulfillment of God's promises and postpone that fulfillment to a future, even a future in which he would not be alive. The satisfaction he personally received was in his contribution to that future fulfillment of others. He shared in that, even though he would be dead to it. Obviously, this gave him tremendous satisfaction and special meaning to his life.

There are three things here to be noted and appreciated about this new philosophy of history. First, Abraham's grasp of the corporate nature of reality allowed him to identify with the community that would experience the blessing promised. Again, this identification was profound and personally satisfying, even before the actualization.

Because he identified with the community to come, the future community for whom the fulfillment would be a concrete experience, the work of his life was given meaning far beyond his personal experience. This is a perspective the church within our Western society needs to recapture.

The second shift in our understanding of history is that it is open-ended. Abraham was free to make choices and to do something new. He could not know what was going to come of his choices for he realized that he could not control the future, however profoundly he had faith in God's general promises. Still, he could not know what would come of his free choice decisions. Abraham never felt coerced. God called, God asked, God directed, but the man himself always was free to make the choices. No stars and no fate dictated his life. The future toward which he moved had never happened before and he had to discover and invent his own way. For all of these reasons the future held promise for Abraham. He moved into it with the vigor and enthusiasm of a free person.

The third matter has to do with the concept or philosophy of time. Heretofore, the nations of the known world saw reality as cyclical, moving in a circular pattern they called history, but a history that wasn't going anywhere. The best example may be the seasons of the year. Year in and year out the seasons are basically the same. That is natural and that is life. Things are fixed; that view feels like fate; fate seems to rule. Everything that has been comes around again. If we contemplate this enough we can grow serene, accept our particular lot, and get in tune with the larger patterns of the beauty and goodness of nature as the gift of creation. Another example of the cyclical view of history and time is seen in the Chinese calendar, in which the patterns of the years are simply repeated in unvarying succession. The cultural examples we have been examining, the Sumerian and Egyptian, demonstrate the point: study the steady pattern of the stars, for the heavens have plotted the life of earth from all eternity; imitate what has already been decided by predicting it and thus accommodate ourselves to our fates.

The meaning of life in a cyclical pattern of history is to be discovered contemplatively. One finds personal fulfillment in resignation to the pattern of nature and in giving oneself to it as an integral and participating part. For most of the ancient world and large parts of the world today time is problematic and terrifying because it changes, it is passing. The goal for many people, like the Greeks and most of the pagan world of antiquity, is to escape the law of change. Time enforces that law. Time, and therefore history, is the most terrifying feature of life. Reconciliation is to be found in contemplation. The message in several of the cultures that maintain the cyclical view of history, and founded in their respective religions, is to practice a form of contemplation, "do not act, but sit." In contemplation one can discover resignation and realize the illusions of time and space. In the contemplation of all that is as passing one can absorb and be absorbed by the unchanging pattern which escapes the law of change and enables the contemplative to come to peace with the cycle of time, with one's own passing, and with the passing of all things.

This was almost universally the concept of time and history until the Exodus community of the chosen people began to express its point of view, beginning with an understanding of Abraham's journey and their story as a people traveling from Ur and settling in the Promised Land, then down to Egypt, and finally, having wandered in the wilderness, to reenter the Promised Land. Things come round in time, but history can no longer be merely a circle, a snake eating its own tail. History, beginning with Abraham, is a journey. History is pictured on a line; it is linear. For the Jew, history is headed somewhere. The goal toward which our lives are offered on the grand journey of the whole People of God makes the life of each person and each generation meaningful and worthwhile wherever on the journey our part takes place. The future is open; it belongs to God who makes things new. Unlike the Greek prejudice toward change and decay, the Hebrew did not consider change something to be dreaded and avoided, something that partook of death and was as unavoidably unfortunate. The Jew knew that change is a two-edged sword, for it was change that took them from slavery in Egyptian society. Change, something new, can be good and creative. From the roots of the Exodus wandering Jews came to see themselves as a pilgrim people. The long history they faced, a history of exile and oppression and Diaspora, only caused Jews and then Christians and therefore all Westerners to embrace this worldview and hold to it with the tenacity born of prolonged experience.

## THE ATTEMPT TO ESTABLISH GOD'S NEW PLAN IN ISRAEL

God graciously initiated the action of deliverance that we are referring to as the Exodus event. However, it is important to note that Israel responded. They were willing to make a serious effort to form their life in accordance with their new identity and purpose, that is, in accordance with that which they were called to be as a community. It is of tremendous theological importance that the Hebrew slaves, as well as Moses, were open to the divine initiative of God's grace. They recognized their condition: they knew their need for a savior. "And the people of Israel groaned under their bondage, and cried out for help, and their cry under bondage came up to God. And God heard their groaning" (Ex 2:23b–24a). "And God said to Moses, 'I have heard the groaning of the people of Israel'" (Ex 6:5). These slaves stood in direct contrast to those whose worldly privileges gave them a sense of self-sufficiency and falsely led them to assume that their privileges were divine blessings.

It is clear what the Exodus event meant to the people who entered into a covenant with God. We witness the birth of a dynamic notion of community, conceived by a people trying to discern the meaning of their divine deliverance from bondage and mediocrity into freedom and a call to universal importance in God's plan for all people and all nations. As time goes on we may add to the list of miracles for which they seek meaning the very continuance of their existence against all odds. Every time they stopped to consider these matters they found it all a little mind-boggling, and thus so was their incredible effort to form the kind of community that would stand, in effect, as a confession of heavenly rescue. They sought to give expression to that confession in forms of worship and community structures. Only a community response of righteousness and justice would maintain the life God had given them as a people, and serve to fulfill their purpose for the world.

The early Yahwistic community moving into the Promised Land and starting to create a society under God's reign had a terribly forbidding job. They were idealistic to the extreme at their best moments, but of course those were relatively few and far between. This was real life, as you and I know it and under circumstances difficult beyond our ken. They were not establishing Camelot. Theirs was the dangerous, tough, grueling labor of colonizing hostile territory. This was the intellectually and emotionally trying effort to form a new nation with a constitution and a united purpose without resources and in a harsh and antagonistic environment. This was an attempt to invent an entirely new way of being a people, a nation, and making it work. Neither the American Revolution nor any other in modern Western history was ever so tough and unpromising. The people murmured. The people rebelled. The people apostatized. The people adapted to Ba'alistic and syncretistic religious ways. The people were every bit as disappointing, difficult, cowardly, and complaining as any leadership, including the magnificent Moses and his chosen successors, could have called forth. There was all of the same human frailty and historical ambiguity that characterizes any human community. Yet they persisted and we still have the legacy. The description of the effort undertaken to establish the covenant community in the Promised Land is idealistic in that the people could not live up to the standard they themselves set, in their worship, in their songs, in their literature and sacred writings, and in their laws and structures. Trying to live according to the early Yahwistic ideals the People of God began a journey still underway. Once arrival is achieved the Promised Land could be recognized as the place where we started. What is remarkable is that such a unique notion of community could not only survive, but also develop and challenge us to this day as the standard.

It is supposed that the slaves who came to be known as Hebrews left Egypt sometime in the middle of the thirteenth century B.C. and that the first king was appointed in 1029 B.C. In that period of time (roughly, 1250–1029 B.C.) the people of Israel wandered for years in the wilderness, fought their way into the Promised Land, formed a league of tribes, and established themselves as the dominant people of the area. Finally, after about two centuries the Jews occupied most of the Promised Land. In that regard we should remind ourselves that the conquest of the Promised Land was more a process of occupation than a military onslaught and uniform settlement. The various tribes moved in with separate actions and different levels of success, grabbing pockets of land where they could, much as settlers of the American frontier moved into land held by Native Americans and claimed entire areas as though it was in their total control. Large Canaanite settlements retained their independence, and everyone intermingled, engaged in trade, intermarried, and fell into all of the other usual courses of interaction. Certainly each picked up the other's ways. Ba'alist religious influences (Ba'al was employed as a general term to refer to the various tribal gods of the Canaanite peoples) lasted well into the period of the Israelite kingdom and the same was true of legal and social influences. One can imagine the pressures and temptations of living in a world in which slavery and the exploitation of others were unquestioned components of the various economic systems, in which there was the constant threat from strong neighbors and empires, in which one was susceptible to the normal human desires that foster oppression, exploitation, and inequality in any society.

Under these most difficult of circumstances an incredible and unprecedented effort was made to create a society based on the new understanding of God and God's purpose for them. The purpose was no less than the redemption and restoration of the entire created order. Israel was to lead the way toward this in-breaking of a divine order into the imperfect structures of this world, which they termed *shalom*. *Shalom* describes the cosmic harmony that would exist if the world and all its inhabitants were reconciled with God and with one another. In Israel's tradition it spoke of harmony, peace, justice, righteousness, and prosperity all taken together. Of course, no human society or human effort was imagined capable of accomplishing this: it was to come eschatologically, that is, history was to unfold purposefully toward God's final goal for creation, especially for the human family. Israel was to lead the way by forming a society that lived out the ideal of *shalom* as much as humanly possible. The ideals for such a society emerged and became indelibly implanted in Israel's faith during its formative period in a tribal federation often termed "the League" or "the Judges."

Perhaps the first feature of this "nation" that an independent observer, such as an enemy, would have noted is that it had no centralized form of government and no ongoing leader. This was a community that did not trust kingship or kingdom, or anything smacking of them. Yahweh was the one and only king. No one could rule in the place of God, and no one could be granted a place of prominence over others. There could be no social hierarchy, no pyramid of privilege and reliance, of dominance and enforced service. They knew that if they had a king and a form of hierarchical government they would soon mimic the other kingdoms of the world; in no time there would be slaves. This was anathema. Consequently the early Israelite tribal community relied on God to provide leadership from ordinary citizens when and where it was needed. When a time of crisis arose, whether it was an internal conflict or a threat from outside, the Spirit of God would come upon someone and call that person to lead the people through that crisis. The system seemed to function like the desert judges of the time of Moses and so these temporary leaders were called judges. The inspired "judge" would then relinquish leadership when the crisis that demanded leadership had been quelled.

The overall scheme for expression of the notion of community to which they felt called, the dominant pattern, was based on *imitatio Dei*: acting toward one another and other peoples as God had acted toward them. Reminiscent perhaps of the way pagan societies felt that they should imitate the heavenly order and designs as best they could discern them, Israel felt that it was in imitation of the true God's righteous action and compassion that they were to live as a new nation. They believed they should create a community of holiness such as would befit the holy presence of their God. The People of God should reflect the inner life and actions of God. This imitation would, of course, reflect the compassionate righteousness of God's justice as it had been manifested in the Exodus. God's justice required carefully constructed systems, structures, and institutions of law. It was necessary to manifest God's nature in government and law as well as in religious observances; otherwise the observances would be empty hypocrisy.

Early Israel was powerfully motivated to create a community patterned after *imitatio Dei* by their conviction that any possibility of a future depended on God's presence abiding with the new community. They had the assurance of God's initiating grace, of God's covenant promise, and of God's utterly trustworthy and steadfast faithfulness. Yet Israel realized its obligation to maintain the people's end of the covenant by fidelity to the new order of life that had been revealed. The people knew they could rely on God's grace and faithfulness, but a hard-hearted response was a repudiation of God's covenant with them and insulting to God's nature. Being called to be God's people required a response that was in keeping with the righteousness and compassion of God. If the people would remain faithful to the covenant, the blessings of God would be fulfilled. If the people were not faithful to the covenant God could not remain with them. Consequently, the desire to insure God's continual and continuing presence in their midst was paramount. They did not believe they could survive as a nation and as a people without God's abiding presence, and in such a case what sort of nation would they be anyway? They had come to understand their dependence on the divine savior who had delivered them from slavery and sustained their life together. The community could be confident in God being with them only if the life they created was a reflection of God's nature and in keeping with the Exodus experience, especially of God's compassionate justice. The God of the Exodus would not look on injustice with indifference but would take action with decisive intervention.

The third motivation for creating social structures according to the pattern of *imitatio Dei* was to manifest God's presence in holiness, majesty, and glory to the rest of the world. They were to represent God to the world, and they were to represent the world to God. This approached an understanding that they had become "sacramental," the earthly link between God and the rest of the world.

Delivered Israel knew all the more clearly its call to fulfill the Abrahamic promise of being a blessing to all nations. This was a people who felt drawn into the universal purposes of God. God's causes were their causes; that is why they existed. What had started with them was to be spread to all people. They saw the need for the redemption of the world clearly enough, and they recognized their role in it. Thus was Israel to portray God's justice to those falling outside its orbit of protection, thus was it to maintain a compassionate openness and offer hospitality to all peoples who entered its territories, thus were its Sabbath "prayers of the faithful" offered on behalf of the whole world. Very early, Israel saw itself as "a light to the nations, a city set upon a hill." The society Israel formed had to contrast with those of pagan societies. No one could exercise leadership, no one could hold power, no one could enjoy wealth and privilege that "lorded it" over another, for they all shared a lowly common heritage as freed slaves.

We should not see in these desires any hint of controversies to come much later in Christianity, especially regarding the Protestant Reformation's conflict over "salvation by grace alone," "faith" versus "works," or "law" versus "gospel." Any such comparison is irrelevant because these early peoples had no concept of individualistic salvation such as drove these questions during the Renaissance. Israel could have imagined only communal salvation, and thus its effort was devoted to the establishment of community structures, laws, and worship. We will find no evidence of personal righteousness being offered as the basis on which the mortal sought to prove worthiness to God, though the psalms lament the derision of society for the righteous. The *imitatio Dei*, the reliance on God's faithful and continuous presence, and the "light to the nations" were not postures to save self. Rather, Israel acted out a response of gratitude. They also understood sin and thus they comprehended how it is not only individual, not only a matter of personal choices, but it is also corporate. The Lutheran bishop and renowned biblical scholar Krister Stendahl has pointed out that the Bible generally does not reflect the inward concerns about righteousness and salvation posed by the "introspective consciousness of the West."[3] Early Israel grasped how sin was rooted in the failures of society to form just structures and equal opportunities. All of this was manifest in community actions: the building of communal structures, institutions, and laws befitting the People of God. They were directed outward in dedication to the construction of a community in which the compassionate justice of God would be lived out on earth, enjoyed by those under its law, and manifested to all.

Early Israel tried to establish an organic or concrete and living connection between the Exodus event and its communal structures. That connection could not be preserved solely by abstract confessions of belief, communal or individual. Biblical faith has always reacted against attempts to spiritualize religion out of the everyday realm of communal life and individual behavior. Beginning with the Exodus event and proceeding through the incarnation, the paschal mysteries, and the varied experience of the church, any such spiritualization has been deemed contradictory to faith in the good news first encountered in the divine deliverance of the oppressed from Egypt. The careful attention of the Hebrew Scripture to law is seen in its persistent recognition of the way the social structures that affect everyday life are a religious concern of the first importance. Such attention was necessary for those who experienced this deliverance and they developed a society inextricably committed to systems of justice, land distribution, use of capital, and treatment of vulnerable classes—institutions implicit in the nature of the God revealed to the liberated.

Israel became a community of faith in all parts of its communal life, seeking to embody divine righteousness and compassion in every facet of life. Religion became a way of life—for the first time in the societies of civilization. This began with community forms of worship. The primary center of worship and of cultic activity was at Shiloh, where the ark was placed. There and in other sites, they rehearsed the redemption drama of the Exodus, celebrated God's presence among them, and offered their sacrifices and offerings as signs of their commitment to the covenant and to their origins. The religious institutions of early Israel did their job in satisfying the spiritual and religious needs of the people.

The Jewish people were given ample opportunity to enter into the sacred time of the origins and to move out of the terrifying time of history. They were put in touch with the whole and with the mystery of the transcendent. Ingrained in the fundamental religious understanding of these people was the grasp of the unbreakable connection between worship and mission. Worship was not limited to cultic activities. The community forms of worship and sacrifice were designed to express and inspire the vocation and the life of the people. Their entire lives were to be a worshipful response to God. So constant and pervasive was the call to worship, not only in the cultic activities but also in everything making up the community life—especially in those systems and structures showing forth the righteousness and compassion of God—that they believed they were called to be "a priestly kingdom and a holy nation" (Ex 19:6a).

It should be helpful to examine some of the concrete features of the society early Israel developed in order to grasp the pattern of life they desired to create. In order to do so we may turn to the Book of the Covenant, the earliest codification of law preserved in the Bible, and consider for our example their intentions regarding the most vulnerable people in society. We see here the Hebrew law in a rough-hewn stage of development. It is very much a mixed bag of newly codified efforts to instill the Yahwistic ideals of the Hebraic League together with the laws and customs of the people of the Near Eastern culture within which they found themselves.

The scattered tribes of the League naturally borrowed from the laws and customs that governed those around them, especially from the Code of Hammurabi. Consequently we are offered two very different blocks of law within the Book of the Covenant. Paul Hanson, in his fine analysis of this work, distinguishes them as a set of case laws in Exodus 21:1–22:16 and a set of codified Yahwistic laws in Exodus 20:22–26 and 22:17–23:19.[4] The case laws are typical of those found in Mesopotamia from the third millennium on down. They are far more harsh and reflective of the privileged and hierarchical ordering of pagan societies. For example, males were treated far more generously than females, slaves were treated worse than free persons, and the poor were allowed to fall through the cracks of society. Even then, there are many reforms made in this section of the Book of the Covenant. For example, in Exodus 21:23–25 we find the famous, and so often misused, lex talonis: "If any harm follows, then you shall give life for life, eye for eye, tooth for tooth, hand for hand, foot for foot, burn for burn, wound for wound, stripe for stripe." Since the most primitive of times the "law" relied far less on a "police force" or on a judicial and penal system of justice than on a system in which tribes, clans, or families would be expected to exact vengeance for a wrong done to its members. Especially since the retaliation was often much greater than the offense, sometimes massively greater, the law hoped the threat of clan vengeance would exercise a deterrent effect. One of the early Hebraic reforms seen here was to abolish the system of revenge and limit clan punishment to the scale of the offense: "an eye for an eye."

However, the second set of laws resonates with a life and culture arising out of the memory of a people delivered, and seeks to institute structures supportive of the divine sense of justice, that is, justice which meets the highest standards of compassion and righteousness. Just as God's initiative sought out the vulnerable, weak, and oppressed in order to raise them up, so these laws look after the poor, the debtor, the widow, the orphan, and those without the rights and protections of citizenship. Let us take three brief but telling examples.

*The Ger.* This important Hebrew word is often translated as "sojourner in the land," or "stranger." Today, the best translation might be "alien." This is the person who lacks the status of citizenship, and all afforded by that status. Even today no class is more vulnerable. In the ancient world the vulnerability was far greater. Sojourning peoples could easily become victims of indebtedness and fall into slavery, for there were no social "safety nets." Without an inheritance, without the protection of an extended clan and family, and serving as the source of the cheap labor needed to make most ancient societies viable, the *ger* was easy to take advantage of and constantly threatened with economic, physical, and spiritual ruin. In Exodus 23:9 the law of this new society offers its protection: "You shall not oppress a *ger*; you know the heart of a *ger*, for you were *ger* in the land of Egypt." The law was not based on some rational principle but on empathy. Nor was the empathy based on some rational principle but on experience. Israel's memory of its past forces it to a kind of understanding born of identification with the fellow human being's predicament. The Hebrew word for "know" (*yd*) is used to indicate the deeply personal knowledge derived from the most intimate involvement with the other person, often used in Scripture to refer to sexual knowledge. The Hebrew word for "heart" (*nepes*) refers to the "essential being" of a person. The commandment could be translated as "You know as you experience your very own identity what it is to be an alien, for that is what you were in Egypt." So, the compassion that God showed to Israel when it was *ger* is to be shown to others when in their land. It is as if the law were declaring, "There but for the grace of God go you. Treat these aliens like God treated you."

*The Widows and Orphans:* From the most primitive of times widows and orphans, especially female orphans, were among the most vulnerable of people. Married women depended entirely on the household of their husband and his heirs. A wife had status in his family only as his wife. An unmarried woman had only her own family, if they could and would afford her. If widowed, a woman was thrust into an ambivalent and insecure space between clans, without claim to inheritance. She was usually considered a liability. If she had no adult children, or if they rejected her, she and her children were homeless. But this was not to be so in the new society of God's people. The Book of the Covenant provided widows and orphans with protection that was both dynamic and concrete by making their well-being the responsibility of the whole community. The tables would be turned on anyone who violated the law by exploiting widows or orphans.

*The Poor:* The poor were the most obviously vulnerable class, living on the borderline between bare subsistence and catastrophe. In no time the poor person could spiral from indebtedness into compounding interest, then loss of property, and finally the bondage of serfdom or even slavery. This was not to be so in Israel. The law provided for the poor and tried to institute ways to help people avoid falling into poverty— or what worse could come. "The Yahwistic community's response to poverty was not limited to adjustments in existing legal structures. It began with the exposure of poverty as a phenomenon that by its very presence called the viability of the entire society into question. Poverty represented an assault on God's order."[5]

In addition to the Book of the Covenant we should make reference to the most radical example of the early Yahwistic attempt to express their ideals in the institutions of their society: the Jubilee Year. This was factored into the repeating cycles of ordinary time that was so important to the Jewish concepts of sanctified time and a healthy life. Each seventh day was the familiar Sabbath, the root concept for sabbatical. Every seventh year was a sabbatical year and it was to be observed in various ways that were very practical, such as demanding the good agricultural practice of periodically allowing the land to lie fallow. The seventh year of the seventh year would be the forty-ninth year, and this was seen as the completion of the Sabbath cycle. To begin the next cycle the entire social system of inheritance and indebtedness, which had built up over the forty-nine-year cycle, was to be wiped clean in order to start all over perfectly fresh. All debts were to be forgiven and all property was to be returned to the original owner. In such a system, no one could build a personal empire and equality of resources and opportunity was perpetuated.

There is more to the Jubilee Year than this brief description offers, but the reality is that there is no evidence that it was ever put into effect. The idea was evidently too radical even for this early Yahwistic community. It does, however, stand as eloquent testimony of the ideals held by this society, whose vision was formed by slaves.

We have examined the roots of the first covenant, often referred to by Christians as the old covenant, as the community of people who experienced the Exodus and began to develop a society based on that covenant as they understood it. When those roots have been neglected the Christian church has been subject to a host of demons. Among them we can count shallow theology, narrow sectarianism, privatized religiosity and amoral individualism, abandonment of social responsibility, disdain for the realm of nature, and anti-Semitism. Most to the point, we see Christianity reduced to a religious establishment happy to bless a social arrangement based on wealth, power, status, and privilege in exchange for its own share; we find Christians counting their blessings in terms of how much better off they are than others. It is now time to see the roots of the old and the new covenant come together in the songs of two mothers, Hannah and Mary.

# HANNAH'S SONG:
# The Meaning of Samuel's Life

Even as the story of Hannah and her child begins we see a constantly recurring symbol of the way the chosen people are identified with slavery. In this instance it portrays how this identity forms the prophetic voice. A barren Hebrew woman presents a slavish image. She was helpless, subject entirely to her master husband, and since she could not produce that which gave her worth (most especially a male) was of value only to the extent of the master's personal regard. The patriarchs were almost always born to such women. The mothers of the patriarchs are often rescued from their slavish condition only by God's grace. In this sense, the first prophet was to be "the son of a slave" who was dependent on God for deliverance. Hannah has been weeping year after year in longing for a son, suffering the ridicule of others and especially of her rival for her husband's affections, and will not be comforted by Elkanah's declaration that she is worth ten sons. But God surprises them. When she gives birth to Samuel, she fulfills the obligations of her prayer and offers him to the service of God under the priest Eli at Shiloh. At that occasion of Samuel's vocational dedication, Hannah is described as breaking into a song of prayer.

The themes of her song in praise of God are the Yahwistic ideals of early Israel. They emphasize the fact that God and the chosen people of God will never give up on these ideals, but that they will be fulfilled because no one is holy like the Lord and the Lord's will shall be done. She sees signs of the reversal of the way things are and of the shaping of the way things are going to be. The words and images are sharp and adamant. This will be!

The hymn articulates the construction of a society formed by a response to God's initiative to embrace the cause of the weak and guard against the powerful oppressor. Its poetry expresses the social vision of the freed slaves. It begins with praise of the holiness and majesty of God. It goes on to declare that the way of God will be the way of the world, for that is the will of the Holy One who is in charge. In this new order in which the tables are turned, the power of the mighty ("their bows") is broken and the feeble are empowered ("the weak are armored in strength"). Equality and the democratization of power are inevitable as the poor and needy are lifted up to rule. The song assures us that this order is in harmony with creation and the cosmic design, over which Yahweh reigns. The source of Israel's strength is God. Violence is no means to power. The lesson to be learned is summarized in the conclusion: "for not by might does one prevail."

For our vantage point, as well as that of the redactor or editor who shaped this story and recorded it in Scripture, the hymn is to be read in the light of what happened in the life of the child this song celebrates. In that light it becomes evident that Hannah's themes not only look back to what has been attempted but also affirm the faith that they will be fulfilled because the Lord wills it. These themes also portend those of the Hebrew prophets in their centuries-long struggle to convert the successive kings and the people of Israel to these ideals, to mold the Israeli monarchy into a kingdom expressive of the God who rescued them as slaves in Egypt, to shape a worshipful community of justice for the cause of the world's redemption.

The most obvious mark of Samuel's life is that he became the first prophet. Knowing this we can read into Hannah's song how the early ideals of the Yahwistic community, now under the guidance of Yahweh's prophets, would survive the dramatic compromise God's people made with necessity, move forth courageously into the new era of the kings, and prevail against any unexpected odds that came at them. Neither co-option nor resignation would characterize the prophetic response, especially to the new situation of a kingdom. The prophets would make sure that Israel would stay on the enlightened path for the faithful in which *shalom* would be the goal and the commitment of each generation would be the justice, righteousness, compassion, and true worship manifested in *shalom*.

The word prophet can be confusing as used in Hebrew Scripture. It is used rather randomly to refer to any number of people, kinds of office, practices, and claims. Nevertheless, there is recognition that reference to *the* prophets is a term of art. It refers to those definitive people called as God's own spokespersons in a recognized period beginning with Samuel and ending at a particular time when the age of the prophets came to an end. The beginning and the end of the age of the prophets is defined by the beginning and the end of the kingships of Israel. Almost all of those recognized as *the* prophets have written texts of their words recorded in Scripture.

Samuel's life, however, was to represent more than the inauguration of the prophetic tradition and this too is to be read into Hannah's song. This complex person was to be the last judge, the last person on whom the Spirit would descend to provide the inspiration for leadership through a crisis. It was when the people realized that the sons of Samuel were not of his caliber and would not be inspired for the role of a judge that they gave up and requested that this last judge appoint a king. In the same way in a later age to come the People of God would give up on the age of the prophets, which will seem to have passed. At this earlier point in their history Israel had to find a way to go forward without the charismatic leadership provided directly by the indwelling of God's Holy Spirit in one called "judge." With the passing of the age of the judges the people had to adapt to new realities. They had to have a way of governing and the only model they had was the dreaded kingdom.

It is important to note this. The People of God have the highest ideals and the faithful are called to give their lives to work for and toward the actualization of those ideals. Yet the faithful must live with the way things are and make the adaptations and compromises that are necessary on the path toward the fulfillment of the ideals. This is part of the dynamic of living both for God's cause of creation by learning to be at home in the world and for God's cause of the kingdom itself. The people of God have to make real and difficult choices all along the way that remain true to both causes, while seeking the ultimate satisfaction of each in the fulfillment of history. This it seems is God's will; certainly it is the way God suffers the process of creation, not imposing or coercing, always working with the realities, taking what is and shaping it in a process in which good comes out of anything, even the cross, for those who have the faith, patience, and imagination to see God's hand at work in the world.

When Mary turned to Hannah's song for her inspiration she did so not only because of the Yahwistic ideals and because of the prophetic tradition, but also with awareness that the ideals of both were yet to be completed. Luke no doubt records the Song of Mary with the final words of Jesus from the cross ringing in his ears: "It is fulfilled." Mary turns to Hannah's words in part because they address Israel's ability to accommodate to a process in which the people maintained confidence in the eventual accomplishment of their ideals, but not in their lifetime or in their situation. Though Jesus will perfect the ideals and "complete" them all—the law, the judges, the prophets, the cultic sacrificial system, wisdom—the cross was not the immediate materialization of the kingdom expected by so many, and, down deep and with real honesty, it is perhaps still disappointing and puzzling to many who claim to be people who follow the cross.

The human effort of the early Yahwistic community to live up to the highest of ideals as a holy nation, to live up to the standards of God, stands as one of the most heroic in all history. They could not do it. We know that early Israel failed to live up to its ideals. It failed to make the Yahwistic notion of community a concrete and historical reality. It came much closer than any other sustained effort in all of history, but even Israel began to recognize that the effort to give birth to *shalom* was one leading into a future climax of history, that the end of the story of their being rescued from slavery and called by God to the redemption of all people would have a different resolution. From this point the hopes and expectations of God's people took different shapes and drew on different images. Never did they, however, give up on these Yahwistic ideals. To this day their effort and the image they had of society forms our best picture of the kingdom of God. Nowhere is this stated more beautifully and confidently than in the texts of the songs of Hannah and Mary and through their careful interconnection.

The calling of Samuel to be the first prophet spelled the end of the effort to establish and live out the fullness of the Yahwistic ideals as they were forged in the early community of the League, for Samuel was the last judge. He gave up the last judgeship in order to become the first prophet and make way for the first king. There is no longer a need for the charismatically called judge once there is a king, but the need for the prophet becomes immediate. There is a sense in which we witness God granting authority over the kingship to the prophets, for it is the office of the prophet that is authorized to anoint the dreaded king. That king was Saul. It was prophetic genius that discerned that David should be anointed the next king. David's line leads directly to Jesus and it is the Davidic kingdom that becomes the model and new hope for the climax of history, the new eschatological vision of the Jewish people, nothing less than that of a kingdom—but God's.

Scripture depicts a dialogue taking place between Samuel, the people, and God, as the realities were forced upon Israel and had to be faced. God and the people came to the mutual understanding that it was going to be necessary to have a king and a kingdom. No matter how hard the people had tried, no matter how reluctant they were to give up their League, no matter how frightened they were of hierarchical rule, their survival was at stake. The Promised Land was in the cross routes of the increasing traffic of trade going east and west. Economic and political realities led them to realize that they could not depend on charismatic judges to resist the pressures from neighboring rivals. The tribes lost confidence in their ability to defend themselves within the governing structure of the League. Finally, they lost the holy ark in battle. The unstable condition was caused especially by the aggressiveness of the seagoing Greeks who had settled along the coastal towns of the area of the Promised Land and were showing determination to push inland. The Philistines had both iron and vastly advantageous iron-age technology. The Promised Land was, in fact, soon to be known around the world as Palestine, after the name of these people rather than the Israelites. The pressures of the situation demanded a new and centralized form of government and leadership. The federation of tribes had to unite. With the coming of Samuel the jig is up. That is why Hannah's song is recorded in Scripture.

The last thing this people wanted, a people who had been spawned by the deliverance from the oppressive rule of a king, a people whose faith demanded that they depend on God to protect them rather than on the might of a ruler who could oppress the people, the absolutely last alternative was to turn to a king. They knew that where there is a king, oppression and the epitome of oppression, slavery, could not be far behind. They knew what all of this meant in terms of giving up on their ideals. Yet, this was the only alternative they could imagine. The last judge, Samuel, warned them most sternly. All that was most dear to the people would be taken by the king to add to his personal luxury and military might, their daughters and sons, their fields and vineyards and olive orchards, and their crops and flocks and herds. The list concludes with the detested prediction: "and you shall be his slaves" (1 Sam 8:10–18).

Yet even Judge Samuel had to relent and become the very instrument to anoint the first king, Saul. What is more important, God finally states that it is the divine will that Israel give up the League and establish a king. In the telling of the story the decision is couched in terms of God relenting to the demands of the people. Perhaps. Under any interpretation, God willed the grand compromise. God instructed Samuel, "Listen to their voice and set a king over them"(1 Sam 8:22a). It was for this purpose that God had given Hannah the child Samuel, that the last judge would generate the prophetic tradition. God responded to the kingdom with the prophets.

Early Israel was quickly proved correct in its dire predictions. The structure required to establish and maintain kingship led straightaway to an absolute monarchy and the same hierarchical stratification of society from which they had been saved. By Solomon's time, only the third king and only in the span of one man's lifetime, the pagan social model was firmly in place in the Promised Land. Indeed it was modeled directly after the Egyptian pattern. To have an idea of the oppression and opulence of the Solomon court while others suffered deprivation at the bottom of a new pyramidal order of society it is only necessary to note that the king took seven hundred wives and kept three hundred concubines. "King Solomon excelled all the kings of the earth in riches and in wisdom" (1 Kings 10:23).The riches would pass from the kingdom all too quickly and the wisdom would come to be recognized in a future passage of Scripture as merely the foolishness of the worldly wise. To the complete dishonor of the Yahwistic ideal, at the extreme bottom of society was a growing class of poor indentured Hebrew slaves adding to the growing ranks of *ger* slaves. The early Yahwistic effort was truly finished with the advent of a kingdom. Soon the kingdom itself would be sundered into the larger northern kingdom, Israel, and its southern kingdom, Judah. In short order Sargon II of Assyria would destroy the northern kingdom, disperse its nobility and main families, still called the lost tribes of Israel, and colonize the area with Aramaic-speaking settlers who intermarried with the Jewish peasants. Their land became Samaria and they were the Samaritans. Aramaic was to become the language of Palestine, including Judah. Judah itself was practically destroyed by the Babylonian Empire and its people were sent into a long exile, finally returning after their unexpected release by Cyrus, the Persian conqueror of Babylonia. Afterward, Israel was dominated by one power after another, never perfectly free to form an order of society of its own design.

Throughout the long history following Saul, David, and Solomon, Jewish kings continued to act more on behalf of their own glory than of the glory of God. Most of the folk themselves fell into the general pattern of seeking their own earthly pleasure, status, and security rather than righteousness and compassion. The history of Jewish kings was one of increasing disappointment.

God chose a unique institution to counter the institution of kingship: the new and entirely unique institution of the Hebrew prophet. There are certainly other missions carried out by the prophets. But it is no coincidence that the age of the prophets comes into existence with the introduction of Hebrew kingship. It not only appeared at the same time, it was part and parcel of the founding of the kingdom. Samuel, who was the last judge and the first prophet, anointed the first king as well as the model king, David. Even more to the point, though it seldom seems to be noticed, the period of the prophets coincides precisely with the period of kingship. One might say that the great enterprise in which the causes of God are being engaged by God's people had entered a new phase in which God had to contend increasingly with these very people, to wrestle with Israel as the angel of God had wrestled with "Israel" in the form of Jacob.

The role of the prophets in maintaining Israel's formative notions of the community's identity and purpose, a notion of community singular in the ancient world, cannot be overestimated. Surely there is little need to review their message and contribution. It can be seen and understood in the Song of Hannah, the mother of Samuel. The message of the prophets is poetic, varied, and multi-layered, but also it is as simple and direct as it is realistic: *if there is no justice there is no God, but only idols of the illusory wealth, status, privilege, and might that human beings tend to assume—wrongly—will satisfy.*

# MARY'S SONG:
# The Meaning of Jesus' Life

Mary learned Hannah's song and, as a young Jewish girl, she must have known it as her statement of faith. This was the song that came to mind when her time came to have a baby in the tradition of Samuel. Perhaps it was Luke who saw the connection. It is explicitly clear that both songs portray the Yahwistic ideals of early Israel and prepare us to hear the teachings of Jesus. They place Jesus in the tradition of the prophets. They anticipate his baptism in which, like a judge of the old League of Tribes and the mighty prophets to follow, the Holy Spirit of God descends upon him like a dove, the very symbol of Israel and the universal symbol of peace, and empowers him. Explicit in the Song of Hannah was the hope for a prophet; implicit was the hope for a king—but a king who was a prophet. Mary's song offers praise for the fulfillment of these hopes.

Like Hannah, Mary sings praises to God who is all-powerful and whose will shall not be thwarted. Mary, too, thanks God for righting all wrongs by turning the tables on the pride-filled powerful while embracing the cause of the powerless. With Hannah, Mary seems to be saying, "though it still seems to be news to most people, I am providing notice that the victory of our God has been won, the promises have been kept, the humiliations suffered by the people of God are being reversed and righted, for the poor and the hungry and the downtrodden have been exalted and given charge." The social vision of slaves is going to be the new plan of God for the world. It is her son who will see to this.

In the very fact of the direct connection of Hannah and Mary's songs, both in substance and in literary form, Jesus is definitively identified as a prophet. Justice was always the central and driving demand of the prophets. The dominant theme in each mother's song reinforces the point. Like Samuel and all the prophets who followed him, the mission of Jesus was to be centered on the establishment of justice. It is that justice of God which only a holy community can establish, and in that day there was no way to conceive of a holy community without a holy king. Jesus is linked to Samuel in that he is the embodiment of the prophetic tradition, and he is linked to David whom Samuel anointed in that he is the fulfillment of the house of David. In a real sense, the Messianic yearning of the people was for a king who would be both prophet and judge/deliverer, the Holy One who would bring about the ideals of the early Yahwistic community through the more advanced civilization and social pattern of kingdom.[6]

Mary's Magnificat fits with the other clever devices in which Luke prepares for the advent of Jesus and makes sure that the Jewish reader is well aware of the sort of person who is about to appear. Note the careful construction of connections between the births and thus the ministries of John, Samuel, and Jesus. John is like Samuel in that he is a prophet and yet far "more than a prophet" (Lk 7:26). John annointed Jesus in baptism; Samuel anointed David. John, in the tradition of the judges of the Yahwistic League, including Samuel, rejects any notion of kingship for the exercise of coercive power or for any form of oppression and violence.

In his own way, Matthew is just as meticulous in drawing suggestive connections and making grand theological points for Jewish readers. Matthew is more concerned to make his case that Jesus is the second but greater Moses figure, one who fulfills the law by perfecting it and living it out. Nevertheless, his version of John's role regarding the tradition of Samuel and its implications for the kingdom of God as developed in the birth narratives and the opening of the ministry of the Messiah suits Luke's construction. Together, Matthew and Luke support and expand on these suggestions with shared images that create the familiar scene of the birth of Jesus. It is pictured in a stable, surrounded by barnyard animals and first visited by simple shepherds of the Judean fields. This is a powerful picture of the Messiah's estrangement from the places and the operators of the powers of this world. The long journey of the wise men from foreign lands and the summary conclusions of the patient and faithful Simeon testify to the universal scope of God's peace inaugurated by the coming of the Messiah and denies any ethnic and national restrictions to that *shalom*. In the same way, the worship performed by the magi is a blatant and clarifying sign to the people of the age that those religions and the societies which rely on such pagan practices as astrology and sacrifice and magic must bow to this king's reign.

The world is being transformed. Matthew and Luke wish to tell us of a birth that is a new beginning for human history. It announces a change in humanity's situation, a new and actual possibility of reversed expectations, a definitive command for things to come. Yet the gospel writers are most traditional in building on the long-established foundation of the Jewish vision: the new beginning has long been yearned for and proclaimed; Jesus is but the new work, albeit the definitive work, disclosing the steadfast faithfulness of God to Israel. Perhaps because it has all been prophesized, the surprising work of God is not supposed to be so surprising, yet it is certainly exalting.

Matthew begins his account of the life of Jesus with a genealogy depicting him as the son of Abraham and the son of David. From there he portrays the early history of Jesus, who, fleeing an eruption of deadly violence against all newborn babies, goes in exile into Egypt and returns, as a recapitulation of the Exodus and settlement events, and then presents him as the new Moses delivering God's new Torah on a mountain, in an address pointedly called "the Sermon on the Mount."

What is this new Torah? It is the message for how to live in the kingdom of God. Modern scholarship has established that the opening statement of Jesus in Mark represents the central theme of his preaching and teaching. "The time is fulfilled. The kingdom of God is at hand. Turn your life around, open your hearts, and believe in the good news." (The Greek word *metanoia* is usually translated "repent." This has become a loaded term, rather limited to a strictly religious focus, individualistic, with lots of baggage. Thomas Cahill argues effectively that the meaning of Jesus is better understood in the corporate terms that would have been heard by the fresh ears of the first century, ears much more attuned to the corporate nature of the sin from which the people were to turn in their social, economic, and legal structures, in their cultural values, and in their actions. The imagery of turning and openness is perfectly in keeping with the meaning of *metanoia*. The "reversal" theme suits the songs of the mothers.) That opening line tells us what Jesus is up to, why he has come. It is the announcement of a new and climactic initiative of God, drawing near to establish the kingdom. This sounds almost like a refrain from Mary's song, and it seems to flow straight out of it. Jesus conformed his whole life to his vision of that kingdom which he, exactly in line with his tradition, believed would create true harmony in creation and the human community that is the goal of history. One can sense his urgency to respond to the new initiative of God to which he felt called. This was the end toward which all prior history was aimed and it was the hope and dream of Israel. Paul the apostle would say that all creation itself was groaning in the birth pains of the kingdom of God, in which those made in the image of God would finally become the children of God.

It is the end of the use of violence as a solution, for violence is revealed as the problem and the cycle of violence is definitively broken on the cross. Too few Christians, much less the world, have been able to recognize this reality, so clear once glimpsed. This is one of the issues of justice to which the church must wake up and to which it must firmly hold. The victim condemned by human society and its religious institutions is proclaimed as Lord. Perhaps the Constantinian Settlement was the point at which violence, particularly on behalf of the state, became acceptable to Christians, perhaps it was the Dark Ages and the need for strong-armed knights to maintain law and order. Somewhere along the way, we joined with pagan society in assuming that violence is necessary: when it is controlled, when it is exercised in the name of justice, when it is imposed on behalf of victims, especially when it is conducted in the name of the Christian god, it is good. Perhaps the church has missed the point Jesus made against violence through acceptance of the cross and in forgiveness of those who put him there. Perhaps we have focused too exclusively on the redemption of sin within each person; perhaps we do not pay enough attention to the way sin is originally described as having grown and spread in human society in the first twelve chapters of Genesis. As we have seen, there the overwhelming picture is one of violence in the name of society and culture. Jesus clarifies the matter and puts an end to it in choosing to suffer violence rather than sponsor it. God-in-Christ calls for a conversion of the human heart in the establishment of a "kingdom," a culture, beyond violence.

Jesus is making his announcement that, in him, the kingdom of God is at hand. This follows readily enough in the tradition of the prophets, but he also is pronouncing himself the last prophet. He had already pronounced the great Baptizer, John, a "prophet," even though the time of the prophets had ended generations before. This is because John has discerned that the new time has indeed come, that the new age of the kingdom is being established. When John meets Jesus he declares to the masses that the kingdom has been established in this man, and that he himself has been preparing the way for him. Jesus acknowledges John's insights by calling him the greatest of the prophets and proceeds to assure him by pointing to signs of the kingdom. But John must wane; Jesus is the last of the prophets and the fulfillment of prophecy.

John had looked to the day when God would break the bonds of sin that enslaved human beings, freeing them to turn their lives around and become God's people in deed as well as in desire. Jesus went home to Nazareth soon after he began his movement and while worshiping in his home synagogue suggested that he was the Anointed One. He did so by issuing his headline statement that "the time is now, the kingdom is at hand" in no uncertain terms. He picked up the Scripture, read from Isaiah's prophecy of the kingdom, and concluded with the assertion that it had come true in their hearing of the words:

> The Spirit of the Lord GOD is upon me,
> because the LORD has anointed me;
> he has sent me to bring good news to the oppressed,
> to bind up the brokenhearted,
> to proclaim liberty to the captives,
> and release to the prisoners;
> to proclaim the year of the LORD'S favor,
> and the day of vengeance of our God;
> to comfort all who mourn;
> to provide for those who mourn in Zion—
> to give them a garland instead of ashes,
> the oil of gladness instead of mourning,
> the mantle of praise instead of a faint spirit.
> Isaiah 61:1–3a

Time and again Jesus is to start with the fact that his was a message of good news to those who have heard too little of it in human society, for example, the oppressed, the poor, those in any need—be it hunger or thirst or clothes. It is to be a time of liberation as seen in the release of captives and prisoners—the very people placed outside the boundaries of society. It is to be a day of healing, for human beings that suffer, such as that terrible suffering of grief over loved ones.

John, stuck away in prison, very humanly still wants to be reassured and sends disciples to ask Jesus directly if he is indeed the One, or if they must wait for another. Jesus tells his messengers to report the signs of the kingdom that they could see for themselves in the healing ministry and in the miracles, that is, in the mending of the created order. Sickness, infirmity, possession, and finally death—all the enemies of wholeness in the life of the kingdom were being defeated. The good news for the poor was an unfailing part of this picture. God's reign of peace and justice was unfolding, the final battle was already in its final phase, and the tide had turned. John was complimented for being able to see all of this.

With the proclamation that the time had come Jesus was to issue the new Torah, the law of the kingdom. Matthew places Jesus on the mount to fulfill the law given to Moses by his own teaching. Just as Moses brings the law down from the mountaintop, so Jesus delivers the fulfilled law, that of the kingdom, from the mount. The heart of the sermon is called the beatitudes, the "blessings." Throughout the sermon we find ourselves going right back to the central issue of justice and using the same literary patterns, themes and references seen in the songs of the mothers. Conventional wisdom assumes that God's blessings are given to those who have good fortune in life while those who suffer, those who are reckoned as worthless in terms of wealth and power and productivity, are without blessing. Thus is the trained and alert reader prepared to discover the same pattern of reversals that by now have become so familiar.

We can think of the list of those to be blessed as the invitation list for the kingdom. It is exactly the opposite from the sort of list the world would expect for an inauguration or the enthronement of a new king. It is a list of those with nothing else and no one else, those who must rely on God's gracious mercy and action. It is a list of those resembling the ones described in the songs of the mothers, Hannah and Mary: the poor in spirit, those who mourn, the meek, those who desire righteousness, the merciful, the pure in heart, the peacemakers, the persecuted for righteousness sake, those who are reviled and falsely berated for the sake of the kingdom, the salt of the earth, the light to others. They are welcomed into the kingdom, and a renewed promise is made for their reward to come. In other words, Jesus is stating the first principles of his message, no doubt taught him at his mother's breast, about the reversal of things, about turning the order of this world on its head.

Everyone who is on the bottom will come out on top, and their reward will match each person's chosen identity, the way each has chosen to exercise personal vocations.

Brother Curtis Almquist, now Superior of the Society of St. John the Evangelist, pointed out in a 1997 sermon to the House of Bishops that Jesus did not speak the blessings of God proscriptively. The preacher of the Sermon on the Mount did not say, if you want God's blessing you've got to go into mourning, you have to become poor in spirit, you've got to be persecuted, act meekly, or be a victim of any sort. But he is saying that if you are a victim of others and of society, God offers you his blessing. "Jesus is saying here—against conventional wisdom—that God doesn't want to *get* you or *forget* you. God wants to bless you. Jesus is simply saying…that if you find yourself in a state of poverty or hunger or mourning or persecution, don't take this as due from God. God will bless you."

In Luke's version (Lk 6:20–26) of the sermon of the new Torah, the same basic series of blessings is offered while Jesus is pictured on the move across the plains of the land, teaching his disciples as they walk. For those who do not get the point, utterly, Luke goes on after Jesus pronounces the blessings to quote a matching series of declarations: "But woe to you who are rich, for you have received your consolation. Woe to you who are full now, for you will be hungry. Woe to you who are laughing now, for you will mourn and weep. Woe to you when all speak well of you, for that is what their ancestors did to the false prophets." The list is enough to give pause to anyone who seeks reward in the present.

Of course, no person is always living as though life is a series of rewards, no matter how fortunate they may be. We all suffer emotionally, physically, and with what seems to be all of our being. We all find ourselves troubled to the depths of our hearts by our sin and spiritual poverty, and simply by the human situation, by our limitations and the way we can't control much of anything. We all need a savior, and Jesus comes to us all—not just to those who ask for him. We experience the forgiveness of our sins to be the great gift Jesus offers us in his death and resurrection. We know our state of sin to be the grand barrier that separates us from one another and from God. We recognize that the failure to institute justice is caused by sin. We are profoundly grateful for the forgiveness we have received. But we must not get lost in our understanding that forgiveness of personal sin is part and parcel of the mission in which creation and kingdom are fulfilled through reconciliation. What can be said for the individual is even more pressing for the church. God's instrument on earth must reform itself so that the world can see clearly that it stands for justice, especially on behalf of those who are not empowered to find it for themselves. The church cannot be viewed as another institution relying on power, wealth, privilege, and status, much less on oppression. Jesus points to the issue of justice without let up and without compromise. It stands at the center of his good news and that fact cannot be avoided. Those who rely on entitlements without siding with those without them will end up being miserable as well as making others miserable. For the person who seeks satisfaction and some measure of happiness in this world, the secret is to join God in blessing those named in the beatitudes. Everyone, including those with "blessings" of prosperity and those who accept the responsibility of power, has a role. God wants each person to be perfectly human now, in faithful obedience to the unfolding will of God who makes all things new. God's will is that justice be done. The reality, Jesus seems quite clearly to be saying, is that the only way to be contented with life is to cooperate and embrace God's will for justice.

Putting today's vernacular in the mouth of Jesus, it would be like speaking to his audience on the mount in these terms: to the little ones he says, "Relax, keep working for the kingdom, embrace and enjoy your life, and trust in God." To the ones on top, "Be careful and be ready to do anything to enter the kingdom. You can be fooled into thinking that what you have is what you want, but believe me, if you knew what I offer you, you would give up any worldly rewards for the peace and joy of the kingdom. Live like you are in the kingdom now: do not fall into the illusion that power will make you happy but side with the people who are in need and must rely on you, avoid oppression and violence of all sorts, forgive people who wrong you even to the extent of loving your enemies, seek God's compassion, justice, and righteousness."

Time and again Jesus sounds just like his mother, and the mother of the first prophet, in his use of sets of sharp contrasts. For example, at one point (Mk 10:35–45) Jesus is approached by two of the disciples most prominently mentioned in the gospels, at a moment when they evidently thought of themselves as more worthy than other disciples. James and John made the assumptions of their culture about the rewards and status of leadership. If Jesus was going to establish a kingdom they wanted the high place in his glory they felt they deserved. Jesus disabuses them of their misconception. His kingdom is not like the Roman

Empire wherein thirty percent of the people were slaves while wealth, power, and privilege was narrowly focused on a few, all of them ruled by an absolute despot sitting at the top of the oppressively fixed pyramid of domination.

"You know that among the Gentiles those whom they recognize as their rulers lord it over them, and their great ones are tyrants over them. But it is not so among you; whoever wishes to become great among you must be your servant, and whoever wishes to be first among you must be slave of all. For the Son of Man came not to be served but to serve, and to give his life a ransom for many" (Mk 10:42b–45). Luke recorded the same teaching, but placed it at table, making use of that imagery: "The most senior among you must become like the youngest, and the presider must become like the one attending the table. For who is greater, the one who is at the table or the one who serves? Is it not the one at the table? But I am among you as one who serves at the tables" (Lk 22:26–27).

This is a new kind of society, one already pictured with the same kind of matching contrasts portrayed in the songs of the mothers. Jesus continually turned to this technique to admonish his disciples throughout the gospels. Again, when the disciples quarreled over their own pecking order Jesus "summoned the Twelve" (Mk 9:35), with all the import of what gathering the Twelve meant, and instructed them: "Whoever wants to be first must be last of all and servant of all." In Matthew Jesus said, "The greatest among you will be your servant...and all who humble themselves will be exalted" (23:11–12). At Luke 9:48 we read: "the least among all of you is the greatest." These contrasts are constantly repeated: served-server; great-servant; first-slave; first-last; greatest-servant; exalted-humbled; greatest-least; senior-youngest; presider-waiter.

Jesus stood directly in the prophetic tradition that said if there is no justice there is no God of Israel. He issued the prophetic theme both that God's mercy is unlimited, and that the People of God are to show compassion to all in need as the representatives of God. God is just and the People of God are to be God's agents of justice in the world. For him, the kingdom is the reign of God's universal justice and there is no room for prejudice, exclusion, rejection, privilege, hunger, oppression, nor any of the "isms" that continue to mark the failures of our society today. The heart of Jesus was especially open to those rejected by others. Everyone is entitled to the protection of the community and everyone is responsible to everyone else, especially those in need.

Matthew depicted Jesus in the unmistakable act of fulfilling the Torah, the law of Moses, with the law of the kingdom, the gospel. It is summarized, if you will, in the beatitudes. The central feature of this gospel "law" is justice. Luke is not as focused on the law, as much as on the divine compassion that demands justice. In each gospel the birth, the proclamation by John that the kingdom is drawing near, the opening proclamation of Jesus that the kingdom was at hand, the baptism, the opening sermon declaring the fulfillment of the signs of the kingdom as predicted by Isaiah, the giving of the new Torah, and the assurance to the imprisoned John that the signs of the kingdom are present in the ministry of Jesus, follow quickly one upon another.

Matthew draws the picture too plainly for any doubt to remain by his representation of the placement and the content of the last sermon Jesus preaches.

> When the Son of Man comes in his glory, and all the angels with him, he will be seated on the throne of his glory. All the nations will be assembled before him and he will separate the people one from another as a shepherd separates the sheep from the goats. He will place the sheep on his right hand and the goats on his left.
>
> Then will the King say to those on his right, "Come, you blessed of my Father, take your inheritance, the kingdom prepared for you from the foundation of the world. For I was hungry and you gave me to eat, I was thirsty and you gave me to drink, I was a stranger and you took me in, naked and you clothed me, sick and you took care of me, imprisoned and you visited me."
>
> Then will the just reply to him, "Lord, when did we see you hungry and give you to eat, or thirsty and give you to drink? When did we see you a stranger and take you in, naked and clothe you? When did we find you sick or imprisoned and go to visit you?"
>
> Then will the King answer, "I tell you the truth, whatever you did for one of the least of these brothers and sisters of mine, you did for me."
>
> Then will he say to those on his left, "Depart from me, with your own curse upon your heads, to the eternal fire prepared for the devil and his angels. For I was hungry and you gave me nothing to eat, I was thirsty and you gave me nothing to

drink. I was a stranger and you did not take me in, naked and you did not clothe me, sick and imprisoned and you took no care of me."

They will also reply, "Lord, when did we see you hungry or thirsty, a stranger or naked, sick or imprisoned, and did not help you?"

He will answer, "I tell you the truth, whatever you did not do for one of the least of these, you did not do for me."

Then will they go away to eternal punishment, but the just to eternal life.
Matthew 25:31–46

Thomas Cahill examines the import of this final sermon in his fine work on Jesus, *Desire of the Everlasting Hills*:

> Matthew's Gospel...shows the public life of Jesus as getting underway with the Sermon on the Mount (and the articulation of the Beatitudes) and closes the narration of this trajectory with a scene no less memorable, Jesus' final sermon before his passion.

> To this heart-stopping lesson, Matthew adds the frightening comment: "Jesus had now finished all he wanted to say."... The Son of Man has become the Ward of all Mankind. Incarnated as the human Jesus of Nazareth, he is after his resurrection the principle of Jewish Justice itself, incarnated in the person of anyone and everyone who needs our help. It is ironic that some Christians make such a fuss about the elements of the Eucharist—bowing before them, kneeling in adoration, because Christ is present in them—but have never bothered to heed these solemn words about the presence of Christ in every individual who is in need. Jesus told us only once (at the Last Supper) that he would be present in the Bread and Wine, but he tells us repeatedly in the gospels that he is always present in the Poor and Afflicted— to whom we should all bow and kneel. It is perverse that some Christians make such a fuss about the bound text of God's Word, carrying it processionally, holding it with reverence, and never allowing it to touch the ground, but have never considered seriously this text of Matthew 25, in the light of which we would always catch God's Needy before they hit the ground. It sometimes seems that it is to church

people in particular—to Christian Pharisees—that these words of Jesus are directed. But the first-century church people, the people of the Way, took this lesson with all solemnity. It gave them their constant focus—on the poor and needy. Though this focus will be abandoned soon enough as Christian interest turns in the second century to theological hatred, in the third century to institutional triumphalism, and in the fourth to the deadly game of power politics, it has remained the focus of a few in every age.[7]

There were, of course, several different notions of what sort of kingdom and what sort of king was to come as the Anointed One. In Jesus came an unexpected answer, another of God's surprising reversals, one which our Messiah very well may have recognized in his reading of Third Isaiah's image of the suffering servant, an afflicted one who in his meekness will redeem his people, that is, ransom them from the slavery of sin. Matthew and Luke view the birth of Jesus as the engagement of opposing forces. They portray Jesus' coming as the occasion for fear, hostility, suffering, and pain. Mary is frightened at the annunciation; Joseph threatens to break off the engagement. Warnings are given to three separate people; there is the treachery of Herod, the exile of Jesus and his family into Egypt, and the horror of the slaying of the innocents.

It is ironic that the joy of the birth narrative also reports such widespread suffering. Perhaps a literary secret and a most profound mystery are being hinted at broadly, one which would become terribly explicit in the life of Jesus: the world must suffer together with God on behalf of the coming of God's kingdom. We have seen Jesus fulfill the law. We have seen Jesus serve as the last judge, the last prophet, and the awaited king. We also see Jesus here as priest. The nativity narrative portrays Jesus as a priestly figure right from the start, one who suffers and sacrifices, one who takes the sinfulness and suffering of the people into his own life and offers it to God. The post-resurrection Christian community came to recognize even in Mary's hymn of praise how Jesus was being identified as the messianic priest. The child proclaimed would be the king and the prophet and the priest of the true Israel; in his personhood was the salvation of the world.

This rounds out our picture of Jesus for purposes of understanding the songs of the mothers, Hannah and Mary. Those who sing with them are ready to recognize and proclaim Jesus as the resurrected one who in his dying and rising has given a new spirit of life to the world, who has regenerated creation, who is the new creation. The early church immediately declared that the long awaited Messiah had arrived and that the long awaited kingdom had begun to unfold in the very midst of this world. The most vivid and definitive sign of this presence of the kingdom is the resurrection. The community of the Jesus movement no longer anticipated the kingdom, the disciples claimed that they were experiencing it. Our age of reformation demands that we rediscover the early church's understanding and sense of urgency, its fervor on behalf of justice.

# THE SONGS OF THE MOTHERS FOR JUSTICE

The central place of justice in the life and ministry of the Christian should be clear. It is impossible to deny. Jesus clearly and passionately articulated this as the heart of his message. Justice, used in the broad or religious sense of the term, is not something for which Christians strive merely out of humanitarian impulses but because of the principal imperatives of faith, because we have in hand our chief marching orders. Nor is justice a peripheral matter to religious observances, spirituality, ethics, eternal life in resurrection, or any other elements and aspirations the church offers. Justice is not one category or one purpose of the faith, among many; justice is not something to work for on certain occasions or by certain people. For example, justice is not to be left to "the prophetic" role—a very convenient category for those who want to avoid the problematic nature of working for justice, and especially when trying to leave justice to others by falsely, so falsely, pitting it over against pastoral concerns.

Yet, somehow, from time to time throughout the church's history and for most Christians today the matter has been pushed onto the periphery. I do not believe there is any one single cause, or culprit, or series of events that dimmed the lights so brilliantly spotting justice in the center of the good news Jesus announced. We will witness certain of these causes when we examine the issues of individualism and clericalism, with the obsession of the former with privatized religion and election-salvation, and the obsession of the latter with narrow and institutional matters of religion. However, the Constantinian Reformation in which the church became established and then had to rebuild after the collapse of the Roman establishment is a good symbol of the failure to maintain justice as a first concern of the church. Since that time the church has too often found itself being co-opted by the powers that be, and trying to co-opt those same powers in the attempt to gain power and influence for itself.

At too many points in our history the institutional church has been a religious agency for the construction of the same sort of pyramidal society that had been shaped on the foundations of the very pagan religions the covenants of Yahweh and Jesus were supposed to supplant. *The Paradise* (1754–1757), a painting by Corrado Cinquinto, reveals how the church and the European monarchical society of the enlightenment were wed. In the painting we see a picture of heaven. It is perfectly balanced and pyramidal. At the top is God, wearing a crown not unlike that worn by the Spanish king, each of whom would have been addressed as "Lord" by the artist. At his right hand is the Son, also wearing a kingly crown. The saints are placed in hierarchical ranks of importance below them and each is offering supplication in the various actions of bowing and kneeling and deference that any observer of court life would have seen performed by dukes and earls and ladies on a daily basis. No one of that age could have missed the point of the painting: this picture of the way things are in heaven was to be duplicated on earth where the kings ruled by divine right in the name of and under the direct sponsorship of God, and where society was rigidly fixed with a ranking nobility and a pyramidal order of society in which those below were subservient to those born to higher stations.

More subtly, the church has had a tendency to turn from history as its mission, oddly enough in the claim that its mission transcends history. Two things invariably result. First, rather than working for a cosmic mission that transcends creation and history, the mission of the church is trivialized; it does not become more than human life, but less; it does not become broader than human life, but narrower. Second, rather than freeing the church from the historical situation, it makes the church captive and servant to the historical situation and to the governments of people in which it finds itself at each particular time and place. Inevitably, the church that tries to rise above history is reduced to a religion and is subjected to offering cultic observances for justification of state actions. Inevitably, worship that hopes to inspire dedication to the mission of the church by rising above the historical without an urgent sense of the way what happens in this world counts and is of ultimate importance obliterates the natural and necessary unity of liturgy and mission.

It is not unusual to see Christians try to relegate justice to a secular concern, somehow secondary to Christianity. Many times during the civil rights debates that had such an impact on my youth I heard people try to distinguish and insulate the issues of theology from those of justice. Some were cynical and manipulative, but many were sincerely articulating what they had been taught as the position of their church. There are earnest Christians who seem to view justice as a topic of public-spirited concern to be addressed at the appropriate time by the church—but only after theological conclusions have been reached in some separate and abstract system of thought. More recently the ordination of women has been formally rejected by some churches on the basis of just such isolated theologizing without the appropriate regard for justice that is always at the heart of theology. I have heard priests and bishops say that they cannot consider the issue of justice because the theological issue has already been resolved in revelation. The songs of the mothers reduce such statements to nonsense. Being informed about our roots and tradition, understanding who Jesus is, it should be overwhelmingly clear that there is no theological matter closer to the cause of the Holy Trinity than that of justice. Justice is God's cause for creation and for the kingdom to come. "Theology" is never in opposition to justice, for God and God's will for human beings is never in conflict with justice. Any good theology must include consideration of justice. Those who pit justice over against tradition or the morals and values of a culture or a rationality that pretends to be unaffected by personal emotions will soon discover that justice will trump such considerations every time.

In the history of Christianity, the issues of justice do seem to get delayed until the time in history when they have "ripened" and are ready to be addressed. Many of the grossest sins of society seem to have been accepted and hardly noticed by Christians for centuries. Then, gradually, after a few alert Christians begin to focus on the reality of oppression and wrong and call the masses to open their eyes, the Christian population seems to awaken and work, and if necessary struggle, for the cause of justice. The list is rather amazing, ranging from war in Christ's name, to torture in the name of truth, to slavery, to women's rights, and on and on. Each wrong seems to unfold and become exposed in the "fullness of time." The church is often slow, not always the first among the society to notice and to battle on behalf of justice, but it can usually be depended on to gird its loins and lead the way in the struggle for just redress.

Many Christians have focused on sin and the need for liberation from this fundamental form of bondage as the primary, and perhaps exclusive, mission of Jesus. Our sinful nature and the various things in our life that hold us back from being able to find personal fulfillment, our inability to realize the love of God and of others, our fears and anxieties and problems are desperately real and immediate to each of us. Sin is terribly real and it does eat us alive, killing our spirit. Like Paul, none of us is capable of doing what we want and know we should do, and we all find ourselves doing exactly what we do not really want and know we should not do. We want to avoid conflict. Christians are perhaps even more reticent to resist evil than others due to our profound desire to be a people of peace and forbearance; there is a strong tendency to confuse the meaning of the cross in terms that make Christians passive in the face of wrong and evil. However appropriate may be our concern with personal sin and anxiety, the church cannot be reduced to the exclusively interior issues of personal salvation, even eternal salvation. Jesus and the long Jewish tradition from which he came begin somewhere else entirely.

Sin results in relational violence. If it is found in the human heart, it takes concrete form in the way people treat people. Sin is introduced in Scripture as inevitably violent and leading exponentially to more violence. Human sinfulness is captured in its essence in social sin, when we find people failing to come together and deciding how to live in community, especially in determining how the least among them will be treated, and establish laws and structures that are Christ-like. On the other end of the scale much depends on how a society decides to treat those who are more gifted, who are given the responsibility of leadership, those who gather more resources and goods to themselves. The Exodus event exposes human sin as the exploitation of people, especially the weak and vulnerable. The response by the delivered community exposes the first line of defense against sin: it is in the establishment of structures for justice.

Jesus understood this. It was primarily what his life was about and it was indeed the heart of his message. If human beings cannot solve the broad issues of social structures in law and in the realms of culture and economy, with genuine care and concern for people who are found in need and oppression, then we cannot take care of the first order of business in which sin is engaged. Societies structured so that people of wealth, power, status, and privilege lord it over others have need for the Judeo-Christian message of Moses and Jesus, for the good news that will liberate the oppressed in that society as well as the privileged lost to whom the "woe is you…" in Luke is addressed.

The first line of battle for liberation from sin is that pointed to so eloquently in the songs of the mothers, Mary and Hannah. What seems to be missed by church institutions that desire to grow and offer their life to a declining number of members is how victories or "miracles" which effect justice in our society would have the power to convert today the way nothing else does. In the society in which Jesus lived the miracle of healing spoke to issues of divine justice and manifested the presence of the kingdom in a way that simply will not affect people in Western society as commandingly. Action on behalf of justice and participation in the transformation of the world are gospel imperatives that will most effectively capture our imaginations today, and that includes the most secular imagination.

The world in which we live does not believe justice is possible. We live in a cynical world of skepticism. In the United States the populace is losing faith even in the politics of democracy, in its system and institutions of governance, as well as the idea of the public servant. The notion of justice seems to belong to the sphere of the miraculous, and where the miracle of justice occurs it has the power to convert, power that in the ancient world belonged to other forms of miracle. Today, if the church were able to stand up to the powers that be and achieve major reform for justice, the citizens of the world would be as affected as John was with the signs of the kingdom Jesus offered him. We can see this even in small victories. The struggle for justice is seen as an effort worth giving oneself to, whereas most people in Western society fail to view most of the activities of the church to which members give themselves as worthy of much effort.

The justice to be found in this world, and while working to welcome the kingdom to come, is best defined by the church in terms of its paradoxical mission: creation and kingdom. We ask how we can fulfill God's will that the human being love this life as it is given to each person as a gift while simultaneously judging it and working with all of our heart and soul to improve it? In Samuel's story, in John's waning, and in the cross of Christ, we penetrate the Judeo-Christian insight that God sometimes wills us to yield to the needs and the institutions and the injustice of this world in order to accomplish what we can in our time and situation, while at the same time God wills that we give ourselves with religious urgency to the establishment of the kingdom.

We have all discovered how we suffer when we stand up and strive against injustice and how we suffer when, like the Yahwistic community and the last judge Samuel, we stand down and adjust to the reality that what should be and what we trust will be, shall not be in our day. All human beings find it difficult to oppose the established norms of our particular society. People manage to do so, but we know that it is neither easy nor enjoyable. It is conflictive and it gets one dirty, it separates people, it draws personal criticism and even rejection. It does require some courage, though that can turn out to be foolhardiness and simply an expression of anger toward society or life itself. Even so, as when Samuel realized he had to appoint the dreaded king, those moments when human beings have to back down from the intense desire to see the victory of justice, when circumstances force us to live with the way things are in order to continue the struggle effectively, require just as much if not more suffering and inner fortitude and faithfulness than taking a stand.

Understanding this, a Christian must never succumb to the temptation of self-deception in choosing to exercise patience in the face of evil. It does take courage to suffer injustice rather than resist the evil that causes it. But too many Christian leaders discover the probity of patience because it is more convenient to wait and pass on the suffering of conflict, rejection, and personal sacrifice to those who follow. Too many Christian leaders conclude that it is wrongful to fight when perpetrators of injustice force community conflict, thereby sacrificing the feelings and the needs of others in order to save their own virtue. It must be admitted that more often than not Christian leaders have taken the passive way out and used patience and avoidance of conflict as an excuse. We take baptismal vows to resist evil, and it is a general rule that patience is no virtue in the face of injustice; passive avoidance of conflict in the face of justice is but cowardice, or even more likely, laziness. Christ was not exercising passivity in acceptance of the cross, nor was he teaching any such thing. Christ took action. He took up the cross. We can only accept the suffering of injustice if our prayers discern God's will to join the grand suffering of creation and kingdom by divinity.

It helps to remember what Samuel and the Yahwistic community did in acceptance of a kingdom. It is especially helpful to recall what Jesus did when he accepted the cross. God will have justice, but the divine love suffers creation the way it is in order to "persuade it" into the shape of the divine will in the ripening of time. Because of God's suffering, and because of our willingness to accept our own crosses, we can accept and finally embrace creation the way it is and love our life as the great gift of God, with the imperfection of injustice. It is largely the taking up of that cross which is the work of establishing the kingdom in due course and in accord with God's time.

There is a conclusion to be drawn from the tradition of the songs of the mothers that cannot be missed except by the most determined and with the most prejudgment. Without justice there is no God, but only the empty idols of power, status, privilege, and wealth. You may have faith, but without the desire for justice you will not have God, and the faith will not be the Judeo-Christian faith. You may have religion and plenty of it, but without the effort to establish "justice in the gate" it will be without God, and the religion will not be the Judeo-Christian religion. You may have a religious community of faith, but without a commitment to justice it will be only one more altruistic institution, probably spending most of its time and energy in search of institutional success, or maybe just survival.

The fundamental Christian understanding of justice, one which also sets forth the proper relationship of the church to the world and the church to the kingdom, can be stated this way: *Christians live for the kingdom of God by immersing themselves in service to the world and become at home in the world by living only for the kingdom of God.* This defines the moral order Christians call "justice," the order which the church must pioneer in its own internal life, the order to which Christians call the world even though the world does not understand that it lives in the new age of the kingdom. The call to reformation is the call to justice.

## ADDENDUM

It must be apparent how very much Jesus was acting, preaching, and teaching within the Jewish tradition, especially the founding vision of the early Yahwistic community, and never left it. It should be apparent how his rejection by his people occurred because of their failure to appreciate what his followers understood about him, because of the offensive nature of his claims as viewed by the various leaders and parties of the Judaism of the day, and because of his failure to fulfill the expectations that had been built up about the Messiah during a time of fever-pitched anticipation. If there is disagreement about the forgiving power of Jesus for reconciliation, there should be no disagreement of significance between Jews and Christians today about the unique vision for human society we have inherited together and about the covenant with God we each claim, and share. The hope must never be lost that these two great communities will some day be reconciled, that our common heritage and religious purpose will lead us to be united in ways which will surprise and delight as only God can surprise and delight by bringing forth the new. The need of each community for reform at this time in history can only help each of us to move closer to our mutual heritage and to our broader commonality. A renewed focus on the mission for justice founded in the Jewish tradition Hannah articulated and which moved Mary to sing out in her gratitude for the coming of the Messiah surely can be the source of a new working relationship and shared prayer.

✦ ✦ ✦ ✦ ✦

## SUMMATION

The call to reformation is the call to justice. If the mission of the church is to serve God in the mighty causes of creation and the realization of the kingdom, then it becomes clear that the nature of human society, and specifically the concern for a just society, is central to the Christian enterprise. Justice, used in the broad and religious sense of the term, is not something for which Christians strive merely out of humanitarian impulses but because of the principal imperatives of faith, because of our chief marching orders. Nor is justice a peripheral matter to religious observances, spirituality, ethics, eternal life in resurrection, or any other elements and aspirations the church offers. Justice is not merely one category or one purpose of the faith among many; justice is not something to struggle for on certain occasions, nor something to be left to certain people. For example, justice is not to be left to "the prophetic" role, presumably within a more comprehensive Christian enterprise. One of our most pressing and urgent tasks, long-range and immediate, is to serve the formation of such an order of society, especially by serving those without privilege, power, status, and wealth—those most in need of a change of heart in the ordering of society—so that they might enjoy God's justice on earth.

In this section we examined the Judeo-Christian insight that God wills us to adapt to the needs and the institutions and the injustice of this world to accomplish what we can in our time and situation. At the same time God wills that we give ourselves with religious urgency to the establishment of the kingdom. This requires a process in which we place our trust in the future that is ours only in our identity with those to whom we offer our contribution. In making our contribution to that future and in our interconnectedness with the ongoing community within the Body of Christ we find our personal meaning and satisfaction even now. What we do makes a difference. The choices and decisions we make really affect the outcome of a real future. To experience this meaning and fulfillment it is helpful (1) if we can lovingly suffer the consequences of the freedom of our fellow human beings and the reality of the way things are in creation with something of the conscious forbearance of God's pure love, especially as seen in the cross; (2) if we can appreciate the corporate nature of reality and our interconnectedness with those who will enjoy the future fulfillment toward which we offer our contribution; (3) if we understand our life as the ministry of Christ: at work, at home, in civic responsibilities, and at play; (4) if we enjoy the other several features of Christian faith in the God revealed in Jesus, the Christ.

The injustice—and the accommodations to it—that devoted Christians must suffer in the process of creation and the materialization of the kingdom can be observed in the difficult situation that called for Samuel to serve as the last judge, the first prophet, and the judge/prophet who anoints the first king and the judge/prophet who establishes the Davidic line. It is most profoundly symbolized in the refusal of Jesus to compel the immediate establishment of his kingdom. Rather, in pure love, Jesus was willing to endure the injustice of the cross. Jesus was willing to suffer the freedom of human beings to reject him and sacrifice him. His action for the great causes of God, creation and kingdom, was not one of imposition but of persuasion and regeneration in the mystical paschal pattern of dying and rising in order to inaugurate the kingdom. He gathered his community of the kingdom to come (the eschatological community we call the church) and invites us to live within this pattern of the paschal mysteries, freed from the sinfulness and mysterious powers that obstruct our ability to love this created order. That is, his community is to live even now as citizens of the kingdom of God in service to its coming and to God's created order.

## NOTES

[1] Joseph Campbell, *The Masks of God: Primitive Mythology*, vol. 1 (New York: The Viking Press, 1959), 146ff.

[2] Ibid.

[3] Krister Stendahl. *Paul Among Jews and Gentiles and Other Essays* (Philadelphia: Fortress Press, 1976), 5.

[4] Paul D. Hanson, *The People Called: The Growth of Community in the Bible* (San Francisco: Harper and Row, 1986), 44.

[5] Ibid., 48.

[6] On a personal note, I agonized over employing the term "kingdom." Like most people today I have become sensitive to all of the connotations people find offensive in it, especially women. Nevertheless, it is precisely because of the offense stored within it that I have chosen to use the word throughout this text. It is an offense that refuses to go away. No one in the Judeo-Christian tradition should ever want to lose sight of the particular history in which the establishment of the original kingdom was an accommodation to the continuing realities that bar us from that very goal and its ideals. There is an irony in the appellation that formed the model for the Christian goal of history. It is irony that remains profoundly important to our understanding of the dynamic between creation and kingdom as God's causes.

[7] Thomas Cahill, *Desire of the Everlasting Hills: The World Before and After Jesus* (New York: Random House, 1999), 245ff.

# III.

# MISSION, BAPTISM, AND GOD'S SUFFERING

Our analysis of the previous reformations leads us to seek the recovery of our self-understanding from the early foundations of the church in Christian mission, in baptismal theology, and in the doctrine of God. We will examine the ultimate mission of the church: God's causes of creation and kingdom. We will compare the identity and purpose of the church as initially grasped in baptismal theology with the more recent tradition of baptism. We will review the original insights about God as revealed in Jesus, which were seen to contradict pagan understandings of divinity; primarily we will focus on the issue of suffering to understand God's relation to us and to Christian mission.

# THE MISSION OF
# THE CHURCH

The mission of the church is not the church. The mission of Christianity is not Christianity. The mission is not religion. The mission is not belief; it is not faith. The mission of the Christian church cannot be secondary to anything, no matter how meet and right, no matter how acute. We must accept the radical and cosmic nature of the mission. Our causes are the causes of God. The causes to which God is committed reflect the inner life of the Trinity. God's causes are creation and kingdom. We are sent by the Lord, as the Holy Trinity sends itself forth, for the fulfillment of creation and the coming of the kingdom in the reconciliation of heaven and earth, and all therein.

When we are grasped by the good news and the church's mission, it is natural to go forward with great urgency to offer this news and this mission to others. Evangelism plays a terribly significant part in the role of the church for the accomplishment of God's mission, but it is not "the" mission. Even the great commission must be recognized as a means to the mission to which Jesus calls us, for surely no one could imagine that our mission would be complete were every human being in the world to be baptized in his name. When we misplace evangelism and make it "the" mission, experience teaches us how we tend to abuse others and the created order, and thwart the kingdom for which we pray. Faith, with right belief, is enormously valuable and the church has a wonderful tradition to offer as well as two thousand years of the best thinking, but the purpose of a faithful community is mission, beyond each baptized member's personal salvation. Religion puts us in touch with God and helps us live for God's will. In the sense that sanity is enjoyed to the extent that one is in touch with reality, it is the purpose of religion to keep us sane, for it is largely through the institutional disciplines and traditions of religion that we are in touch with all of reality including ultimate reality. Nevertheless, it cannot be said that Christ became incarnate and gave his life in order to establish a religion. The religious nature of Christianity is a means to the mission, not the mission itself.

It can be surprising that, after two millennia, the church does not enjoy a generally accepted theology of its own nature and mission. Surely, it is surprising how difficult it is for members to talk together about the church in any depth. Even when we seem to be using the same language about it, we invariably find, if we check, that our language means very different things. The truth is that the quality of our commonly held definitions and concepts is inadequate to engage in the level of dialogue we know is needed. Members have a troublesome time trying to help Christians who disagree with them understand and respect the positions they take on issues that divide them. This is true even when we engage people with whom we hold the broadest and most traditional agreements, those sharing the same branch or denomination of the church. We cannot grapple with our most honest questions about the identity and purpose of the church, and most of our problems and conflicts have to do with different understandings of identity and purpose.

This lack of an ecclesiology (the technical term for a theology of the church) is not a product of the broad and long-standing denominational divisions within the church, or of those divisions that preceded or transcend denominationalism. The fact that there is disagreement about the nature of the church among its different branches and traditions has little to do with the denominational division matter. Today, even within each tradition, there is insufficient common understanding or commonly held language about the church for helpful dialogue between people who disagree.

There are many defining statements that can be made with broad assent. We can talk about "the Body of Christ" and "the People of God," about the visible and invisible nature of the church, and about the sacramental, prophetic, and evangelical functions of the church. At the same time there are many statements we can articulate to nuance our distinctions. We can talk about the salvation of souls and the establishment of the kingdom of God, about our personal relationships with Jesus Christ, and about works and faith. We can identify issues that separate Christians regardless of denominational lines. These issues range from how to fully include women, homosexuals, and children, to how to read and apply Scripture, to how to resolve particular moral questions about the beginning and ending of human life. But when we try to explore questions about the identity and purpose of the church that not only accommodate our agreements and our differences, but also help us deal with them in terms of mission, we quickly find ourselves frustrated. The reality is that we do not have a metaphysical system that can serve as a foundation for a common theology of the church in today's world.

Perhaps we will be handed a theology for the future ecumenical church by some new Thomas Aquinas who will perceive how to apply a rediscovered philosophy of a new Aristotle, but I do not believe it will be soon. As was the case with the Gregorian Reformation that finally produced the medieval synthesis as articulated by Thomas, I believe the process in which we are engaged is necessary to our development of a commonly held ecclesiology. A synthesis will come, but we will have to muddle our way through to it and the process will feel messy enough. The synthesis will emerge only as a common vision emerges.

## COMMENTS DURING A DISCUSSION OF CHRISTIAN MISSION

A concrete result of theological confusion and lack of definition is found in a lack of vision and mission. Christians are not sure how to make a difference, however you define that difference. A number of comments made during some of my Sunday morning visits to parishes in the Episcopal Diocese of New Jersey at adult forums illustrate this frustration. The topic was mission. I asked the participants to avoid talking about church growth, and to deal with how we can make a difference for the world and for God's kingdom, how we can affect history with "His Story." My paraphrase of some of their comments follows:

> I feel like I am caught up in a grand and interwoven system in which powers and principalities are in control and I am helpless to do anything for the common good. There is so much poverty, crime, greed...the facts are overwhelming. I think about how many children die because of bad water, how many babies go to bed hungry every night, and I don't think I can do anything about anything. The world's economy seems to have a life of its own, and it is impossible really to help the needy except with Band-Aid activities. Justice and peace are ideals too elusive to even dream about. I just go to church, repent, tithe, try to be kind to my neighbors, and live according to Christian values. What else can I do?

✦ ✦ ✦

> Those of us who are African-American keep our eyes on heaven to come. That's where we will get our reward—not here. We have been slaves, and even now we know prejudice and oppression white people don't even think about! But,

we can look forward to our reward in heaven, and don't think that isn't real. The more it seems you won't get your reward in the here and now the more important it is to know you have a promise when the angels take you to your rest. No, we can't just wait for heaven, because we know how it is when you need justice. We know how it is to have to depend on others to get justice. We work for justice now for ourselves and for everyone else too. Our eyes on heaven and our feet moving for equal opportunity and peace and justice—that's how we want to picture making a difference.

My daughter was so normal. Just sensitive, that's all. She took a semester break from college and went to work in Haiti. The poverty overwhelmed her. She was never the same. She said she couldn't get the images of starving children and dying animals out of her mind. She said she didn't want to live in this kind of world. My daughter went to work for the church and ended up committing suicide.

Don't we see how lucky we are? We live in a free country with prosperity and every kind of opportunity. We have everything going our way. Of course there are some better off than others. There will always be the poor, and who knows why some people suffer illnesses, and aren't as intelligent, and don't get as many blessings as you and I have been given. Let's do what we can for them, but let's not spend all our time complaining or losing sight of how great things are. Let's appreciate it and give thanks to God for our many blessings. Let's enjoy our one life. I would be denying my Creator if I didn't enjoy this one life, this gift.

I am really more hopeful about the future than ever before. The free market is going to create more wealth than the world has ever seen and new technology is going to "democratize" it, that is, the world's resources are going to be more equitably distributed than ever before.

♦ ♦ ♦

No one ever will be completely happy or fulfilled. We all have to suffer and live through our share of tragedies. But that's just the way it is. We had better not waste our time hoping for a utopia. The kingdom will only come in another world, not this one.

♦ ♦ ♦

It all comes down to the individual. Each of us has to decide. The church gets all fouled up and off track when it tries to do things in terms of the collective. We have to be pastoral. We can't be so focused on issues. That just gets us into controversies, and that gets in the way of doing our job as Christians. Our job is to save souls.

♦ ♦ ♦

I recently heard a politician lamenting the fact that our youth are not voting or participating in the political process. He said that people 30 years old and younger are serving their civic community more than in any previous generation, especially those in need. But they are doing this in ways that are direct, hands-on, and one-on-one. They are serving in soup kitchens and AIDS centers, building homes, and tutoring younger students. They are doing all sorts of things we think of as ministry, but they see no reason to engage the structures of society through laws and regulations and broad policies—or even through voting.

♦ ♦ ♦

I have always agreed that this world is a vale of tears through which we must move without much hope or expectation of anything much. It is like we are being tested. But we do have our reward to look forward to: eternal bliss.

When asked, "What does it mean then to say that 'the meek will inherit the earth'?" the speaker responded:

Statements like that are sort of a biblical code about heaven's blessings, just like talking about the kingdom of God is really talking about the reign of God in each person's heart. I'll tell you what I think it means: The people who ought to be worried are the ones who have all their rewards here in this world.

The hard work reflected in this kind of remarkably open and high-level discussion is indicative of the lack of theological clarity in today's church. The people of God are willing and well intentioned, but are left foundering in perplexity and bewilderment. We are all but immobilized and despairing about what should be and can be done to make a difference, much less "*the* difference."

Whatever the outcome, for the moment, I believe that we need to recognize three core insights of the early church that are particularly relevant today. And we must be able to understand each other when we talk about them. Perhaps eventually they will prove to be of significance in the commonly accepted ecclesiology to come. For this work they will be important in our exploration of the tasks forming the agenda for this generation: community, ministry, and justice. We will offer preliminary definitions of God's two causes, of baptismal theology and of the suffering of creation and kingdom.

# SEEDS OR FRUIT, CREATION OR KINGDOM

There is a total Instruction as well as specific instructions from the Light within. The dynamic illumination from the deeper level is shed upon the judgments of the surface level, and lo, "former things are passed away, behold, they are become new."

Paradoxically, this total Instruction proceeds in two opposing directions at once. We are torn loose from earthly attachments and ambitions—*contemptus mundi*. And we are quickened to a divine but painful concern for the world—*amor mundi*. He plucks the world out of our hearts, loosening the chains of attachment. And He hurls the world into our hearts, where we and He together carry it in infinitely tender love.

—Thomas Raymond Kelly (1893–1941), American Quaker[1]

There are several stories in Scripture about seeds and their fruition. In each case it is assumed that the purpose of a seed is to blossom, and in this will be its fulfillment. The blossoming of the seed produces something considered more valuable, such as food. Paul uses this climaxing process in his powerful analogy of the promise of resurrection. He reminds us that the seed's fruition is impossible unless it dies as seed. Only then may it issue forth into what he assumes it was created to become. In the same way we are to die in our created nature as human beings in order to blossom into our eternal being in heaven, our true destiny.

Jesus talked several times about the seed and the blossom into which it becomes transformed. In at least one instance he applied the planting of seeds to illustrate for his disciples their evangelical task. It can be argued that the very foundation of civilization had occurred in the discovery of a way to obtain a steady and healthy human diet by controlling produce from the planting of seeds. In the long and fitful development of farming, a process of sowing and reaping, people began to assume that seeds existed to bear crops for the use of living creatures. Seeds that did not blossom were considered wasted otherwise. Just so, Jesus tells us how seeds that aren't planted deeply but scattered on hard soil are likely to be picked up by birds and taken away, while seeds planted in the shallow soil are likely to fly away in the wind or yield produce prematurely. In either case, there is no harvest for the laborer and the laborer's community. This is an important analogical lesson for the spreading of the good news he proclaimed about God's kingdom and, as Jesus points out in his inimical use of parable, it is to be learned from basic farming principles any listener can still understand.

In the order and workings of creation, there is another side to all this. For the purposes of creation as they slowly evolved and revealed themselves through the eons, it is the fruit, flower, and grain that exist in order that the seed may survive and flourish and be more broadly distributed, not vice versa. The clever plant developed fruit, flower, and grain with the characteristics of beauty, smell, taste, and nutritional quality. These attractive features provided sufficient incentives for birds and bees and bears and all order of living things to carry produce away from its plant, and to open it somewhere else for the exposure and distribution of the smaller seed which it surrounds, the thing of true value for the survival of the species of the plant.

So dexterous are plants at accomplishing their evolutionary tasks of scattering seeds that some can selectively attract diners who will accomplish the job for them and simultaneously ward off others who will do it incorrectly. The Chiltepine chili pepper plant, *Capsicum Annuum*, went to the trouble of making a fruit for consumption and then filled it with toxic chemicals. The capsaicin chemicals adversely affect animals of the southern Arizona desert, like packrats and cactus mice, that destroy the seeds when they eat the fruit and thus prevent their dispersal. This keeps unhelpful creatures at bay. "Good guy" consumers that promote the spreading of seeds by excreting them whole, like the curve-billed thrasher, suffer no ill-effects of the toxic chemicals in the fruit and eat up.

It was especially important for creatures like birds to carry the seeds away from the immediate vicinity of the plant, not only for survival of particular species of plants, but for the placing of floriculture via random scattering and selection, and ultimately for the development of the ecological system upon which earthly life depends. Consequently, nature created the process of producing something as desirable as food and flower to serve as a vehicle for the seeds, rather than creating seeds for the production of plants with useful food and beautiful flowers. The birds and the wind are only doing their job in nature when they scatter the seeds, which otherwise would have been wasted, or would go only to serve as our food.

As we contemplate the purposes of seeds and fruit, and of birds and farmers, and meditate on the scriptural analogies, certain questions present themselves. These questions have to do with God's role for us as human beings and as Christians. And they simultaneously point us to God's grand purposes—creation and kingdom. For what are we created? What is our human purpose? What is the mission we were created to perform? Are we placed here in God's image in order to enjoy creation, in order to act in a kind of partnership with God and contribute to the process of creation, in order to become fully human? Or are we given human life in order to blossom into eternal life in heaven and thus are called to serve that which is to come, namely, the kingdom of God? In an oblique way the analogies of Jesus and Paul raise the issue of how the life of the world and the life of the kingdom are related.

I propose the following conclusion: Our causes are the very causes of God. The causes to which God is committed are those that are fundamental and ultimate, cosmic and radical. They are creation and kingdom.

The church is the link that joins the two. That is a fundamental definition of the church. "Christ-like," "in-Christ," "the Body of

Christ," "the sacrament of Christ and the kingdom," "representing Christ"—however a tradition may wish to put it—the church is that human institution of the earth and of the kingdom which unites the two, holding each sphere of reality together, representing the world to the kingdom and the kingdom to the world. The church serves in the "new age" of the uniting, in preparation for it. The goal of the church is the final joining of creation and kingdom in the return of the Christ, the ruler of each dominion, at the culmination of time. There shall be a new heaven and a new earth and "God shall be all in all" (1 Cor 15:28). We contribute to the causes of God in each generation by giving ourselves in the ministry of Christ for the fullness of creation and kingdom for each and all.

The key difficulty, perhaps especially at this particular moment in history, is due to the fact that Christians find the relationship between world and kingdom paradoxical. God wills us to be at home in the world; God calls us to recognize that we are in exile. God wills us to embrace human life, our specific life, the way things are, as the most precious gift; God calls us to critique the world and change it most radically. God wants us to value what happens here because it really counts; God wants us to live for the long term of eternity, as though heaven is what really counts, rather than for the satisfaction of the moment. God wills that we become fully human; God wills that we yearn for our eternal destiny. God wills us to bless this world; God calls us to judge the world.

A great twentieth-century saint, Albert Schweitzer, noticed this paradox and recognized its import. He observed first the defining importance of the way different religions deal with world-affirmation or world-negation. Schweitzer was primarily seeking to form an ethical system by which to live. He was open to any ethical expression. It became clear to him that different religions line up with a posture that is either positive or negative toward the created order. He counted Hinduism and Buddhism as major religions that negated the value of the world in favor of a reality outside of and transcending creation. He found world-affirmation in the Hebrew prophets, the Chinese thinkers, and in modern thinkers. He found that Christianity expressed both world-negation and world-affirmation according to the theological postures taken at different periods of Christian history. However, Schweitzer decided that Christianity is fundamentally world-affirming because the only reason it turned away from the world in favor of an order transcending creation was to transform the world and prepare for the kingdom of

God. The good doctor recognized that this dedication to the created order and the order of reality transcending it is what made Christianity unique among the world religions. The incarnation had brought the world and the transcendent together, had joined the creation and the new creation to come in the kingdom. Thus by reconciling the paradox in his own mind he was able to follow the ethical way of Jesus, for "only the ethics which is allied to the affirmation of the world can be natural and complete."[2]

Dr. Schweitzer's insight offers the key to the discussion in this entire section. Christianity is affirming of this world, totally devoted to creation as we have received it, as well as to creation as it will be fulfilled. At the same time Christianity is affirming of heaven, totally devoted to the transcendent, the realm of God together with whatever other forms of existence there may be and of the "afterlife" for human beings. It is affirming of each because it is committed to the transformation of this world to conform to the kingdom in which a new earth and a new heaven are joined.

In order to serve God's causes of creation and kingdom it is necessary to serve each equally without cheating one or the other. We have to learn to hold each cause in dynamic, dialectical tension with one another. For example, the church must maintain the urgency of establishing the kingdom in siding with those who suffer due to deprivation, prejudice, and oppression. We cannot be satisfied with the status quo. At the same time the church must celebrate and live as a community defined by the fundamental attitude of thanksgiving, the eucharistic community of the church. We do our best for each of God's causes by focusing on the other. *We serve the kingdom most effectively by immersing ourselves in service to the world. We serve the world most effectively by living for the kingdom.* When we try to serve one without the other, or have one as the ultimate end over the other, we find that we are acting out of despair.

It has been said that Western culture no longer holds a shared Christian faith but that it possesses a strong Christian memory. This is akin to the famous statement attributed to Gandhi that he found Christianity to be the most attractive of the world religions, and perhaps true, but he saw no evidence that it had ever been tried. Because of our cultural memory most of us assume that we understand the gospel, whether or not we are committed to it. One of the important differences between the gospel and our cultural memory of it seems to be the widely held view of the cosmos that is limited to two dimensions: life in this world and an "after-life" which may be heaven or hell.

The gospel presents a rather more complicated and more promising cosmos, one that makes Christianity unique. In Christ, heaven and earth have been joined:

- We live in this world;
- We live during the rule of the Christ in the realm of God's kingdom, which we pray to come, but which is present for us even now;
- We look forward to the kingdom to come as the consummation of Christ's rule in which God's will shall be done on earth as in heaven;
- And we look forward to eternal life in the community of heaven.

God initiated creation. Christ regenerated this original creation in the redemptive events of the incarnation, the cross, and the resurrection, and thus Christ inaugurated the new age of the kingdom to come. Christians live in and work for the completion both of creation and of the kingdom that has been established but which we pray to come. That is, Christians are called to embrace creation as it is offered to us and at the same time Christians must work to see the kingdom established on earth, joining heaven and earth in a new heaven and a new earth.

## CREATION AND KINGDOM AS THE CAUSES OF GOD, HUMANITY, AND THE CHURCH

Let us start with our understanding of God and God's purposes. We know the causes for which God is in action because they are stated specifically and clearly enough in Scripture and because they are so very obvious in the broad patterns, movements, and parameters of the Christian story. The causes of God are creation and kingdom. We usually refer to each as God's own: God's creation and God's kingdom. It is for these two causes that the foundations of the universe were laid. It is for these two causes that the Word of God became flesh and Jesus gave his life. It is for these that we pray. Sin becomes a barrier that separates us from God and from God's creation and from God's kingdom. In the forgiveness of Christ we are reconciled, and it is that reconciliation we offer to the world.

Because we are to make God's causes our own, the causes of humanity and of the church are defined in these terms. In creation and kingdom we find our mission and know our destiny as human beings. The church's role is to unite heaven and earth; just so the church is to further creation and welcome the kingdom.

Human beings share the two causes of God. The decision to participate in these causes, consciously and intentionally, brings meaning to each moment and each effort, and it gets us past the suffering we must endure and, through God's grace, use.

Each person who comes to life in this world has to make a decision, and the Christian choice is to be at home in the world. We are to embrace human life, our specific life, as the most precious gift of God. We are to take special responsibility for that gift, accepting life the way it has been given to us, and living as fully as possible in concert with the world God gave us. One of the special roles of humanity in creation is to serve as God's stewards of the good earth and of all that is. We have been placed here on earth in God's image as caretakers and representatives. Stewardship is such an integral part of our makeup, our being and identity, that we experience it as a need.

There are many important ways in which human beings serve the creation of which we are a part. There are many vocations in all spheres of society, for all of life is precious and is God's. We are creative and at our best we seek to create in cooperation with the ongoing act of creation that is God's. Christians believe that it is by immersing ourselves in the very stuff of creation, not by escaping it, that a human being meets and experiences God. Rather than separating us from divinity, the world mediates between God and humanity. The entire sacramental system of the catholic family of churches is grounded in the incarnational reality of the faith and in the experience of Christian believers that it is in the material of the earth that we discern the transcendent. It is in the ordinary that we find the extraordinary.

Creation is still in process. It is called history. The world is history, not merely an unchanging stage on which the story of humanity unfolds. History is open because God, who has been revealed as the Holy Trinity, is love, and love is open to the freedom and experience of the beloved. Love is spirit taking shape in history through the delight of communion in freedom with others. The Spirit of God at work in the world creates a plenitude of opportunities for its expression as love, including those of conflict and those of reconciliation.

While history is open, it has a beginning that provides it with definition and a defined goal toward which it moves. It moves at the will of God and that means at least in part, and perhaps decisively, it moves in the free decisions of human beings. The Triune God is continually persuading human beings with the full power of love itself to move in the directions of the Creator's own will, the will of pure love. Love is powerfully attractive: pure and uncorrupted love ultimately will prove to be irresistible. Love is determined; pure love is determined absolutely. Put this way, it is clear that the faithful can rest assured that the purposes of the will of God shall be achieved. God has loved the world so much as to redeem it, regenerate it, and bring forth its new creation. God did this in Trinitarian response to the love emerging in the world's experience through the creation of new forms of love in the incarnation and the paschal mysteries of the dying and rising of the Christ. The love of God draws humanity into the redemption, the regeneration, and the new creation. The kingdom of God itself is coming to be in the history of the world. The kingdom only will be definitively present with the second coming of the Christ. The establishment of the kingdom is what history is about. That is, history is about the coming together of the creation and the kingdom. In this fulfillment is the ultimate goodness of the earth. This, and no less than this, is what Christians are up to in partnership with God.

Scripture tells us that sin started when human beings desired something of the earth for what it is apart from God, and apart from the purposes for which God created it. When the web of relationships was broken between creation, humanity, and God, humanity "fell." Another way of saying this is that we try to find our cause for creation within what the early church called "this age," or "the world," alone. We are dissatisfied and unfulfilled in the limited nature of life as we have received it. We cannot fulfill our purpose. We cannot find our peace in God. We cannot find our home in the world. We do not live according to our promised destiny. Principalities and powers seem to rule our lives and all of creation. Yet, like Adam and Eve, we seek to control our own destinies, to create our own meaning for the totality of our life, and to find our own satisfactions. In pride and in despair—the two sides of the same coin we know as original sin—we seek to justify who we would will ourselves to be. In our freedom we choose to allow the rule of the powers of evil. Even those of us who should know better, even we who have been told and can pass on the story of the People of God, even we continue to desire the world and things within it for what they are in themselves without God. Most of us, most of the time, forget that it is in the created world that we can find God, and that life is about God.

Nevertheless, human beings experience the love of God, often most profoundly within the very depths of sin and failure. We know our need for redemption, and sense that we are capable of regeneration. We seek to uphold the true order and characteristics of creation, even as we know this life to be in conflict with its own internal laws and nature. We recognize the value of our freedom and so we seek the liberation of those who are oppressed, the empowerment of those who cannot exercise their freedom creatively. Religion, in many guises, has shaped powerful visions of the way things might be were human beings to be fully redeemed. The vision of Jesus was built on that of *shalom* and grew into that of the kingdom of God.

The cause of humanity for creation becomes the cause of its destiny. That is, our human cause and the cause of the church are not limited to this world. The kingdom is also our cause. The kingdom of God belongs to everyone as destiny and thus as purpose. This is part and parcel with humanity's cause for the material universe and thus for liberation, justice, and peace, for the kingdom is now part and parcel of the world. This is the good news Jesus brought us as the Christ. To those who know only of "this age" it is hidden because it is still unfolding; through the eyes of faith it is apparent and already operative. Christ died primarily because people, especially religious people, could not tolerate the idea that we can live as though the kingdom is present. The first proclamation of Jesus that "the kingdom of God is at hand" had to be rejected. This news, of course, still is being rejected.

Humanity's cause is properly the kingdom. Humanity is to seek the transformation of the world of "this age" in accordance with the kingdom so that humanity may be what it was created to be and so that each human being may become the person they were created to be. The world of "this age" may not know of the good news about the kingdom, or it may not believe it, but intuits enough about the purposes of creation that it wishes to adopt the signs of the kingdom as its cause. We all yearn for the blind to see, for the lame to walk, for the deaf to hear, for the oppressed to be liberated, and for a moral order of justice. Many humanitarians devote their lives to working for these needs and desires.

The church was founded to serve the cause of creation and the cause of the kingdom on behalf of God with a consciousness, motivation, and grace that the rest of humanity does not yet share, that, by the grace of God, all of humanity might come to embrace its true nature and realize its true aim. In this way God, humanity, and church will become one in purpose. We dare to claim that this already has been accomplished, though it is yet to come that God's will shall be done on earth as it is in heaven. From the interior life of the Divine Trinity it was the Word of creation who became the champion of redemption and founder of the kingdom, who embraced the created order from within, who became fully human, who called together a community of disciples to represent God in the uniting of heaven and earth, who was executed by humanity, and who was raised into heaven to reign over creation and the kingdom. In other words, the gospel is all about Christ's "victory" for the Holy Trinity's causes—creation and kingdom.

In the light of the incarnation and the resurrection, the world of human life includes the kingdom of God as the reality that frames it, gives it meaning, and defines its destiny. The church is to serve the world on behalf of God, proclaiming the good news that the newly proclaimed kingdom of God is the one thing worth living for, the "one pearl of great value" for which anyone would sell all they have (Mt 13:46). It does this in the world by gathering the community that understands that we are already living in the "new age" to come and which seeks to live accordingly, Christ-like.

Creation and kingdom are the causes of God who is Trinity, and they can be described in those classic terms. Creation was for the One who was to be called the Son of God; the Son was the agent of creation; the Son was given to the created order for its redemption; the incarnate Son has been raised to reign as Lord of creation and of the kingdom which he established; the Son will offer the kingdom to the One to whom he prayed as heavenly Father when his prayer is realized at the completion of creation. According to God's purposes from the beginning of the foundations, when the kingdom comes heaven and earth will be reconciled.

## CONFUSION ABOUT CHURCH, WORLD, KINGDOM

This is all straightforward, orthodox, and perhaps familiar. However, it is in articulating God's two causes and in comprehending the interrelationships between God, church, world, and kingdom that we run into the most difficult misunderstandings, disagreements, and divisions within the church. This is not the case only in today's church. It has always been so. I suspect that every heresy that has presented a serious internal threat to orthodoxy is rooted in the failure to grasp and hold to the many subtleties and implications of the relationship between creation and kingdom. For example, there have been countless attempts to develop a Christian spirituality without founding it in creation, and it is common to see Christian conceptualizations disconnect redemption from creation theology. Certainly, the world is confused about the causes of God and the purposes of human life. But faithful and knowledgeable Christians exhibit confusion as well, with significant consequences.

One example is what I call "oops-theology." The basic assumption of oops-theology is that the incarnation is a correction of creation. Accordingly, the sending of the Christ was an emergency measure by a desperate Creator, a God mechanistically enslaved to certain juridical rules of heavenly "justice." Human beings had to be saved from creation because it had gone wrong, making people subject to sin. This sort of thinking is preoccupied, if not obsessed, with issues of election-salvation.

In oops-theology the scenario begins with the declaration of God that creation is good. However, when Adam and Eve commit the original sin there is a shift in the divine appraisal, as though God could be imagined to say, "Oops." This begins what is taken to be the long Old Testament story of God's efforts to save human beings from themselves and from what is wrong with their predicament. After each effort fails, God is left saying, in effect, "Oops," and going back to the drawing board. This happens again and again, but nothing seems to work. These salvation efforts are initiated with a mix of punishments, as Adam and Eve are cast out of the garden, followed by special protections. It proceeds to a new start by drowning the world in a great flood, it picks up steam with the election of a people, and finally tries out various special gifts that are presented to the chosen people: the law, the Promised Land, a kingdom, a royal household, the prophets, wisdom literature, the lessons of exile, the Bible, and apocalyptic promises. Oops, oops, oops, and more oopses. Nothing seemed to work until finally God sent his only begotten to become human and offer himself as a sacrifice to pay for the sin of Adam and the children of Adam. "Whew."

Perhaps oops-theology is too cute a term, but is it not all too accurate a description of what most people assume? In the second century Irenaeus found himself countering this kind of thinking in its rawest form: docetic gnosticism. This was a heresy so powerful and threatening that it forced the third-century church to settle on a canon of Scripture, defining which gospels and epistles would be considered Scripture and which would not, with the specific purpose of excluding the writings of Gnostics. The root idea Irenaeus attacked in his great work *Against Heresies* was the Gnostic prejudice toward material creation. Gnostics pictured human beings as souls trapped in matter, from which they could be saved by escape into pure spirit. As a spiritual being each soul could advance by successive stages into the highest heavens, which is where souls belong. The way of salvation by escape from earth into the heavens depended on obtaining certain knowledge that was secret and hidden from the uninitiated. Thus we have the title "Gnostic," a Greek word referring to those who "know" as opposed to those who do not. Certain Gnostic groups tried to co-opt Christianity through a reinterpretation of the incarnation in which Jesus was portrayed as the savior of spiritual knowledge. For anyone who accepted their premises, God could not become flesh. God "incarnate" could only appear to be human within a disguise of flesh. It was claimed that this spiritual being came from heaven; he was given the human name of Jesus and a human body that could suffer crucifixion for the purpose of imparting to his entrapped followers the special and secret knowledge necessary for spiritual salvation from creation.

Irenaeus detected the theological issue on which hinged the controversy: the orthodox Christian understanding of how redemption is related back to creation. The incarnation did not oppose, contradict, or overcome the faults of creation. Rather—and here he coined an original term to define the concerted and concomitant nature of the two grand actions—the incarnation *recapitulated* the creation in the inauguration of the kingdom to come. Without making consistent use of that term, orthodoxy would continue to employ this basic concept to affirm the absolutely unique Christian view of reality. From the beginning God had two causes: creation and kingdom. They are brought together by the redemption secured through the incarnation. In the end, creation will find its consummation in the new creation of a new heaven and a new earth.

The incarnation was not a new idea of a God desperate for solutions. The outcome of the world is established within the depths of reality. From the beginning the source of all life was created out of the dynamic of love, with love's freedom for the other and love's openness to the future, yet toward an end that was anticipated in the mind of

God and was inherent in the laying of the foundations. The initiative act of creation prepared for the redemptive joining of the divine life with that of humanity in the Christ, for the regenerating paschal mysteries of the dying and rising of the Christ, and finally for the completion of the first promise of creation and the consummation of the rule of Christ in the coming of the kingdom. The created order was designed for the rule of the incarnate One to come, who is God and human, bringing together creation and heaven. New existence is indebted to Christ from before time and forever.

If oops-theology and ancient Gnosticism are considered rather far from the mainstream—though I would disagree and claim that they are each most highly relevant in today's society—we may look to a theologian as brilliant, as broadly acceptable, and as highly influential as John Calvin to consider how common the failure is to recognize and tenaciously maintain the befitting relationship between creation and kingdom.[3] According to Calvin, God descended into the manhood of Jesus not for the sake of the inner life of the Trinity—that absolute community of absolute love passionately going out of itself for the others of creation—but for "the sake of our dullness and weakness." That is, "without the sin of man, the Son of God would not have become man." Calvin's understanding of Christ was limited to that of representation and function. Thus did Christ represent both God and humanity and so, on the cross, was able to reconcile humanity's sinfulness with divine justice. Thus does Christ have two functions in Calvin's system: forgiving transgressions and overcoming the consequences of sin. Just so, God is only in Christ in his particular form in order to bear the guilt of sin and to take it away from created reality so that human beings may stand justified before the face of God.

This limited view of an emergency-Christ leads to a few problematic conclusions. First, like almost all emergency measures the logic leads to a view in which Christ is a temporary measure as well. Take, for example, the oddity of Calvin's inevitable conclusion that Christ will in due time become superfluous. In Calvin's terms, the Father handed the divine rule to the Christ when he sent him in the flesh, but since the reality of the Christ exists solely for the problem of sin it will end when the kingdom comes and the Son returns the rule to the Father. The redeemed will depend immediately upon the rule of God himself. Calvin was not thinking of the annihilation of Christ in person, but of a transference of the divine rule from the humanity of Christ to the divinity of Christ, as it retreats, if you will, into the Trinity. Mean-while the man Jesus enters the hosts of the redeemed. The logical extension of this reasoning that began in the emergency-Christ pre-sents all kinds of problems for an understanding of the incarnation.

The spiritualist view of the way things will be when the kingdom comes reveals something of a prejudice about the created order itself, and there is little wonder that Puritans lurked just around its corner. In Christ we know that God is not only otherworldly, but also this-worldly; God is not only divine, but also human; God is not only rule, authority, and law, but also the event of suffering, of liberating love. We are not to acknowledge these revelations about God, as we discover them in the incarnate Christ and then suppose that they are temporary, limited somehow to a certain period of time. Calvin's view of the end toward which history is headed leads to his conclusion that the mission is the *restoration* of the original creation rather than the *completion* of the original creation in the *new creation* of Christ. Nothing new has come into the world with the incarnation vis-à-vis the original creation. The two causes of God achieve only the final purpose in the kingdom. Calvin's view has no final purpose either in the Christ, in the incarnate One, in the God with us, or in the regeneration of creation by Christ.

## PARADOX

We began in consideration of certain rogation analogies. Even at that point we found ourselves making careful distinctions in the course of discovering definitions about the nature and purpose of seeds and fruit, which are more complex than had been assumed. Our rumina-tions suggested some of the same thought processes about the purposes of God. Indeed, we uncovered a fundamental theological definition. Now it is necessary to consider how we have also uncovered a funda-mental theological distinction.

The definition is of God's two causes, creation and kingdom, and the distinction is between them. The definition is not whole without the dis-tinction; that is, the distinction between them is a major component of the definition. The definition requires a distinction between each cause as well as between God's activity on behalf of each. The defini-tion and the distinction contain what theologians might call the reli-gious dialectic inherent in the gospel of world-negation and world-affirmation together with otherworldly negation and otherworldly affirmation. For example, the gospel simultaneously judges the world and blesses it; the gospel refuses to let us live for the next world without living for this world.

Both the definition and the distinction are unique to Christianity. What we have uncovered is one of those things that makes Christianity different from other religions and philosophies, that takes this faith beyond any other system of thought and prayer and way of life. Because the church exists on behalf of God's causes, it is the distinction that defines the church's mission. It is also the defining distinction between the purposes of human life for the Christian, that is, between the purposes of serving each of God's causes.

We are taking note of a grand though subtle matter. It seems deceptively simple, but it is complex. It requires precise logic to formulate in even crude fashion. It goes to the very depth of the most profound and vexing questions of existence. Finally, it is mystery.

For example, the definition instructs Christians that we are to become at home in this world. Yet it also informs us that we are in exile. Creation theology teaches Christians to espouse this world and love it the way it is, all of it, including tragedy and suffering. Some would even suggest that we not only are to acknowledge but to accept the shadow parts of our selves, the reality of sin, and evil itself. By doing so we are to make our fundamental attitude toward life one of thanksgiving. At the same time Christians promise to resist evil, strive for justice and peace, and make the world aware of how badly, and just where, human society fails to reflect the compassion and the righteousness of God. With God we declare the creation good, yet we proclaim the new creation, a new heaven and a new earth. We work to build strong, vital, and influential church institutions but those same communities regularly sing ritual songs of lamentation, songs that yearn for the radical overturning of the order of society based on status, power, privilege, and wealth. We define ourselves as servants to society while devoting our life to the replacement of this society by the kingdom of God on earth.

With little attempt to sort them out, most of us faithfully and sincerely accept each of these teachings, and many other claims for mission that stand in juxtaposition to one another. I think most of us believe all of them, but have little idea how we can hold them simultaneously, much less live them out coherently. Most of us, most of the time, choose one side of the equation and offer sincere adherence to the other as an ideal—one we may or may not hope other Christians are fulfilling.

## Consider just a few examples:

- Our goal is to become fully human as Jesus was fully human.

- We are to become at home in the world.

- We are to embrace and enjoy creation as gift, even that which we experience as bad, wrong, and hurtful, even the reality of evil.

- Life in the here and now is truly real and truly counts. Reality is our "friend."

- Suffering is redemptive and necessary for creativity.

- Life in Christ is especially and most profoundly joyful.

- We are to love creation so completely that our fundamental and defining attitude toward life is one of gratitude.

- We are to be incarnationally immersed in our particular human situation and identified with the society.

- We are to build effective and successful church institutions with maximized resources to exercise power, influence society, and serve those in need.

- Our goal is to overcome our humanity in the perfection of heaven.

- We are to recognize that we are in exile, "sojourners in the land," pilgrims on the way to our true home in heaven.

- We are elected for salvation from our fallen condition and from the world's evil.

- That which takes place in heaven is more important than what occurs on earth and dictates earthly reality.

- We all must suffer, without regard to righteousness or sinfulness.

- We must deny instincts and urges and work at morality in order to live as Christians.

- We are to be prophetic critics of the world. We are to work to establish the kingdom in place of society as humanly constructed.

- We are to be studiously detached from society and serve as the advocate of minorities, those oppressed, and those on the margins of society.

- The church is not to conform to the world, especially to the spirit of the world in a materialistic age, but instead must offer a countering gospel about transcending spirituality.

Let us begin by recognizing that the confusion results from the actuality that the distinction between God's two causes is genuinely a paradox. Then let us not forget that a genuine paradox is logical. There are cases in point when Christians seem to give in to what would otherwise be a contradiction and call it a paradox. That is, when two doctrinal truths seem to contradict one another, and yet the faithful remain confident that each must be true—indeed, the truth of each may be deemed necessary for the faith—we often allow ourselves to declare them a paradox. We also often acknowledge each as transcendent mystery. We may blame the frailty of reason and the limits of human knowledge for our inability to resolve the contradiction. This allows us to hold to both truths simultaneously without having to reconcile them or give up one of them. Actually an unresolved conflict of belief should not be viewed as genuine paradox, but as an inexplicable contradiction. Perhaps we can say that such a discrepancy is a "suspended paradox," awaiting resolution when logic and knowledge will be able to resolve the polarized truths and hold them in proper dialectical tension. At any rate, just as Christian mystery is always revealed, so a genuine paradox is always logically reconcilable.

A famous example of a genuine paradox is the fact that light is both corporeal and non-corporeal. Until this was established, experiment after experiment had been conducted to prove each respective theory over the other. One experiment would prove beyond scientific doubt that light is composed of non-corporeal waves, and the next would prove beyond scientific doubt that light is composed of particles. Because these were considered contradictory results, the conclusion that both could be true was not accepted. Thus, the experiments continued. Albert Einstein examined the facts and realized he needed to rethink the make-up of the universe. His theory of relativity reconciled the truth of each experiment's conclusion and, explaining how, left us with the paradox that light can both be and not be corporeal.

Genuine paradoxes are reconcilable if we are able to reason through to the bottom of their logical conclusions. The process of logical analysis for doing this actually conforms to the fundamental structure of paradox, the dialectic. The advances of modern logic, together with the discoveries of modern science, are forcing us to acknowledge the way two opposites often must be held together in dynamic tension, in the balancing of complementary poles, if you will, in order to speak the truth. The balancing of complementarity is necessary for logic and for the make-up of reality.

The deep questions of human living, the sort of questions which have fascinated philosophers from the time of Heraclitus, have usually involved what many have thought of as dualities: such questions as of "the one and the many," of "faith and reason," of "being and becoming," of "subject and object," of "matter and spirit," of "universal and particular," of "actuality and potentiality," and of "necessity and contingency." One way to resolve each question has been to defeat one side of its duality, to abolish it as artificial. People have tried to say that faith can-not be real, that potentiality is only a concept that exists in the mind for purposes of anticipation, that becoming is only a way of looking at the rapidly passing states of actual being. In present terms, we have seen the church try to claim allegiance to one or the other, world or kingdom, and slide off into various forms of ecclesiastical life, which are unsatisfactorily one-sided and one-dimensional. There are those who have denounced the world in the name of eternal heaven. They range from those who claim to have been given prophetic notice of a date for the end of the world to a variety of pietists who view this world as a testing ground or a mere shadow of reality, to the oppressed who can see no hope or meaning in this world—and the elite who do not wish, or will not bother, to offer them other hope or meaning. There are those who denounce—or who at least disdain concern for—the heavenly life to come or any remote future fulfillment, demanding utopia here and now. They range from political progressives who see the correct political agenda as the church's mission to liberal Protes-tants who think of Jesus merely as a teacher and example while doggedly continuing to pin their hopes on a philosophy of progress.

The other way to resolve the dualities is to see them as mutually interdependent correlatives. We may find the truth not by taking one pole to the exclusion of the other, but rather by taking both poles in combination, opposites held in tension such that if one pole were to go away the reality of what we are holding would go away. Indeed, the very positing of either polarity implies or suggests the genuine other. To illustrate this we can point to anything from a coin to the make-up of electricity. One way of referring to such polarities held in the dynamic tension of a whole is to call them a paradox.

The paradox of God's causes is perfectly reconcilable and its unity can be explained as well as sensed. The very positing of either the cause of the kingdom or the cause of creation implies the genuine other in the Christian consciousness. Intuitively, Christians know each needs the other. This unity is apparent even as we contemplate our analogy to the evolutionary purposes of seeds and fruit. Though Mother Nature developed fruit for seeds, rather than vice versa, it is equally true that fruit, flower, and grain play a major role for the creative process in and of themselves, and that seeds are valuable to grow food despite the fact that this was not why they evolved. Even farmers and eaters of what they reap all have a highly significant role to play for Mother Nature. It was only over a tediously long period of observation and lots of trial and error that human beings learned how to use the tools of evolution for themselves and their needs; the hope of humanity is that we can use them for God's purposes as well. We have learned to scatter and design the pattern of seed planting in a way that enhances the beauty of the world, and we have the ability, if we develop the will, to feed the people of the world. Hopefully, we can work in partnership with God for the cause of creation when we sow and harvest and beautify our environment. We have faith that we can intentionally cooperate with nature, though it is always dangerous to intervene.

## DIALECTIC

The easiest way to explain the unity of God's two causes is to recognize that our mission is to work for both without cheating for one or the other. We are to become at home in the world while striving for the kingdom to come on earth as it is in heaven with a genuine sense of urgency. We are to bless life in this created order and help each person love what is, no matter what outside circumstances the individual has to face. At the same time, we are to work to improve the circumstances for each and every one as much as possible, especially for those who suffer, those who are in need, those who face prejudice, the poor, the less gifted, the less endowed, the less empowered. We are to accept the way things are while remaining alert and active in service to the plight of others, especially where justice fails.

## Therefore:

- It is not acceptable to ignore issues of justice in the name of evangelism or some other facet of Christian mission, especially if institutional success is more at heart than anything else.

- It is not right to reduce the gospel to "religion."

- It is not suitable to refuse relevant Christian dialogue with society in order to hide from internal controversy and conflict.

- It is fitting to proclaim the salvation promise of splendor and bliss in heaven.

- It is appropriate for pastoral leaders to help their parishioners find comfort in the faith, especially in such a storm of change and flux as confront Christians today, and to know God's love without demanding that they take particular positions on issues at controversy in the church.

- It is meet and right for leaders to demand a high water mark for Christian community in terms of corporate engagement, hands-on ministry, education, liturgical effectiveness, stewardship, and commitment to all other standards of the kingdom to come.

- It is the truth that shall set us free, and it is never good pastoral counseling to buffer people from the pain of reality.

- It is not acceptable to be an angry and hate-filled person in the name of peace and justice, and to ignore institutional needs in the name of ideals.

- It is not right to reduce the gospel to a system of behavior, an ethic, perhaps even forgoing prayer and contemplation in an activist pursuit of social goals.

- It is not suitable to adopt the issues society has deemed timely *carte blanche* as the church's agenda in order to be relevant and without careful and prayerful discernment of the mind of Christ.

- It is un-Christian to preach heaven as a way of avoiding the causes of God for creation and the kingdom to come on earth.

- Good shepherds must make it clear to the flock that the only way finally to obtain the peace and self-fulfillment they seek, and to achieve the Christian joy they desire, is to give themselves sacrificially to issues of justice and in ministry to the needs of the community and those in need.

- The builder of community must be pastorally sensitive to the realities of process, individual differences, and personal feelings—and especially of the equal value of each and every person.

- The pastor must promise to be there with the person who must face the truth and serve that person by offering himself or herself together with the larger, ultimate, and freeing picture of the truth.

The issue is not creation vs. kingdom; the issue is holding creation and kingdom together and maintaining the sense of drive and urgency that Jesus himself demonstrated with his passion for each. We can err by making too much of creation and of being comfortable in the world, especially by accepting our place among the powers that be, and we can make too much of getting through this world as though it were a test that we want to pass in order to be promoted to the next world of perfection. Perhaps the most offensive misunderstanding is to believe the created order is evil and that heaven is the only acceptable desire. None of this takes either creation or kingdom seriously enough, for creation seeks to be fulfilled rather than superseded, and the heavenly kingdom seeks to be established rather than put off.

Interestingly enough, we best maintain each of God's causes by focusing on the other. *We serve the kingdom most effectively and most sincerely by immersing ourselves in service to the world. We serve the world most effectively and most sincerely by offering ourselves to the kingdom.*

It is in our preparation for the kingdom to come that we find ourselves at home in this world. It is in service to this world that we enter even now into the kingdom that is coming. We are given freedom from the bondages of the world in order to be slaves to the freedom of the kingdom; we are liberated from the world in order to offer it the salvation of God's kingdom. For the student of logic, this is the same dialectical double negation that lends reason to the Christian cosmology of world, heaven, and kingdom. That is, there is no salvation in this world; there is no salvation apart from this world; salvation comes in the kingdom in which heaven and earth are joined.

The church is distinctive from the world, free from it, in order to serve it. Thus, the church is to transform the world, making it more transparent to the kingdom and preparing for the kingdom's coming. At the same time, the church is distinctive from the kingdom, though it is God's people seeking to live in community under God's reign and to make that reign manifest. The Holy Spirit is not self-contained within the earthly Body of Christ; the church *does* participate in human sin. The value of the distinction between the church and the kingdom is that the church is able to offer the world the salvation of Christ by being incarnationally immersed in it. In service to the world the church is the sacrament of the kingdom.

At first blush, one may suppose that the church serves the kingdom primarily by keeping its sights there, by being otherworldly. Alternatively, one may suppose that the church serves the world by immersing itself in the earth, caring for mother earth, helping people, and seeking to improve society. In fact, the church's role is far more complex. The dialectical dynamic of the relationship is such that each pole of the contrariety is served simultaneously whenever the church is being the church—whatever the direction of its focus and however intentional that focus may be. The crucial matter, for "the church to be the church," is that it intentionally serves both the kingdom and the world, refusing to fall into the temptation of supposing that one or the other is the only appropriate object of Christian concern, or even that one has priority. Indeed, there is a sense in which the dialectic operates with more clarity when it moves in the exact opposite way of what may be assumed on the surface. The church most clearly serves the world by offering it the salvation of the kingdom, and the church most clearly serves the kingdom by immersing itself incarnationally in the concrete and ordinary matters of the world. The way the church and its members prepare for the kingdom and enter into its life even now is by serving the world, and the way the church and its members find a home in the world is by living for the kingdom to come. The intention of serving both kingdom and world is observed with more certainty when the focus is on one, with the awareness that it is the other pole of the contrariety, which is actually being served most directly. Thus the church mediates between kingdom and world.

## THEOLOGICAL EXAMPLES

In order to understand the dynamic of God's two causes, we need to distinguish and define them. This requires that:

- We fathom the validity and truth of each cause as stated;
- We appreciate the polarity of each cause in tension with the other and the appropriate, logical nature of this unity in tension;
- We comprehend the danger of confusing the causes or of choosing one ahead of the other;
- We agree with the necessity of working for each paradoxical cause together and simultaneously.

Perhaps it would be helpful to survey two examples of how both of God's causes are held together in doctrinal consideration and in actual practice. One worthy goal of the inspection might be to gain some better "feel" for the matter.

## CHRISTMAS

An example of the Christian grasp of the paradox of the two causes of creation and kingdom can be seen in an examination of the traditional understandings of Christmas, that is, in a theology of the incarnation. There are at least three broad approaches that have been taken to comprehend and live out the import of the incarnation, each suggesting a basic conception of the Christian faith and each speaking to fundamental human needs. The first approach focuses on grace and addresses the question of human sin. It emphasizes divine love and humility, God's love seeking to reconcile us to the world, that is, to creation as we experience it. The life, teachings, and compassion of Jesus demonstrate that unfathomable love.

John's conceptions of love and Paul's descriptions of grace are developments from this theme. It provides an answer to the question of how sinful human beings can be justified to stand in the presence of a righteous God and the question of what will happen to the promises to Israel: the gospel of reconciliation by the grace of God. The incarnation is the union of the gracious God with sinful humanity. Human freedom is found in being an agent of grace and love to others, in being a servant of Christ. Lutheran theology has particularly focused on this approach with its central insight: justification by faith. Viewed from this perspective the incarnation leads to the cross, where the divine suffering takes away the sin of the world.

The second approach addresses what our era has thought of as the existential and epistemological questions, that is, questions of the meaning of existence and of the source of knowledge. The root supposition is in the joining of God and creation: the Word became flesh, God became human, the infinite became finite. This gives a new and unique interpretation of the human situation, one that overcomes our predicament. In the words of Irenaeus, "God became human that we might become divine." He also said, "The Glory of God is a living human being." We can know God because the incarnation has made the divine self present to us and in us. This provides the faithful with an authentic response to the radical skepticism and anti-historical thinking of the Enlightenment. It also provides an authentic response to existential angst: life has meaning because God enters into it. Human beings have freedom in that we can choose to conform to the divine will manifested in Jesus Christ. To be free is to take on the maturity of Christ Jesus.

Theologians find Paul and Augustine particularly helpful here. While Luther is more associated with the first approach, this too speaks profoundly to the issue he raised about justification. The Lutheran theologian Walter Bouman makes this point with a fine insight. He begins by noting that while a monk Luther confessed obsessively, but Luther did not confess his sins as his mortality. He knew that our works could not justify our immortality, for we shall all die. The good news, Bouman reminds us, is not that Jesus is immortal, but that he is beyond death. In fact, the incarnation and the resurrection are taken together as the good news: Jesus *is* mortal *and* he is *beyond* death. This justifies our mortal existence, for his victory over death is ours. This in turn provides meaning to the works we do. As Bouman concludes, "Christians are assured that there is more to do with our lives than preserve them." In this second approach the incarnation is seen as leading to the Easter victory and giving it the fullness of its meaning: the resurrection triumph over death and despair.

The third approach sees the incarnation as redemptive and regenerative. The focus is on God's righteousness and compassion, which demands justice and peace and makes it possible through the promised kingdom. This approach claims that God intervenes and identifies with the oppressed and needy for the transformation of the world. The heart of this perspective is Christ's proclamation that "the kingdom of God is at hand," and his gathering about him of the poor, the sinful, the marginalized, and all forms of the outcast. The nativity songs of Mary, Zechariah, and Simeon make it abundantly clear that God's action is for the upheaval of the social order in order to make way for a new and more just plan of human community. God has sided with the oppressed and will redeem the world by means of the lowly. What is at stake is history, the purposes of God for human life. What gives life its greatest meaning and satisfaction is participation in the cause of the kingdom of God, for this is what history is finally about. The present is to be seen in the light of the promises to Israel and the expectation of the new work of God. Human freedom is found in the ability to be human now in a community in which the human potential of each and all is accessible. Jesus was fully human.

In these three very traditional approaches to the meaning of the life and ministry of Jesus can be discerned quickly the need for an agenda of reform. To begin with, the concerns of the first two can be and have been all too easily reduced to individualistic issues of the salvation of souls, even if this was not the original intention. The need to concern ourselves with the corporate dimensions or implications of the incarnation immediately presents itself. Second, the first two approaches give little priority to the *activity* of God, to the ongoing activity of God as present, here and now, and consequently they do not foster a sense of the urgency of mission or ministry that would make any real difference in the here and now. Christian life can become simply a matter of "religion," which is hardly distinguishable from any other religion. It is relatively easy to see the popularity of Enlightenment deism here, especially in the individualistic new world of North America. It is also clear why preachers know that they must limit their Christmas sermons to the themes of the first two approaches, and—because these themes can so easily be sentimentalized and even reduced to religiosity—why Christmas sermons are so often dreaded by preachers.

The point is that each of the three approaches needs the other two to explain the incarnation and make it fully and comprehensively meaningful for the church. The actuality is that the first and second approaches are so often dominant that they exclude the third. The consequence is that a form of Christianity arises that does not appreciate the communal-historical understanding of the gospel. This is one thing that has gotten us into trouble: a church that calls only for *passive* and *private* affirmations about the grace of God and the knowledge of God. The first and second themes have become recast in such a way that they have lost their power to convert while the genuine gospel is domesticated or perverted and missed altogether. For example, Christians seem to have accepted the modern philosophical challenge of the question of knowledge with the naive assumption that our affirmation of the knowability of God will satisfy the divine mission. This suggests that atheism is the big problem the gospel has to overcome and if that problem is solved we can be content. That is, if theists could prove the existence of God, or if enough persons could claim to have had personal experiences of God, we could be vindicated. This ignores the reality that for most of human history God's existence was assumed and yet the mission of the church remained to be accomplished. The fundamental issues of mission are the concerns for where and how God is acting and how the People of God can remain faithful to that action.

An acquaintance once told me that mysticism is the only genuine goal of religion. What was sadly obvious in his life could be anticipated in his statement: he had no religion, no tradition, no community, no celebration, no support, only a lonely job of religious thinking and private piety, that offered him little evidence of personal spiritual beauty. The father of existentialism, Søren Kierkegaard, identified one side of this fallacy by pointing out the obvious: an argument that could decisively prove God's existence would produce neither an experience of God's reality nor any action by God. The pre-monastic desert fathers revealed early on the other side of the fallacy by acknowledging that they could never know if their private experience of God was actual experience or something else, perhaps even an experience of the satanic. Their strong suggestion was to assume that an experience is demonic unless concrete proof subsequently reveals that it is of God.

Removing the theme of personal love and grace from the theme of ultimate fulfillment and fruition opens the way to eschew the present work of reconciliation in favor of a more convenient preoccupation with heavenly salvation or an apocalyptic ending of space and time. In such a situation the church is reduced to dealing out justification through cheap grace with little faith. It amounts to a refusal to see the world as the realm of God's reconciling work, and leads to a denial of any missionary hope for the world.

Jesus demonstrates the power of the rule of God, amazing and provoking those who do not want, as well as those who despair of, any change in this world and who therefore are committed to the standing order. It will not do to give the ultimate interpretation of the incarnation a merely temporal explanation, such as the idea that the kingdom began and has advanced to certain degrees with Jesus, and now moves gradually but inexorably toward its culmination in a future world. This opens the door to the liberal fallacy of progress as well to postponement of the present need to a future time. Moreover, the neutralizing if not despairing supposition that the present time is unredeemable ends up blessing the present state of affairs by default while the church commits itself to waiting for heaven or a future age.

I cannot help but think of Billy Graham, a dominant church figure from my youth, as an apt example of how otherworldly preoccupation and conservative socio-political views inevitably combine. While he was describing our evil age, he never bothered to deal with the greatest evil of his day by meeting with his fellow Christian, his fellow Baptist, his fellow preacher, the other leading religious leader and Southern neighbor of his day—namely, Martin Luther King, Jr. To imagine the reconciliation of differences they could have accomplished and peoples they could have represented is staggering. One cannot help but wonder what would have happened if, instead of spending his time with presidents and preaching all over the world, the Rev. Dr. Graham would have crossed the North Carolina-Georgia state line to meet even once in public with the man who undoubtedly will be remembered as a saint.

It is my understanding that historically Lutherans have tended to concentrate on the first two approaches: those that emphasize the questions of sin, existential meaning, and knowledge of God over grace and God's presence to us. Beginning perhaps with the work of German Lutheran theologians in the mid-sixties, Wolfhart Pannenberg and Jürgen Moltmann, Lutherans have emerged as leaders in the third approach, which focuses on the ultimately redemptive effect of Christ's life and ministry.[4]

Walter Bouman, one of the Lutheran leaders in formulating the Lutheran-Episcopal intercommunion agreement, has gone so far in his consideration of the third theme as to redefine the whole question of how Lutherans commonly have distinguished Protestantism from Catholicism.[5] Paul Tillich, a Lutheran theologian of note who preceded Pannenberg and Moltmann by a generation, defined the fundamental Protestant principle in comparison to the fundamental Catholic principle. In Tillich's view, the Protestant principle is that nothing takes precedent over the individual's relationship to God in Christ, not even the church. On the other hand, he said, the Catholic principle is the belief that the church is necessary for the individual's relationship to God in Christ. This follows the definition of the antithesis between Protestantism and Catholicism offered early in the nineteenth century by Friedrich Schleiermacher: "The former makes the individual's relation to the church dependent on his relation to Christ, while the latter contrariwise makes the individual's relation to Christ dependent on his relation to the church."[6]

Bouman finds greater room for intercommunion between Anglicans and Lutherans in an expanded understanding which redefines the question. He says: "The way Schleiermacher defines both Protestantism and Catholicism does not do justice to the relationship between Christ and the church. If one asks whether the church is necessary to come to Christ, the Protestant/Pietist answer is negative. The ultimate consequence is American revivalism, where a very small percentage of those who make decisions for Christ ever find their way to a local congregation, or radio and television evangelism that "saves" individuals who come to Christ as they listen in their homes but who never seek a relationship with a local congregation. Catholicism, by insisting that outside of the church there is no salvation, is equally wrong." The issue is posed inappropriately.

> We must ask whether there is a necessary relationship between Christ's messianic mission and the church. The answer is that the church belongs necessarily to Christ's messianic mission both as its goal and as its continuing agent. It is essential to change the question....If we give appropriate attention to the eschatological approach to the-ology...we will be able to move past...the sterile alterna-tives."[7]

Bouman goes on to articulate some of the features of what he calls the "newer" eschatological approach.

> The Gospel has to do with the Reign of God inaugurated by the crucified and risen Jesus, the Messiah. Because the Gospel has to do with the Reign of God, a messianic com-munity belongs essentially to the Reign of God. To believe that Jesus is the Christ = to believe that the Reign of God has begun = to be made one new humanity (Eph 2) = to live a life worthy of the calling to which you have been called, that is, unity (Eph 4).[8]

To preach Christmas is to preach the presence of the kingdom of God, to affirm that everything is possible at this time. To preach the presence of the kingdom of God is to trust and hope in the God who will surely fulfill the promise to Israel. Christmas is a profound celebration of the refusal to despair over the possibility of the reconciliation of heaven and earth, to give up on the healing of individuals, to cease praying for the peace and justice of God's compassionate righteousness.

## RELIGION VS. GOSPEL

We may take another example of creation and kingdom in the subtle relation of the Christian faith as gospel and religion. Christians recog-nize their faith as a religion. At the same time, many theologians claim that Jesus utterly discharged this role of the sacred once and for all and faith in him transcends religion as it has always been understood. Perhaps the best-known proponent of this latter position is Karl Barth. Most

Christian thinkers consider the gospel religious but distinguished from other religions in the sense that it redefines what the term means.

My own definition of religion, or at least of the value of religion, can be put in modern psychological terms. Religion exists for the sanity of the world's people. It is religion that enables us to stay in touch with all of reality—including the sacred, that reality which is unseen and cannot be directly experienced by the senses but which provides ultimate meaning and purpose to people beyond the banalities and finite limitations of the world. We understand that to the extent that we grow out of touch with reality we become insane. Consequently, to the extent that we are out of touch with ultimate reality, to the extent that we are out of touch with the fullness of reality including God, we are wanting in full human sanity. Religion provides a means for us to stay in touch with the realm of the sacred and maintain our sanity. It should go without saying that false religion has the capacity to make us especially insane, perhaps fanatically and self-righteously insane.

Mircea Eliade has provided a grand and compelling vision of religion, identifying that which is shared by a vastly different range of religions throughout world history.[8] Interestingly enough, Eliade, himself an Eastern Orthodox Christian, offers a sharp critique of Christianity as it is practiced as a religion. Religion makes the sacred available to people. The sacred is any part of the transcendent realm of God or the gods, what Christians conceive of as the kingdom of heaven or what the Greeks conceived of as Olympus. However, the sacred is universally available as an experience of the foundations underlying the nature of being.

Eliade's vision assumes that the sacred is hidden but is available to people in rituals, myths, symbols, archetypes, sacrifices, and various mystical occasions, theophanies, and hierophanies. The sacred can somehow be experienced as saturated in special objects, special spaces, and special periods of time. The sacred can be experienced through their medium. The center of the world, the sacred mountain, the sacred rock, the sacred tree, the sacred building, the sacred city, animals and crops of sacrifice, and the sacred myth of the make-up of the cosmos in its many variations are examples of the sort of earthly channels that are often employed for the separated and pervasive power of the whole. The sacred is also to be experienced in various forms of appeal to the supernatural by shaman-priest-type personages whose direct empowerment by the divine is accepted by the community. Additionally, though Eliade does not emphasize the power of the verbal in presentation, relying more on the content of oral myths and stories than on expression, no one who has fallen under the spell of gifted preachers, orators, and storytellers can fail to appreciate the power of a speaker to evoke the sacred.

For Eliade, the sacred comes as an eruption of power sensed and experienced as the whole and as purely given, yet it must be chosen by intentionally separating the medium from the ordinary time and space and material of history. This is key. Eliade believes the sacred is known only in a space and time separated from ordinary time and space. History must be separated from the supernatural in a realm on the other side of the ordinary world, though ordinary reality is used as the medium for the all-in-all power of the sacred. For Eliade, the separated, saturated realm of the sacred is experienced through the actions and words and objects that repeat the time of cosmic origins. This, he says, is the true time. The true time of the origins is made available through the repetition of the archetypes, the symbols, the myths, the rituals, and the rites of the origins. It rescues us from the "nightmare of history" and the "terror of ordinary time." Ethics is a moot consideration relative to the experience of the sacred. The separation from the ordinary is even a separation from ordinary ethical realities, even the righteousness of the person seeking holiness, for the sacred empowers beyond the good and evil of ethics.

Eliade is highly critical of the failure of Christianity to do its religious job, leaving a Western culture hungry for experience of the sacred. We moderns do need to be freed from the banalities and illusions of a world increasingly seen as simply profane. We Westerners, perhaps especially Christians, need the corporate ritual experience of moving into the realm of the sacred, what we know as God's kingdom. Christians need to employ symbols and sacraments much more fully and daringly so that the sacredness they offer may be more genuinely experienced. There is ample evidence of spiritual hunger going unsatisfied in our churches. There is undeniable evidence of increasing interest in Eastern religions precisely because they are considered "mysterious," and this in turn is due to their focus on the sacred outside of the ordinary of time and space. There is unavoidable evidence of how attractive the redis-covered religious truths of pagan practice have become in "new age" religion, literature, and art. Pagan religion has been made all the more engaging due to the injustices and the condescension with which the practitioners of paganism have been and continue to be treated. Notice our driving search in the arts for an atemporal and ahistorical myth that might save us from the "nightmare" of the here and now, that might take us beyond the banalities and "terrors" of our history and our fear of nature. And is it not true that contemporary commentators increasingly talk about our society in terms that verify the proposition that human life lived out of touch with the sacred produces insanity, in individuals and in a society?

Eliade surely is correct in pointing to the genius of Eastern Orthodoxy as the Christian tradition that does the best job of offering its membership an experience of the sacred. Orthodoxy is oriented toward participation in the sacred and transcending whole, that is, toward the cosmos, toward aesthetics, toward the kingdom and the glory to come —thus making an effort to have the glory more transparent here and now. One cannot help but notice how its worship is not trapped by the demands of ordinary time or of individual attention to the words and performance of ordained leaders, not nearly to the extent of Western reliance on the charisma of ordained leaders. The Orthodox style for Christian living is shaped more by worship, by icon and art, by communal myth, by sacred symbols, and by cosmological theologies. In ritual and myth there is a maximized sense of separation from the ordinary together with a rich appreciation of our "divinized" humanity. They recognize the values inherent in religion and the religious desires of the human spirit.

The Orthodox are at once more casual about worship, allowing the participant to move in and out of the liturgy in a more leisurely and more extended experience, and more expectant of the intensity of experience. Alexander Schmemann once expressed to a class his exasperation over the Western preoccupation with the concentration that demands a long attention span by exclaiming, "I love my wife, but I don't think this requires me to stare straight at her for an hour with all the attention discipline can muster, in which case I would indeed flee and refuse to do that again for at least a week. You Westerners! You need to learn to be with God together. Take your time, relax, enjoy. If you grow bored, go to an icon; if you grow hungry, bring a bag lunch; if you grow sleepy, take a nap—If Jesus comes we'll wake you up."[10] Yet the expectation is that the congregation will move together into the realm of the Spirit of God, into a taste of the kingdom itself, moved the way human beings are when we view great art, listen to Beethoven's "Ode to Joy," or rise to our collective feet at a touchdown.

Finally, however, we can see that religion in and of itself does not provide the means or the will to hold together the tension between what the gospel has revealed to Christians as creation and kingdom, or to sufficiently value both of God's causes. If we may return to my definition of religion as that which keeps us in touch with the fullness of reality, including ultimate and transcendent reality, it is clear that the gospel claims to transform the role of religion. In the incarnation the sacred becomes so readily available that it is in the ordinary that we find the extraordinary, the transcendent, and the infinite. Therefore, Christians are called to embrace this world of space and time and history, rather than escape from it into ultimate reality.

Other religions seem generally to accept the assumption that in this world there are certain matters that are sacred or religious and others that are secular, that is, concerned with this world only. However, for Christians, if the original usage of the term "secular" is properly employed, there is nothing in the world that is secular. All is sacred—the incarnation itself assures this. When the members of the early church coined the term "secular" they would not have been able to imagine participation in a part of life that was secular and in another part that was religious. The Christian did not have a "secular life" and a "spiritual life." For the baptized, all life was spiritual and sacred. The early church invented the concept of the secular in order to define the difference between the church and everyone else. The church lived in the "new age," the age of the kingdom to come, the age inaugurated by the Christ. The secular society did too but didn't know it, and continued to live as though they were in the old age. The early church used the word "secular" to refer to that part of society that as of yet did not know the gospel—news that we already live in the "new age" of the kingdom.

The new gospel demand is that the primary expression of one's religious experience and commitment now be found in fidelity through word and deed in this time and this history to the God who wills the freedom of justice for society, for history, and for a new future. The gospel understanding of the term "secular" now emerges, as employed in popular parlance today, not as that which is "not religious" or "non-sacred," but as the common term for action outside of the institutional life of the church where the experience of the personal God of Christ must be expressed in new action for justice and radical neighbor-love.

We can see the dynamic quite clearly in the purpose of sacramental worship, in the careful connection between liturgy and mission. We may take as our examples the sacraments of the Eucharist and baptism. We use the most ordinary and everyday elements of water, bread, and wine—indeed, elements with deep and important roots in the evolution of our humanity and of the human community. Our purpose is not simply to separate them out from the ordinary to be saturated with the divine presence and become the medium through which we experience the sacred. Our purpose is to grow in our ability to see God in water, bread, wine, and all other ordinary elements of the earth. We partake of the Eucharist not only to taste of heaven—after all, we ourselves are already the Body and the Blood of the Christ—but also to take and love the world as God's cause and thereby be nourished to serve it. Our liturgy expresses and inspires us for our mission. This keeps us sane. The church, the people who are gathered and raised into heaven by the incarnation and resurrection of the Christ, are called not only to become conscious of how we are united with sacred reality. We are to see in it the beauty, righteousness, compassion, and justice of God's own divine life, and in this perception to act to transform the world to what we see, to conform to the beauty, righteousness, compassion, and justice of God. Putting the same thing another way, the gospel and its liturgy is about the divinization of creation. The incarnation stamps all of the created order as sacred with God's kingdom as its destiny.

At this point it is important to emphasize that this good news is not offered without dealing with all of the religious insights, including the "terror of ordinary time" and the "nightmare of history." The gospel casts light on this world, and in that light we know the world is not our true home. We know that no one can expect to find ultimate meaning from time and history. We know that no human effort, no civilization, no culture, no land, no religion, no society, no institution, not even the church, will satisfy our longing, for they will be exposed to each of us as sinful, contingent, and ambiguously caught up in both good and evil. We know all life to be contingent and our social structures to be arbitrary. We know all philosophic wisdom as foolishness, and all theological speculation as "straw." We see our human weakness and the fundamental nature of our sinfulness in full exposure. No one in touch with reality, much less the fullness of reality, could miss the violence, the injustice, the vicious lies, and the perversions of decency inflicted by the corruption of power, by the obstinacy and self-centeredness of human beings, by even the best and most well-intentioned efforts of an

always ambiguous society. We know the meaning and impact of alienation and are left with it. We do not know ourselves, and we find ourselves struggling with instincts and desires that are experienced as natural. We hunger for food of eternal life and yearn for spiritual beauty.
We suspect our nostalgic craving for the sacred cosmos of our origins.
We suspect our desire to turn faith into superstition, magic, and manipulative illusions of personal power and success. The gospel will allow us
no pretensions. We are left only with faith, no certitude.

The world's real ambiguity is recognized: it holds possibilities for
both good and evil. Religiously, the world's reality is dialectic: the ultimate
incomprehensibility of the self, of society, and of history against the
hope for a really new and comprehensible future; the estrangement and
sin in self and in society against the significance and goodness of history;
the radical negation of the world against the radical affirmation of the
world. The gospel reveals the profound trust and loyalty that God's
people are to have for the world, but it also exposes the realistic distrust
and suspicion God's people have toward it.

Because the gospel forces us to undergo the radical and disorienting
experience of world-negation we are driven into its radical world-
affirming nature. It begins with discovering the nature of the Creator,
the God of Jesus. In the gospel the sacred is revealed as a self, the living
and triune God who is personal, gracious, acting, judging, and proclaiming. This one God acts in the events of ordinary time and history, and demands that human beings act on behalf of the divine will and
in union with the incarnate and risen Christ. The primary expression
of faith in this God is in the power of a liberated hope in the cooperative actions of God and humanity in ordinary history and in ordinary
time, cooperation expressing itself in historical action and not only in
repetition of the actions of the origins, cooperative action to free the
neighbor, cooperative action for justice for those who cannot act on their
own behalf, for a future end not identical with but fulfilling of our par-
adisal, participatory origins. The gospel calls us into a community
responsible for history and for the world. We discover that our particular
history is not illusory or only partially real, but that what we do and
what happens to us truly counts. The here and now is real.

Finally, the distinction between Christianity and religion is not
just that creation has been made sacred. One might identify the Christian
conception of the heavenly kingdom with the religious conception of
the sacred and conclude that the cause most valued by religion *per se*,

put in Christian terms, is the heavenly kingdom. Certainly, the exclusion of the world from the experience of the sacred except for certain separated and exceptional objects would seem to belittle God's cause for creation. Nevertheless, this would be an oversimplification of the matter. In the Christian understanding the kingdom of heaven will enter the created order not only to complete creation so that God's will may be done in each sphere, but for the sake of a new heaven joined to a new earth, "that God may be all in all" (1 Cor 15:28). In the new heaven and the new earth, humanity will achieve our full identity before God, and the absent God will come to complete identity in the world. The ultimate goal is the endless play of redeemed and liberated creation in the immediately present glory of God himself. Only when ultimately joined by creation and made new will the heavens rejoice in the way that the gospel promises.

> Then comes the end,
> when he hands over the kingdom to God the Father,
> after he has destroyed every ruler and every authority and power.
> For he must reign until he has put all his enemies under his feet.
> The last enemy to be destroyed is death....
> When all things are subjected to him,
> then the Son himself will also be subjected
> to One who put all things in subjection under him,
> so that God may be all in all.
> 1 Corinthians 15:24–26; 28

## CONCLUSION

Fruit, flower, and grain evolved so that seeds would survive and scatter, allowing the ecological growth and spread of plants according to the pattern of natural selection. The produce of seeds, however, was immediately appreciated by Mother Nature for their contribution to living creatures, and assumed their important place in the ecological whole of life on earth. We may assume that the Creator had both results and the dynamic interplay in mind from the beginning. In a small way this points us to an understanding of the two grand and long-range causes of God's commitment to creation and kingdom. This process is the creative process of love in its openness to the future, and expresses the inner life of the Holy Trinity. The church is given the most difficult and most exciting task of linking together the concrete reality of each cause, the world and the kingdom. The difficulty is due in part to the fact that human beings find the relationship between world and kingdom paradoxical. On the one hand we are to be entirely grateful for the world, bless the world, and in it find our satisfaction and our fulfillment as human beings. On the other hand we are to critique the world and change it most radically; we are to work to replace it with the kingdom itself. The church must constantly discover in each situation how to maintain the urgency of establishing the kingdom to critique the way things are, siding with those suffering due to deprivation, prejudice, and oppression. At the same time the church ministers to help people accept the way things are with the genuine satisfaction of enjoyment and to live in a community defined by the fundamental attitude of thanksgiving, the eucharistic community. We see the effort to maintain this dynamic in our theology of Christmas, and in the exercise of religion.

# WATERFALLS AND SPRINGS, FONTS AND OILS:
## The Identity and Purpose of the Church

"Dad, I don't want to go to church this morning. I don't think I want to go every week. Sometimes I'm going to do something else."

The dreaded moment had arrived for my friend Tom. All devout parents know they can expect the challenge about church from their children. Actually, it is probably necessary that most children who are "given" the faith of their parents, godparents, and congregation put it aside for a time in order to reclaim it when they are ready. Only then can most young people profess the Christian faith as their own. How the challenge is handled at the time it is presented is an important moment for the family.

Tom had known something was up from the moment his teenage son had failed to be on time for breakfast. As the rest of the family had gone about their normal Sunday morning routine the boy had remained in his room, not stirring. Finally, as everyone else was ready to leave, the teenager appeared and made his announcement.

"Son," Tom replied softly, "church isn't something we do. Church is something we are."

Tom did not have to talk to his son about the importance of worship, about commitment, or about why it may or may not be important to gather regularly with the community. He did not have to talk to him about this or that reason for being there when the community gathered, or what Sunday meant in the liturgical scheme and human round. Tom had surprised himself as well as the young man in what he had to say, and suddenly the young man could see both who he is and what the church is. That meant everything. He turned around, went back to his room, and got dressed to go with his family.

Tom's son had been well taught and he knew what the church is, as well as who he is. He understood anew. I think there are many of us who need to understand anew what the church is, and who we are. This identity and purpose is implicit in our baptism.

When the church is internally driven to reform by comparison of its originating traditions to its contemporary traditions, it is logical that the first point of comparison should be baptism. The defining theology of the church, and perhaps of any institution, should be discernible in its system of initiation. This theology of baptism is articulated in Scripture and in the early traditions, but until our Ecumenical Reformation began it had become terribly obscured. It is possible to summarize our reformation as an effort to recover our self-understanding inherent in the church's theology of baptism. When we understand baptism in the fullness of its implications, the particular issues of reform will sort themselves out coherently and we will be capable of making a decision about each.

The primary baptismal element, water, presents two very different images that speak to the two fundamentally distinguished understandings the church has held toward baptism in its history. During each stage of the church's life, a theologically elaborate explanation for the meaning of baptism has been presented, but what is actually learned by the mass of membership is what they see, feel, and experience in the actual performance of the services in which they participate. Participants can discern for themselves the values we assign to baptism by our actions, and in our actions can be perceived that which the church truly values. It was Alfred Adler, one of the four fathers of depth psychology, who said that we should not, and usually do not, watch a person's lips to believe what they say—we watch the feet. An American president who changed his mind about a promise not to raise taxes is not the only person to have this lesson haunt him; people have long known that it is what we actually do in worship, not what we say about it, which counts.

I believe we can capture what has been conveyed in one or the other of two basic images of baptism. They have been the basic and controlling images for our sacramental theology and perhaps even for our theology of the church. As basic and controlling images we can call them "paradigms," and the movement still taking place from one to the other can be called a "paradigm shift." This is a term that contemporary theological circles find increasingly helpful as the pervasive nature of the current change becomes better understood. It is a term that suggests gigantic, long-lasting, and important shifts in the way we see reality, such as is caused when, in the slow movement and recycling of planetary crusts into its hot interior, the plates of the earth's crust shift slightly and the world wakes up to new changes and new appearances on the surface of the terrain such as mountain chains, lakes, ice, and so on. These great changes seem to take place rather suddenly, and sometimes violently, but they have been underway for long periods. When a paradigm shift occurs what was a "given" in one era is hardly conceivable in another. The paradigm shift we are considering is one of the most important for our movement into a new era, a shift in which we are returning home from a prodigal image of baptism.

## WATERS CASCADING

For centuries the dominant image of baptism has been one in which its waters cascaded from heaven. It is the image of a grand sacramental system for all human life, regulating even the availability of eternal life for human beings. These waters contain God's power and the power is poured out of God's life. One might say that the waters contain God's grace. Without their cleansing power God's grace is unavailable to individuals. Without their imposition in the name of the Trinity the sacraments of the church must be denied, and of course, the sacraments of the church are necessary to salvation, that is, to heaven.

In this dominant image, the flow of the waters from heaven to earth is controlled and administered by the clergy. It is as though the ordained control the divine spigot and have managed the flow of a waterfall down to a trickle. The clergy are a hierarchy set apart from the laos (the baptized, the People of God) and through the act of ordination have been given divine power to perform the sacraments. Ordination is itself a sacrament and from it comes the authority for the exercise of ministry and thus the authority to govern the church, which is in itself a form of ministry. The ordained clergy are the dispensers of the objectified means of grace. The rest of the *laos* as a whole are relegated to the role of passive recipients of grace and clients of ministry. Ordination controls baptism, instead of subjecting itself to baptism as the source and governor of all ministry.

Under the controlling image in which water is poured down from heaven and managed by clergy, baptism is reduced to an act on behalf of a single individual, through a single minister, and for a singular purpose. This is apparent in the liturgical action itself. The individual is the person being baptized, the minister is the clergyperson performing the liturgical act, and the purpose is heavenly salvation. The focus is on removal of original sin for a person, clearing the way for a life opened to the possibilities of salvation. Fundamentally, what is to be observed has something to do with the preparation of an individual not so much for life on earth, as for life in heaven. The most important thing is to avoid hell. For much of history infants were baptized quickly for fear that they would die and not be taken into heaven because the mechanical action of baptism had not "saved" them. Fear in its many forms, ranging from social embarrassment to superstition, remains as a dominant motivation for the ceremony and it is given a prominent place throughout the rite and ritual. For life here and now, the important thing is that certain cultural norms be observed.

There is little expectation demonstrated that anything else is happening to the life of the person being baptized. There is almost no sense that anything is happening to the baptizing community, or to anyone else present or absent. There is little understanding conveyed that the community has anything to do with the person being baptized, other than adding a member or welcoming the "newest Christian." Even with the recent revisions and reforms, our baptismal liturgy presents a clear mental picture in which the person being baptized is the recipient of ministry rather than the initiate empowered for ministry. There is no sense that the life of the community and the human life of a person are being shaped in the liturgy, and in what should be careful and thoughtful preparation for it. Probably there is no goal of spiritual formation for either the person or the community. It is doubtful that anyone at an infant baptism will think about the implications of their vow to adopt the baby as a community, with all of those attending responsibilities.

Few people will have a thought about the responsibility of the community to the person being baptized, and precious few baptizands, or their families and godparents, will give real and serious consideration to their responsibility to the community to live in accord with what is supposed to be happening to them, that is, to be seen in some measure as a living sacrament of the living Christ.

For centuries justice on earth went unmentioned in the rite of baptism. What do the waters of baptism have to do with that? What does religion have to do with that? What does spirituality have to do with that? Even today, as a bishop of the church who regularly asks if the baptized will persevere in resisting evil, strive for justice and peace among all people, and respect the dignity of every human being, I wonder how often the people affirm these actions and attitudes without really registering them.

The liturgical act of baptism is trivialized. There is little real excitement, and probably none of what excitement there is has to do with the presence of the transcendent. Instead, since the one being baptized is usually an infant, the event too often is geared more toward cuteness and pleasantry, rather than meaning—much less exhilaration. Almost no one identifies with the one being baptized, nor is it likely to occur to anyone that this is largely what the service is about, though many people will identify with the parents or grandparents and, if it is known to be of precious sentiment to some part of the family, many will appreciate the ample gown in which the little one will be hidden. This is in actuality a family event, with others present and genially supportive.

Validity, in and of itself, becomes the preoccupation in such a system. The question about baptism becomes simply, "Did it take?" The image of baptism as waters pouring down from heaven manifests a highly mechanical system that borders on the magical. The programmed actions of the priest in connection with the liturgical prayers are what count, for if it is done properly and with the right intentions the event occurs in heaven and therefore cannot be undone by anything on earth. It matters little where or when the act is performed, or who is involved. It will work just as well on any Saturday afternoon in a corner of the parish church with a limited number of family and friends present as during the eucharistic feast on Easter Sunday. It is not important what use is made of the liturgical symbols except to mechanically insure validity. For example, Baptists have insisted on immersion only because this makes it a valid baptism, not because of the meaning it symbolizes, elicits, and effectuates for that community, not because of how it forms the community and challenges the person. The bottom line quickly became whether or not a baptism is valid. Too much of this attitude remains with us, and must be reformed.

## WATERS BUBBLING UP

The other image of baptism is one in which the waters of God's grace are bubbling up from within the earth. These waters are available as basic and necessary elements of creation for us to go down into them, go down into our mother earth as though buried, that we might be born anew, rising up from our earth's womb with water flowing down transformed faces and bodies. Rising with Christ, the redeemed receive the messianic anointing which reveals them as citizens of the kingdom, and not only citizens, but queens and kings of the kingdom of God— in this life and in the eternal life that begins now. In the liturgical action we are given to understand that the heavens are opened, the angelic hosts are gathered, and God is acting in history to reconstitute and shape the Body of Christ. Heaven, whatever its images and creatures, and earth, just us folks gathered around some water, are joined. The community may well move into the threshold of the kingdom and experience what it knows in faith. The baptismal liturgy is geared with an overabundance of symbolic and ritualistic tools capable of being employed to express all of this and so much more. As the paradigm shifts and Christians increasingly experience the opportunity and the sheer joy of what is to be an adept, we will begin to do a better job with more abundant and more imaginative uses of ritual and symbol.

This alternative image of baptism portrays a spirituality that is positive, arising out of joy, affirmation, conversion, acceptance ,and incorporation, rather than from rejection, fear, and guilt. This image opens upon a universe created by God and offering God's own life for those entering into the paschal mysteries of the incarnation. It is an image that grasps the connection between creation and redemption as designed in the foundations of the universe. It expresses the gratitude of humanity for our ability to enter into God's life in and through this world. This sacramental reality, the full abundance of God's grace, bubbles up from creation itself, for the redemption of creation.

Everyone rising from the waters of baptism enters into the full power of the dying and rising of Christ. Sentiment is set free, yet is governed with the sobriety of the limit of creation. Baptism not only prepares for life in this world, it discloses the future and prepares the person and the community for the full force of death. Death must begin in this life, death to all that holds us back from the glory of God, dying to sin until we die to this world. Paul declares, "Do you not know that all of us who have been baptized in Christ Jesus were baptized into his death?" Martin Smith points out the fact that baptism was not always reduced to a family "christening service." There was a time when the people of God found their authentic identity at the heart of the baptismal mystery. He imagines the way that the early church understood the experience of baptism as a "force-field for transformation....The bishop, in effect, stood in the community at the font and the table and said to those who approached, 'Beware, you are entering a force-field for transformation. If you get too close you will die. But if you want to die, draw nearer, and we will show you how wonderful it is to die, how urgent, how painful, how costly, and how necessary if we are going to find new life.'"[11]

Original sin is the "sin of the world" which we cannot avoid, a condition all human beings experience, one which we do not choose but which we nevertheless willfully and knowingly fall into by concrete acts and chosen attitudes. Every person is born into the sin of this world and is in need of salvation. With baptism this need is set within a context; it is the promise of resurrection in this world and in the world to come. One may say that conversion is the continuing pattern of all Christian living, just as it is the pattern of the Christian year. The lifelong preparation for death and dying, as symbolized in baptism, is to enter into heaven. The waters cover the face of the new earth, and heaven and earth are made one.

Faith is a necessary condition for the sacrament of baptism, even in the case of infant baptism. An infant is not psychologically capable of the intentional act of faith required, but since the child's relationship to parents, godparents, and the parish community is a real part of the person of the child, then faith also belongs to the child. Infant baptism is the celebration of the grace of being reared in a Christian family and in the Christian community of which the family is a part. The child's faith is a given, becoming a part of the child's development. Infant baptism presupposes that the child will, in fact, be reared in the faith of parents, godparents, and the local parish community. If parents and godparents cannot vow that they will carry out this design of raising the child in an environment of practiced faith, then baptism is meaningless and trivialized. That is the worst thing about the practice of baptism as we have known it: it is trivialized.

*Baptism is a matter of community as well as individualization.* At baptism each person enters into the reality of the church, gaining a corporate identity and genuine individuality within the Body of Christ. The intrinsically corporate nature of baptism discloses that the human person is, by nature, made up of relationships. A social animal anthropologically, each human being is his or her relationships. The individual (the person stripped of all relationships) is an abstraction; only the relational person exists as actualized. Baptism makes this manifest. The event is not merely for or about an individual—it is for and about the community. Thus baptism transforms both the individual and the community. Formation of the community into its baptismal identity is the most important reality of baptism. In the preparation and in the event itself, both the person and the community are shaped at the most profound level of identity.

Baptism expresses grace as social and interpersonal, given in and through the life of the community. Salvation is the process of becoming human as Jesus was human. It is the process of satisfying our relationship with God and our neighbors. Baptism is an intentional celebration of a person's conversion from the illusion of self-sufficient isolation to life in the Christian community. That is, salvation is the acceptance as a community of the call of Jesus to welcome God's kingdom by being the servant of creation. Baptism is the creative sign expressing the universal unity to which our Lord calls the church. The church takes each baptized person into itself, reconstituting and forming itself into the Body of Christ. In our formation we discover anew that church is not simply something we join or go to, it is something we are.

*Baptism is a matter of ministry.* It is baptism that is the source of ministry and authority in the church. In baptism each member enters into the fullness of the ministry of Christ and of the church that represents the Christ. The baptismal commitment of each member is to welcome the kingdom of God by incarnationally serving the world and to become joyfully at home in the world by serving the cause of the kingdom. This ministry of service begins in the effort to shape the church in accord with the act of baptism, that is, to make the reign of Christ manifest in the life of the congregation as a pioneer of the kingdom. The cause of the kingdom of God is an order Christians understand as justice, an order in which there is harmony, peace, and love in and between human beings, creation, and the Holy Trinity. We pray that this becomes a reality in the church, at least to the extent that it can be seen by the world.

Church is not simply something we go to and do, but what we are. Because of what we are, we are sent to do much. Baptism confers the power, authority, and responsibility of ministry on every baptized person. This includes but it is not limited to those who are also ordained into holy orders. Ordained ministry is never separate from or independent of the ministry of the baptized. The special power, authority, and responsibility the ordained receive come from the baptismal waters and are never disconnected from the power and authority of the community that has shared those waters.

*Baptism is a matter of justice.* In baptism the vision of the way the church links heaven and earth, of how the causes of creation and kingdom are the charge of the church, is most manifestly clear. It is professed and believed in faith that the church and its earthly membership are joined in the uniting of heaven and earth. The good, truth, and beauty to be enjoyed in God's reign of justice are hinted at so strongly in the liturgy that they can be sensed; a yearning for that realm of justice is elicited that cannot be extinguished. For those who experience this vision of a new heaven and a new earth the baptismal vows mean everything, and the desire to persevere in resisting evil, to strive for justice and peace among all people, and to respect the dignity of every human being becomes a gospel imperative. For the person who experiences the reality of baptism, the accountability to God becomes a driving motivation in life, and that accountability is on behalf of the creation and the kingdom.

This ministry of service begins in the effort to shape the church in accord with the act of baptism, that is, to make the reign of Christ manifest in the life of the congregation as a pioneer of the kingdom. The cause of the kingdom of God is to welcome an order Christians understand as justice, an order in which there is harmony, peace, and love in and between human beings, creation, and the Holy Trinity. The baptized pray that this becomes a reality in the church, at least to the extent that it can be seen by the world.

When it becomes understood that in baptism the many enter into the one ministry, that of our Lord Jesus, that each member is grafted into the fullness of that one ministry, then clericalism and ecclesiastical elitism are lost causes. The ministry of all the baptized and the full inclusion of all baptized people into all forms, areas, and orders of ministry are understood as fundamental to realizing the meaning of being baptized into one body and one ministry. No baptized person is to be rejected, marginalized, or excluded from the sacraments, the governance, and the full responsibility of the church. In the same way, when baptism makes its powerful claim that we are one, a united ecumenical church becomes a driving desire.

## THREE EXAMPLES OF THE EFFECTIVENESS OF BAPTISM

### GENEVIEVE

One of the first baptisms I celebrated as a priest was that of Genevieve, the daughter of Vickie Moreland, a childhood friend from my hometown. Genevieve was born just about the time I was settling in as rector of Grace Church, New Orleans. Vickie's husband, Richard, was not a believer, and so he was content to have an old friend of his wife and of her family do the baptizing. We had one conversation in their home (with memorable homemade onion soup) in preparation and while it was both intellectually interesting and socially enjoyable, Richard positioned himself at a distance from the event—except for his excitement over an occasion in which his daughter was to play the central role.

I was concerned because I knew everyone, not just Richard, would not be able to be close to the baptism. The font was situated in a corner of the worship space at some distance from the pews, and could only be seen by the five or six people who could gather around it. When I expressed my concern, Vickie agreed to let me use a common washbasin, to be held by an adult lay reader, Wilson Shoughrue. We positioned the bowl at the head of the center aisle where a fair number of people in the pews could see something of what was happening to Genevieve. I invited the children to gather around us so that they could see. However, when it was actually time to pour the water on Genevieve's head I realized that the small children really couldn't see anything except the bottom of a container in Wilson's hands and a baptismal gown in my arms. On impulse I asked Wilson to lower the bowl he was holding as a font. Twice more I asked him to go lower until he finally just looked at me with a blank face and knelt down on the floor. Down to my knees I went with him with the baby in my arms.

Suddenly the whole church heard the sharp little voice of a toddler say, "Mama, it's a real baby!" There was appropriate laughter, but I knew something important had just happened. I poured the water three times in the name of the Trinity, and then again on impulse I asked another child, whose face had been thrust in between mine and Genevieve's, if she would like to bless the baby. She dipped her fingers in the water, made the sign of the cross on the baby's forehead, and said "God bless you, Genevieve." Another child immediately leaned over and kissed her on her forehead. I stayed put and so did Wilson. Each child took their turn doing something by way of a blessing, most of them using the water. I promise you that Genevieve carefully looked each child directly in the eyes. When I stood up I had the sensation that each adult face I looked into had tears on it. I know the parents and godparents did. I offered them the opportunity to bless the baby, and they did so with a special tenderness. Then, without prompting, Wilson moved the font forward to the front pew, and I followed with the baby. A very old lady slowly and awkwardly, but ever so lovingly, dipped her fingers in the bowl, marked the baby, kissed her, and said, "God bless you, my child." Slowly, taking our time, every person in the church made their way close enough to the end of their pew that they too could participate, almost all using the water and blessing the baby with use of her name. Tears were flowing freely. Smiles lit every face. It was a tender moment, a liminal moment.

When the service was concluded everyone was a bit dazed. Wilson remarked, "*That* baby was baptized." His wife Mary Ann said, "Boy, I'll bet this congregation makes sure she gets a good Sunday school education. They will treat her like she is their collective daughter." "You're right," I reflected, "Christians always say words of adoption, but this time I think this child was rather genuinely adopted."

Just before the service began the next Sunday, a man noticed Vickie and the baby and asked about "the father of Genevieve." Vickie explained that he was at home. The man got the address and left to fetch him, saying, "He doesn't have a choice. He baptized her with us; he's got to be here with her—and us." He brought Richard back and he never left. Within two years Richard was the senior warden of the parish. Vickie served as president of the Day Care Center Board and president of the Women of the Church. Even so, they were both always known best as "Genevieve's parents." Genevieve still has her baptismal banner hanging over her bed as do so many children who followed her to the baptismal font at Grace Church. It reads: "Genevieve, I Have Called You By Name, and Claimed You As My Own."

## Theresa

I was serving as rector of St. Mark's in Palo Alto. When the family of four, Paul and Theresa and their two girls, appeared and asked about baptism, everyone was especially thrilled. The program for preparing adults for baptism had already become a vital part of the parish life, and the parish was always on the lookout for interested adults. The parish decided to use the ancient Latin name for the program, "catechumenate." Our catechumenate was rather simple. Those interested in baptism met regularly, at least every Sunday morning following the sermon and during the remainder of the service, with a group who were called catechists. However, these catechists knew that they were merely fellow inquirers who were committed to helping the candidates for baptism discover and explore their deepest questions. They used the weekly Scriptures read in the service and the sermon as their basic material and they engaged in some hands-on ministry for justice. Their ministry was to be reflected upon in the light of the Scripture. Anything else could be a part of the work of a group, as long as it was agreed upon. Clergy participated as called upon.

Paul and Theresa were pleased to join and participated with enthusiasm. Our program had no definitive beginning point and no designated end, though the liturgical observations followed the related patterns of the seasons. Once people enrolled, they joined and moved through the seasons with special liturgical actions, the prayers of the congregation, and support for the group. When someone said they were ready, usually after some six to nine months, we had a baptism at one of the four appointed celebrations: Easter, Pentecost, All Saints' Day, and the Baptism of our Lord. Easter had become so popular that many people decided to wait until then, even if they felt ready for baptism prior to that season. Paul and Theresa and the girls opted to wait for Easter.

Juan Oliver was the priest responsible for our catechumenate. He was present one night during Lent when Theresa began to cry in the midst of a group session. She couldn't stop crying long enough to explain, and her crying escalated into incoherent and unbroken sobs. With considerate pastoral care she finally was able to catch her breath, and, with a great deal of embarrassment, explain. She could not be baptized at Easter. She wasn't ready, because, as she said, "I don't think I am ready to say that I can die for this faith, and I know I am not ready to let my children die." She went on to describe how she had been reading the material they were sharing, especially information from the early church. It was clear that people who decided to be baptized might at any moment be challenged and sent to their death. Their families usually went with them. This was not academic, not just history. Theresa had learned that there were more people martyred for their Christian faith in the twentieth century than in any other century, more than in all the other centuries combined. She could not be sure what lay ahead for her, much less for her children. How could she place them in harm's way when she wasn't even ready to place herself in such a position?

The reader may be able to imagine the faces of the people of that congregation on the next Sunday morning when Juan and I stood beside Theresa and Paul and explained that though they would continue in the catechumenate, they had postponed their baptismal plans for the time being, because they weren't sure they were ready to die for the faith, or to let their children die for the faith. More than that, perhaps, the reader can imagine the effect on the congregation all during the next year as the preparation and exploration continued and the prayers were offered. For the family did not give up, but continued with the process of formation in the catechumenal program. More than Paul and Theresa, the congregation was being formed in baptismal theology in most concrete and meaningful terms. Then, at dawn on the Easter Vigil, each member of Paul and Theresa's family came up out of the font with the waters of burial and new birth in Christ rolling down their faces and dripping from the hems of their robes. Generous amounts of luxuriant oil were poured over their heads and flowed down their faces, interrupted only by the sign of the cross on their foreheads marking them as Christ's own now and through eternity, no matter what might happen. Their catechumenal group of fellow inquirers took them into the sacristy and massaged their heads, necks, and shoulders, dried them off, helped them change into their new robes of the righteous and led them back into the assembly to great applause and the kiss of peace passed all around. The reader can imagine the effect on the life of the parish.

## Amanda

When Amanda's mother became pregnant, Cindy asked if she could participate in the catechumenate in preparation for her daughter's baptism. That made good sense to everyone. At a point, however, she and her husband decided that adult baptism by choice was the better alternative for their daughter. Participation in the catechumenate continued happily, as did the pregnancy, birth, and rearing of Amanda. This happy young child quickly became a highly valued member of the community.

It was during the Easter season of her third year that Amanda greeted me at the appropriate time during the eucharistic liturgy, opened up her arms with a big smile and demanded: "Peace me!" I should have seen what was coming. It wasn't very long into the next fall that I was once again approached by Amanda while communion was being distributed. She had Cindy by the hand and was obviously leading her to where I stood. She said to her mother: "Tell him." Cindy looked odd, not displeased and not puzzled. She replied, "You tell him." Turning to me, Amanda drew herself up and declared, "I want to be baptized. I want communion and I want to be a Christian." Was a four-year-old mature enough to make a decision for Christ? Obviously so— for one who lived as Amanda did in a committed Christian community and in a family with their values.

# GOD: The Suffering of Creation and Kingdom

There has always been a curious gulf in Christianity about how we are to behold God. Our accepted tradition of piety draws one picture about the God to whom we pray, while our accepted tradition of metaphysical theology draws another that contradicts it. It is as though we are to pray one way and think another. Theology has taken the absolute nature of God, with characteristics like omnipotence, omniscience, immutability, and perfection, to mean that God cannot be affected by anything in any way. That is, in God there is no room for growth; change is an unacceptable notion; suffering is impossible; and no adjustment can be made to the future that is already known. There have been significant exceptions, especially in the nineteenth and twentieth centuries, but the vast majority of the schools of theology have held the line firmly that God cannot suffer or be moved by anything outside the divine life. It has taken some rather fancy philosophical footwork for the giants of our tradition, notably Augustine and Aquinas, to explain how God can love and yet remain unmoved and unaffected by the relationships of love, or how God can receive and answer prayer since the future for which prayer is offered is already known, God's mind not being subject to persuasion. Perhaps most of all, theologians have struggled to explain the prayers of Jesus in the Garden of Gethsemane as he asked to be spared if possible and then reconciled himself to the cross he was about to bear—and to the cross itself.

Meanwhile, the traditions of asceticism, common piety, and mysticism went in exactly the opposite direction in appeal to the God of the Exodus and of Jesus Christ, the God who is revealed in Scripture as intimately available and involved in history. We worship, adore, and praise God in confidence that our offerings of thanksgiving are received and enjoyed. Of course, theologians also had to reconcile Scripture with the long-standing philosophical presuppositions about the attributes of the absolute nature of God. In each case they have had to do this conceptual work of reconciliation without losing any of the divine involvement and care of Scripture and piety. It has not been easy for these greatest of our thinkers and others of us can only respond with awe and gratitude for their efforts. Without going into my own thought processes that lead me to conclude that they have ultimately failed, let us just say that I will side with piety and Scripture. I opt for God who is capable of being an intimate, a friend, and a comforter.

There are a few things relevant to the issue of suffering that I think important to establish. For example, we need to offer a more expansive and dynamic grasp of ontology, of our understanding of what it is "to be," in order for the developing age to appreciate the Christian story. What is the meaning and the actualized essential reality of "being," as in "to be" anything: God, a priest, a fertilized egg in the womb, the all-time home run hitter, art, the good, the truth, anything? Existentialism has been overwhelmingly dominant throughout the twentieth century. It is a significant addition to our understanding, and we will, as we need to, continue to appreciate and use its many insights. However, in addition to its inherent individualism, one of the existentialist assumptions that has gone largely unquestioned, even as we left the rather static world of Newtonian physics and grew accustomed to the dynamic nature of the universe, is an understanding of being which remains far too fixed and rigid. Our grasp of being must reflect the creative becoming that is exhibited in the world of human experience. Being is too set and independent without the needed element of relativity. For example, no love, whether it is the love of neighbor from the great commandment, or love in which sexuality plays a part, or love between God and human beings, no love can be a "thing," a "being," in a static pattern or form. Love is spirit at work in the here-and-now of life, taking form and actualizing in a continual process of becoming. Acknowledgement of the dynamic nature of being opens the door to our understanding of the suffering that must be a part of any becoming.

## GOD'S SUFFERING

The following observations about God follow logically from the thesis that God suffers willingly. Perhaps they will serve to clarify the ideas being expressed about the divine nature by putting more flesh on them. While ever controversial in certain circles, each has made a significant contribution to the tradition in both its theology and the common piety.

*God is love.* Love is experienced by human beings, and if we believe God is love then we can draw certain conclusions about God based on our experience. For example, let us say that we accept the classic definition of being-itself as a synonym for ultimate reality. Except as sheer mystery, being-itself has no meaning apart from the forms of being we encounter in our shared experience as human beings. If there are other aspects of being we have no way of knowing them. We do know love as spirit that takes form in human experience, in time and space and history.

*God suffers creation; God also suffers the coming of the kingdom.* In human experience love must suffer. It must interact, for love presupposes beings that can both give and receive in relation to one another. Acted upon, love is responsive and empathetic and open. Suffering, in its fundamental or ontological sense of "being acted upon," is a requirement for all love. Love has as its goal the enjoyment of communion in freedom, that is, the enjoyment in freedom granted each to the other in a relationship of communion. The intention of love leads toward the fulfillment of freedom in communion. In the divine life this intention is always present for that is the goal of creation. God must be open to the future of the beloved's freedom, and God must suffer whatever that future brings out of the free actions of the beloved. God must have ways of receiving and responding to what happens in the world, since God has chosen not to control but to use whatever happens in the world for the purposes of love.

*God is absolute and God suffers absolutely.* I believe one of the ways to say that God is absolute is to say that God suffers absolutely with and for the creation and the kingdom. These are the causes of God, and God is willing to give the entire Trinitarian self to the causes as well as to each and every beloved. God absolutely and perfectly loves the whole of the creation and of the kingdom, and each part, each creature, is loved as though it were alone in the universe. The empathy of God is absolute and perfect. Love accepts the suffering that comes with the freedom and openness to the future it wills for the beloved, for itself and for the relationship. Creation and kingdom are processes that must be suffered.

*The sign of the cross is definitive.* Suffering is complex, one of the mysteries of created life. Everyone suffers. No suffering is good; suffering is to be resisted at all cost and, where possible, eradicated. God does not will suffering. God helps the beloved creatures to resist suffering; God helps the beloved creatures to endure suffering; God promises that the sufferer will personally prevail. All creatures can endure suffering in part because God is with them in solidarity and empathy, suffering exactly what they suffer and, as well, what the empathetic lover must suffer. God helps us take suffering and use it creatively; in history God even turns it into the positive; in history God even turns it into the good, the true, the beautiful. Creatures can choose to join God in the suffering of creation and of the kingdom "by taking up the cross." Suffering can be creative for the sufferer, the source and occasion of growth and spiritual maturation. When suffering occurs in the resistance of the suffering of others it is an act of love and it is of service to God's causes. The great ethical question is how human love is to serve God. We labor for the kingdom in which there will be no suffering.

This can be very confusing for Christians, who focus on the redemptive and creative nature of suffering. Let me place the matter in a different context. I take it as axiomatic that anything good is potentially terrible, and in direct proportion. The reason we face any opportunity for good with anxiety and even fear is that it contains the proportionate potential for how awful things will be if the good isn't fulfilled, turns, and goes wrong. Every mature bride and groom knows this reality only too well. However, though there is terror in good, there is no good in terror or in the terrible consequences that potentially are contained in the good. The suffering that can be used to produce creativity and personal growth contains the same dynamic. We must not desire or impose suffering in anticipation of the good that can come out of it. We must learn to embrace our suffering, but we are not expected to seek it, desire it, or enjoy it. The cross of Christ was awful, the worst that human beings can do. It is good because of what God made of it, but it remains the sign of what must be overcome.

*Creation is an act of love that is ongoing in what we call history, for it is only in suffering that love creates that which is new.* Creation is not some act that occurred once and for all until the fixed reality we call the world comes to an end. (1) We cannot even think that way any longer, for we have developed a radical historical consciousness. This is so even if we think of the time of creation in cyclical terms. (2) This perspective doesn't suit what we know about love in human experience and, in particular, in the experience of God's people.

(1) Contemporary human beings have a radical historical consciousness. We think of our life and our world as involving a real freedom, as having possibilities as yet unrealized, as having an open-ended future to be shaped partly by our own decisions. We can only define ourselves as being in history. We are each a being with a past, a present, and a future. In our minds truth, meaning, intelligibility, and existence have the character of events that are in process and cannot be retained as a reality like objects we can take hold of more than once. Return to a thought and it will be reshaped. Revisit an insight and it will have a new and fresher look. Look back and the nostalgia will frighten as well as thrill. This is due to our awareness that what is past cannot become the same again or be brought forward except as a contribution to what has become and is becoming. The truth of Faulkner's insight, "The past is not dead, it is not even past," is brilliantly, frighteningly, and hopefully pictured in the contemporary historical consciousness of his own characterizations.

This historical consciousness of having been somewhere and of going somewhere is more than an incident in our intellectual history; it is a revolution in our sense of life. We have a new sense of time and of becoming. The context of history in our minds is the world in evolution, an image for eons of time, for the gradual emergence of all that is, an awed humility before what is to come, and openness to what else there may be beyond our knowing. All of us have come to think scientifically and thus we all take the world as a progression of possibilities that have come into concrete actuality.

This sense of history does not depend on a belief in progress as the way history moves. Few people have retained such idealism in the face of twentieth-century experience. The historical consciousness can be nihilistic, pessimistic, or realistic. What has changed and is true for those who might be more hopeful, as well as those who are doubtful about the future, is the sense of what kind of options there are and where we must find meaning if any is to be found. Time and history cannot be treated as merely a stage for real things, they have to be treated as real as real can get, an ingredient of being itself.

Freedom and history must be intelligible as real aspects of being. What we do in the here and now, in this person, in this history, in our actions, must count. We cannot have some things which we know to be taking place here on earth discounted because they don't match what we believe or hope or suppose may be going on in another realm, like heaven. All temporal things must be real, not something less than real that are overcome in some other life reality.

(2) God's love takes form in history, not simply in the abstract. God's love responded, and is responding, to the reality of human sin. God suffers the reality that the human spirit is subject to the distortions, alienation, slavery, and perversities of the finite freedom of human existence. The history of God's love creates domains of reconciliation. Mercy, forgiveness, reconciliation, and regeneration are not simply ideals of love; they are the rendering in historical forms of the love of God and of what God is doing in human life.

God's action in the cause of creation involves the divine suffering. God's longing and agonizing over the world must take form in acts of love. In its freedom and openness to the future, the love that is God creates its own history in the actualizations it takes. Love changes shapes, is found in history in new ways, brings into being new forms of itself. The incarnation is the great action of love's responsive and creative history. The love of God *becomes* the suffering, self-giving love actualized in history when, in one person of the eternally outgoing interrelationship of Holy Love in the Trinity, the life of God becomes incarnate to share the human lot, to suffer the limitations of human existence, and to die in finite existence that the world might be regenerated, or if you wish, reconstituted, or if you wish, recapitulated. That is, the world is reconciled to the original purposes of creation in the joining of a new heaven and a new earth. Love in history becomes His Story, the story of Jesus of Nazareth.

*The issues of justice are dealt with in history, moving toward and preparing for the kingdom of God to come, not in a single action in which all sin and evil are resolved.* The Christ has come and the kingdom is established, yet the ways of an evil world persist. The kingdom will become the reality of the world and of heaven only through the persuasive action of God in history. First it had to become a choice, then it had to have its way through a history of choices. This reality simply conforms to the way love seems to work in a world in which it must suffer creation, in which it must have a history. Love persuades instead of imposes. Though the Christ has come, the array of possibilities must be arranged for human choices in history so that we are gradually persuaded to welcome the kingdom. Everything could not have changed and been established as a new reality at once with the cross, for then it would have been imposed without the freedom with which God created human beings.

Christians immediately recognized that they belonged to a new order (Rev 22:5; 2 Tim 2:22; 1 Pet 4:2; 5:1). Yet, just as immediately, it was recognized that the radical work of love implicit in the new age remains, in a strange way, hidden. One only has to read about the conflicts in the early church as they are revealed in Scripture to understand the disappointment and puzzlement the first Christians suffered over having to await the actualization of the kingdom in the time and space of history. So it has been since. It seems that in each generation the church has to struggle with its issues of evil, make its contribution to the kingdom's coming. Sometimes it seems as though the church is terribly slow in recognizing the existence of evil, only awakening with a shock to grasp how awful is some behavior or institution that had previously been accepted, perhaps even valued. Consider the issues we now consider an intolerable evil but toward which the People of God once acted as though they were blind to anything at all wrong: torture, slavery, and the subjugation of women. The list can be depressingly long. That is, it is depressing until one realizes that this is the dynamic of love at work taking form in actual history. All the ethical concerns that have grown in significance throughout Christian history are in part at least implicit in the new life of the gospel, but they are not explicit, and the reason for that must be sought in the historical situation into which the gospel came. Creation has become the new creation in Christ. The new creation in Christ is the subject of history and it is subject to history. The revolution of the kingdom is a permanent revolution that must work itself out in history.

*God is patient, loving not only out of consummation, but also out of the suffering of loyalty not-yet-fulfilled.* Our society is so driven by consumerism and so spoiled by instant gratification that we can lose sight of love's self-satisfaction in patience and loyalty. We tend to look at love's consummation and think we have seen the whole. That, as any lover knows, is ridiculous. The faithful, even courageous, waiting for consummation not yet realized is one of the ways love realizes itself. It is the suffering of the not-yet in the gift of the other's freedom. In the not-yet is to be found a form of communion that expresses love quite richly and enjoyably—and nobly. Of course, this is so because of love's confidence that the ecstasy of the fulfillment is to come. To call it love's foreplay would miss the point and perhaps take us astray, but not entirely. Perhaps the better analogy would be to see God as a pregnant mother, bearing her children with love's anticipation and her sustained loyalty to a humanity and a created order yet-to-be, but bearing life with potential so secured that it participates in actuality and can be experienced in development.

*The loyalty of love suffers compromises and accommodations with the not-yet state of the beloved and the beloved's circumstances.* Love is not very idealistic and has little room for sentimentality. Absolute love will suffer and be satisfied within the process of history with less than perfection. God, who is Love, desires our welfare even when it means allowing us to accommodate ourselves to the finite realities we confront in our own time. We are asked to remember simultaneously where we are going, the way things will be, and to work for it with the passion and urgency portrayed in the prophets. Even in the prophets we can see how God communicates the divine willingness to suffer the compromises and accommodations due to the realities the beloved faces, both in the beloved's human weakness and in the social limits of humanity.

I remember being told by Rabbi Heschel, the former professor at Union Theological Seminary and broadly recognized scholar of the prophets, that the student who understands Amos and Hosea taken together understands the prophets as whole. Amos was a simple man who accepted the call of God to stand before the most powerful people of his day, including the king and religious leaders, and accuse them in no uncertain terms of their failings and of God's demands. He warned them especially of the coming Day of the Lord, when all would be put right, that is, the righteous would be raised up and the guilty would be judged. His calls for justice in God's name ring down through the centuries with a beauty and passion that speak as movingly today as they did almost three millennia ago. No one who has listened to Martin Luther King quote his words in the sonorous tones of his "I Have a Dream" speech will doubt that: "Let justice roll down like mighty waters, and righteousness like a never-ending stream" (Am 5:24).

Hosea declared his message eloquently enough to qualify as one of the great spokespersons in history, but his most effective communication occurred through allegorical actions. The most poignant statement was in his faithful marriage to Gomer, a prostitute. Time and again, Gomer would stray; but without fail Hosea would forgive his wife and take her back. Hosea chose to suffer Gomer's infidelity. He claimed that this was the sort of relationship God had with the chosen people. God was like a faithful groom married to a faithless people. Nevertheless, God had chosen his bride, Israel, loved her, and would never fail to forgive her. God would remain faithful no matter what. Together, Amos and Hosea provide us with an image of God as the creator who loves us so greatly that we can be suffered to exercise our freedom wrongfully and faithlessly. Yet, we are called in no uncertain terms to live according to our highest ideals and to work for our longest ranged and most demanding goals for human life.

*The concrete actuality of human community, in which each person is interconnected with every other person and shares a common subjectivity that is ultimately rooted in God, provides a means of fulfillment for each person, at whatever point in history they live, in anticipation of history's culmination in the kingdom come.* There are many reasons why the corporate nature of reality forms the basis for satisfactions no individual alone can enjoy.

The comprehension of the Creator's nature which gradually emerged in the Jewish religion led to the insight that history is not cyclical; it is a linear reality leading to things that are new and fulfilling for the Jewish people. Even in a history notable for suffering, this satisfaction has proved very real for vast numbers of Jewish individuals. Christians especially appreciate the meaning their ancestors found in anticipation of the Messiah and the restoration of the Davidic kingdom. This expectation was translated with the coming of Jesus and has proved meaningful to the lives of countless Christians.

Needless to say, with the rise of individualism and the concomitant diminishment in our grasp of corporate reality and community in Western culture, so has the personal stake in the crowning of history declined. Signs are appearing, especially in the sciences, but also in theology and philosophy, of a renewed regard for the corporate nature of reality. With them, there is renewed interest and hope in the final expectation and the fulfillment it can lend to Christian lives dedicated to the transformation of human society and who consider themselves participants in that human community to come.

✦ ✦ ✦ ✦ ✦

# Summation

What is there in the model of the early church that we must rediscover in order to accomplish our reformation? Among other things, there is a pressing need to come to a common understanding about the identity and purpose of the church and resolve certain incompatible understandings about the nature of God, in particular about God's relation to the world. In this section we examined:

- The mission of the church as the two causes of God: creation and kingdom;
- The identity of the church, especially the authority and vocation for ministry: baptismal theology.
- The absolute relativity of God: the suffering of creation and kingdom.

*1. The mission of the church is creation and kingdom.* The church is the link that joins the two. That is a fundamental definition of the church. "Christ-like," "in-Christ," "the Body of Christ," "the sacrament of Christ and the eschatological sacrament of the world," "representing Christ"— however a tradition may wish to put it—the church is that human institution of the earth and of the kingdom which unites the two, holding each sphere of reality together, representing the world to the kingdom and the kingdom to the world. The church creates in partnership with God, as God's stewards, and the church welcomes the kingdom. The church serves in the "new age" of the uniting, serving in preparation for it. The goal of the church is the final joining of creation and kingdom in the coming of the Christ, the ruler of each dominion, at the culmination of time and history. There shall be a new heaven and a new earth and "God shall be all in all" (1 Cor 15:28). We contribute to the causes of God in each generation by giving ourselves in the ministry of Christ for the fullness of creation and kingdom—for each and all.

The difficulty is due in part to the fact that human beings find the relationship between world and kingdom paradoxical. God wills us to be at home in the world; God calls us to recognize that we are in exile. God wills us to embrace human life, our specific life, the way things are, as the most precious gift; God calls us to critique the world and change it most radically. God wills that we become fully human; God wills that we yearn for our eternal destiny. God wills us to bless this world; God calls us to judge the world.

In order to serve God's causes of creation and kingdom it is necessary to serve each equally without cheating for one or the other. We have to learn to hold each cause in dynamic, dialectical tension with one another. For example, the church must maintain the urgency of establishing the kingdom in siding with those who suffer due to deprivation and prejudice and oppression. We cannot be satisfied. At the same time the church must celebrate and live as a community defined by the fundamental attitude of thanksgiving, the eucharistic community of the church. We do our best for each of God's causes by focusing on the other. We serve the kingdom most effectively by immersing ourselves in service to the world. We serve the world most effectively by living for the kingdom. The church is distinctive from, and free from, the world in order to serve it. Thus is the church to transform the world welcoming the kingdom of God. The church is not the kingdom, though it is God's people seeking to live in community under God's reign. Thus, distinct from the kingdom, the church is able to offer the salvation of Christ to the world by being incarnationally immersed in it. We can see the effort to maintain this dynamic in our theology of Christmas and in the exercise of religion.

*2. One way to summarize the reformation in which we find ourselves is to recognize that fundamentally it is about the recovery of the church's theology of baptism.* Once the full implications of baptism are understood the particular reforms follow with coherent inevitability. For example, when it is understood that in baptism the many enter into the one ministry, that of our Lord Jesus, that each member is grafted into the fullness of that one ministry, then clericalism and ecclesiastical elitism is a lost cause. The ministry of all the baptized and the full inclusion of women into all forms, areas, and orders of ministry are understood as fundamental to realizing the meaning of being baptized into one body and one ministry. In the same way, when baptism makes its powerful claim that we are one, a united ecumenical church becomes a driving desire. I believe a case could be made for each of the other issues of the current reformation that will eventually prove legitimate as a component in the recovery of our self-understanding inherent in baptism.

One way to distinguish between the examination of the first notion regarding the theology of the church, that of creation and kingdom, and the examination of the second notion, that of baptismal theology, is to recall how our reformation is driven by two forces, external and internal. It may legitimately be acknowledged that the encompassing and controlling issue of external reform is the relation of the church to the world and to the kingdom. The mission of the church is naturally outgoing, service from the church to the world. However, it must be remembered that the first way to serve the world and the kingdom is to serve the church in its role as linking the two, as when justice within the church is served. The encompassing and controlling issue for internal reform is baptism, with its implications for ministry, community, individuality, authority, governance, and all aspects of the church's identity and purpose. Nevertheless, the authority for ministry which is directly in mission to the world and the kingdom is found in baptism.

3. *The long and uncontested tradition of our piety together with the revelation of Scripture inform our understanding of God as the creator and friend and comforter who suffers with and for creation.* We pray in confidence that God is responsive. We worship, adore, and praise God in confidence that God's life receives our offerings of thanksgiving. Love accepts the suffering that comes with the freedom it wills. The empathy of God, who is known and revealed as Love-itself, is absolute and perfect. Creation and kingdom are processes that must be suffered. All creatures of creation suffer for the cause of it; suffering is a part of created life itself. Creatures can choose to join God in the suffering of creation and of the kingdom "by taking up the cross." Suffering is complex, one of the mysteries of created life. Suffering can be creative, the source and occasion of growth and spiritual maturation, and helpful to others. All suffering is to be resisted and, where possible, eradicated. We labor for the kingdom where there will be no suffering.

The following observations follow from our understanding of suffering:

God is love. God suffers creation. God also suffers the coming of the kingdom. God is absolute and God suffers absolutely. The sign of the cross is definitive. Creation is an act of love that is ongoing in what we call history, for in its suffering love creates that which is new. Contemporary human beings have a radical historical consciousness. God's love takes form in history, not simply in the abstract. The issues of justice are discharged in history, moving toward and preparing for the kingdom of God to come, not in a single action in which all sin and evil are removed. God is patient, loving not only out of consummation but out of the suffering of loyalty not-yet-fulfilled. The loyalty of love suffers compromises and accommodations with the not-yet state of the beloved and the beloved's circumstances. The concrete actuality of human community, in which each and every person is interconnected with every other person and shares a common subjectivity that is ultimately rooted in God provides fulfillment for each person, throughout history, at the culmination of the rule of Christ in the kingdom come.

## NOTES

[1] Lorraine Kisley, *Ordinary Graces: Christian Teachings on the Interior Life* (New York: HarperCollins, 1992), 95.

[2] Albert Schweitzer, "Ethics for Twentieth Century Man," *The Saturday Review of Literature*, vol. XXXVI, no. 24 (June 13, 1953).

[3] See *Joannis Calvini I Novum Testamentum Commentarii*, ed. A. Tholuck, vol. V (1864): 226ff.

[4] "Eschaton" is the term theologians use to refer to the time when the climax of creation will occur in the completion of God's purposes at the end. How long this end-time will last is not at all clear, any more than what it will be like or when it will occur. The fundamental notion is that the universe was not created to last forever, but to reach certain purposes that will confer meaning on every life and every effort leading up to and contributing to the eschaton. In our tradition the statement of Jesus at the time of his death on the cross is an eschatological statement: "It is finished." The sense was not "It is over" but "It is accomplished."

[5] Walter R. Bouman, speech before the House of Bishops meeting, Kanuga Episcopal Church Conference Center, March 7, 1996.

[6] Freidrich Schleiermacher, *The Christian Faith* (Edinburgh: T. & T. Clark, 1948), 103.

[7] Bouman, House of Bishops speech,16.

[8] Ibid.

[9] See Mircea Eliade, *The Myth of the Eternal Return* (IV/66) and *The Sacred and the Profane* (IV/2).

[10] Alexander Schmemann, *For the Life of the World* (Crestwood, N Y: St. Vladimir's Seminary Press, 1973), 67.

[11] Sermon before the House of Bishops of the Episcopal Church, 1998.

# IV.

# *MINISTRY*

One of the original contributions I hope to make in this section is a single coherent and systematic theory of ministry. Those developed in the Gregorian Reformation and in the Protestant Reformation no longer genuinely satisfy any component of the church, rather they continue to divide, and increasingly get in the way of mission. Indeed, no feature of the church was as responsible for the conflict and division created in the Protestant Reformation and Catholic Counter-Reformation as the dissatisfactions and disagreements concerning ordained ministry. Reformation that seeks unity and coherence for the future must rediscover that the authority for ministry is baptismal, with ordained authority subject to the authority of the baptized community instead of vice versa. While this was one of the primary objects of the Protestant reformers, their knowledge of the early church was inadequate, and they were only partially successful. The source of the authority for ministry and governance is, of course, God-in-Christ. The reigning Lord places the authority for ministry in the hands of the community. It does not emanate from a hierarchy of the ordained, who are granted special insight and power from God apart from and independently of the community.

At the same time, the ministry requires a sacrament of order. Sacramental order was protected by the Catholic Counter-Reformation, but in the limited and crippled way the hierarchical clerical orders acted on the basis of an authority derived apart from and exercised over the community. A major part of the explication of this section will clarify the threefold order of ordained ministry and its relationship to the entire range of the church's ministry as the sacrament of order. We will not fully realize the ministry of all the baptized, the *laos*, until we understand and reform the ministry that orders it. The sacrament of order expresses the nature of the church. It does so in the powerful, pervasive, and definitive way that sacraments confer meaning: symbolically. Because the sacrament of order has been obscured for so long, except in theological theory, so has the nature of the church been obscured, except in theological theory.

# A SACRAMENTAL UNDERSTANDING OF THE WORLD AND MINISTRY

Because we hope to view the full picture of Christian ministry, this inquiry will address, at least by inference, the ministry of those Protestant churches without a sacramental system, that is, churches that do not consider their worship and ordained ministry as sacramental. However, the part of this explication that addresses ordained ministry relies upon a sacramental understanding. Consequently, this appeal is primarily to the churches that believe God has created a sacramental world. The vast majority of active Christians participate in a sacramental system. Their family of churches, which may be referred to as the catholic family of churches, includes the Roman Catholic Church, the Eastern Orthodox churches (Greek, Russian, Armenian, etc.), the Anglican Church, and the Lutheran churches (certain branches are more sacramentally founded than others, e.g., in the United States the ELCA is more sacramental in its life than the Missouri Synod).

These communions have a sacramental view of reality, and sacramental theology is central to their understanding and experience of the faith. Christianity is an incarnational faith. In Christianity the physical and the spiritual are not separate or in conflict, as in some other religious perspectives. The sacramental churches explain this in radical terms: it is in the physical that the spiritual can be experienced most concretely; it is in the ordinary that one can discover the extraordinary; it is in the stuff of earth that one can find the transcendent. The physical and the spiritual are inseparable. The world of sensory experience—all that we taste, touch, smell, hear, and see—expresses and reveals the spiritual. This is why God can be experienced in a sunset, on a mountain top, in a trout stream, while listening to a symphony, playing a game, or participating in drama, and most of all, in personal relationships. The ordinary conveys truth, beauty, and the good. The ordinary conveys the very presence of God. This is why God communicated the nature of divinity by becoming flesh.

Jews and Christians have always understood that it is through the world that God relates to human beings. Scripture opens on a picture in which God offered creation as a banqueting table for human beings, so that merely eating of the earth would be communion with the Creator. Even after we broke fast and consumed something not created for our use, something we wanted for its own sake and not because it related us to the Creator, God sought reconciliation with human beings by entering into the world. God limited neither the divine revelation nor divine communication to the medium of the spiritual; God did not visit people solely in prayer and contemplation and mystical communion. It was in the incarnation that the separation caused by sin is overcome and that the church is given the divine food that, again, grants us communion with God. Because of our sacramental theology we do not separate experience into sacred and secular; we do not segment the temporal and eternal, the spiritual and the material, church and world, Sunday and the rest of the week.

When the churches that view life as sacramental consider the fullness of the ministry of the baptized, including the reasons for sacramental ministry, it is to the theology of baptism that our thinkers turn to begin the initial process of reasoning. That is, the tradition of sacramental theology is the discipline that supplies the most suitable and most directly helpful methodology for analyzing this subject. Other disciplines, such as historical and philosophical theology, contribute necessary insights but these fields of study are not the most directly applicable.

## THE IMPORTANCE OF WHERE TO BEGIN

Where one chooses to begin consideration of the church's ministry is important. First, when the church starts with ordained ministry and individual authority it can place an overweaning importance on them. Many of the divisions within the church appear to be based squarely on differences held about the ministry and authority of the ordained. It would seem that churches allow this to define their entire life, especially as it determines ecclesiastical polity. On this single basis, entire communions, many being composed of millions upon millions of people through several centuries, are declared by others to be outside the life of the "true church." None of their myriad actions for the mission of the church are considered "valid" because they are performed by and under the authority of a ministry "invalidly" ordained. Different denominations can agree entirely on the mission of the church and find precious little room to quarrel over theological differences, but when the question of ordained ministry is raised, obsolete preoccupations with validity and antiquated historical wounds suddenly loom unassailably between them. Once we start with ordained ministry and the authority held by individuals in ordained office we find it too difficult to maintain our perspective that mission dictates ministry, instead of allowing ministry to dictate mission.

Secondly, when there is no consensus about the meaning of ordained ministry—and this is so today even within each communion—confusion reigns. There are broad agreements and well-defined disagreements, even across denominational lines, but the effort to render precisely our grasp of ordained ministry and authority is the captive of perplexity more than of common understanding. Issues that had been considered satisfactorily explained and settled once and for all have suddenly become increasingly controversial. The inclusion of women in ordained ministry, celibacy, and clergy "conversions" from one denomination to another give long-standing controversies new life and open up new areas of bewilderment and agitation for the whole family of sacramental churches, Eastern and Western.

Take as an example of the confusion regarding ordained ministry, especially apropos the gap between theory and practice, the claim of certain Western branches of the church to have a threefold order of ministry. These churches have articulated neither the distinctions nor the unity of the three orders in terms that apply to the actualities and make sense to the people of this day and age. In fact, there is only silence concerning the interrelationship of these three orders. Where perhaps the interrelationships have been theoretically articulated they certainly have not been demonstrated. Yet, despite the lack of articulation and actual practice, the church must harbor such resolute theological reasons to display the threefold order of ministry that its meaning resides very deeply, almost at the bottom of things. There seems to be a gut level of insistence that will not go away.

In actuality, the Western churches have long acted as though there were one ordained ministry. For Protestants it is "the minister." For the Roman Catholic and Anglican churches it is "the priest." We do not lack literature concerning the priesthood or the role of the minister, but there is little consensus. There seem to be few who can claim to possess a consistent concept of that distinctive vocation, few sacramental theologians who wish to define with theological precision the relationship between the priest and God and between the priest and the community. If there is a lack of theological consensus or understanding regarding the priesthood, there is almost a vacuum concerning the diaconate and the episcopacy. Most Christians are left with vague notions about servants and apostles. In actual practice, though not in theory, bishops are viewed simply as more authoritative priests. This is so perhaps especially regarding administration and decision-making but also in terms of the power to perform sacraments. Lutherans accentuate the administrative emphasis in the way that bishops are elected to terms of office; there is no Lutheran diaconate as of yet. The Roman Catholic and Anglican deacon is usually a priest-in-training, or is considered a minor priest—one who cannot perform the sacraments. The Roman Catholic Church was primarily responsible for getting the restoration of the diaconate underway following World War II, heroically motivated by leadership that came out of the concentration camps of Germany. However, more than for any other reason or purpose, as the Roman Catholic diaconate has developed it has been used as a badly needed opportunity to obtain more clergy from the ranks of married men, and it is increasingly narrowing into a clerical caste of priest-helpers or substitutes. The Anglican renewal of the diaconate is exciting and hopeful, but those who have been involved in this movement recognize how far it is from being shaped into the force for service that rings in tune with the songs of the mothers, as the diaconate is envisioned. In fact, this is too much to ask of the diaconate without the general renewal and clarification needed for all three orders of ordained ministry.

Our approach will be to begin with the central issue of mission. We will seek an understanding of ministry as the actions we take on behalf of mission. We will look for patterns and principles.

# THE MINISTRY

There are certain principles crucial to understanding what we mean by ministry, and in particular sacramental ministry. And there is a pattern that is key. We must look first and always to Jesus. All ministry is that of the risen Lord. The minister is always the resurrected Christ himself. We must never lose sight of this fundamental understanding; our line of reasoning must never vary from this track. The church ministers on behalf of Jesus. The church is the sign of his presence in the world; the church is commissioned to continue and complete the ministry of Christ. This is indicated in the commonly used term for the church, "Body of Christ," and by commonly accepted claims of the church that it represents the Christ. The *laos*, the People of God, is sent as an agent and ambassador of the mission of God. Already we identify a first principle: **Ministry is representational.**

The Christ was incarnate for the most grand and cosmic and time-less of purposes. His redemptive ministry was assured from the very foundations of creation. In the mysteries of the incarnation and resur-rection everything stirred, the whole of creation turned, the universe is made new. His ministry, in particular his death and resurrection, rec-onciled heaven and earth and through him is the advent of a new heaven and a new earth. We have been summarizing this all-encom-passing mission in the terms "creation" and "kingdom." **The scope of ministry that represents Jesus is to be cosmic, universal, and across all time.**

The risen and cosmic Christ whom the church represents on earth is never to be considered apart from the human being from Galilee who was executed during the reign of the Roman Emperor Tiberius. This man did things. Jesus of Nazareth functioned as the Christ. Jesus exercised his personal ministry. He intended his func-tions to do something for the people to whom he ministered in action and word and to mean something for all time and in all places. The extent of his consciousness is open to discussion, but his intention to act on God's behalf in a very special role is apparent. Increasingly we will see the importance and the complexity of the principle revealed: **Ministry is a matter of specific functions and it is a matter of intentionality.**

When we begin to consider what Jesus himself actually did, per-haps the first thing we notice is how Jesus of Nazareth went about gathering his community and sending them out into the world to rep-resent him as his agents. He called them into a society not only for the benefit of each other, for fellowship, for mutual support, for celebra-tion, or for tending to logistical matters. He gathered them and sent them to exercise a ministry on his behalf. He gave them his authority and his blessing. This pattern of gathering and sending began straight away in the gospel story, immediately following his baptism. On the very day of the resurrection he charged his disciples with his mission. Finally, the gospel story concludes with his commissioning just prior to taking leave of earth. The story of the rise of the church in Acts and the epistles begins with the sending of the disciples into Jerusalem to perform the earthly ministry of the risen Lord. The ministry of Jesus was, in large measure, to gather and send the church on his universal mission. The church always must remain loyal to this original calling and sending of his community for mission. **The ministry of the church is to be *loyal* to the original pattern of *gathering the faithful* and** *sending them on the universal and timeless mission* defined by the life of Jesus.

The grand and cosmic ministry of Jesus was down-to-earth and localized. Jesus healed. Jesus forgave. Jesus blessed. Jesus empowered. Jesus reconciled. The healing and empowering blessing of God was offered for the transformation of human individuals, communities, and people, so that they could live according to the genuine purposes of their creation. Those who received this ministry found themselves living with a certain fundamental posture toward life. That is, in their experience of reconciliation, followers of Jesus were grateful, they were faithful, and they were worshipful. They formed a community whose inner life of faithful and worshipful gratitude manifested the reconciliation they experienced personally, experienced with one another, and experienced with God and the created order. Jesus called his community together in a worshipful, compassionate, and just society in which the beatitudes were the rule, a society in which the early Yahwistic ideals were realized, and he commissioned them to work for the full realization of that society, the kingdom of God. **Ministry is *reconciliation* through the formation of communities of thanksgiving in which is offered and manifested the *blessing of God for healing, forgiveness, and empowerment*. These communities work in society to welcome the justice, peace, and reconciliation of the kingdom.**

The ministry of Jesus took form in humble acts of service, concrete and "hands-on" wherever he saw human need. The preexistent Christ "did not regard equality with God as something to be exploited, but emptied himself, taking the form of a slave, being born in human likeness. And being found in human form, he humbled himself" (Phil. 2:6b–8a). Jesus explicitly said that he came like one who was to serve at table (Luke 22:27). At first it seemed that Jesus understood his personal mission of gathering the whole people of Israel to be limited to his own heritage. Gradually he turned north into Samaria and began to demonstrate this universal notion of his mission in acts of service to any and all. Unlike Samuel and the Israelite community seeking to establish a society reflective of the holiness, compassion, and justice of God's own life, Jesus was never in any position to minister through the structures, institutions, and laws of his day. In their tradition formed in the early Yahwistic ideals, however, Jesus made it crystal clear to his personal followers how they must follow the principles of justice in the vision of *shalom* and he called all who would listen to that new plan for human society in which service of others is the rule—not lording it over those without equal might, position, and resources. Jesus expressed his identity in use of his unique gifts for service. He identified the life of service as the ordinary and fundamental way of carrying out the stupendous mission in which heaven and earth are reconciled. In concrete acts of service offered to those in need, Jesus renewed the creation and manifested the presence of the kingdom of God. **Ministry is *service*. It is exercised in humility. It is concrete and hands-on. It is offered to those in need, especially those who cannot find justice for themselves and on their own, those who are weak, sick, lonely, poor, suffering, oppressed, and marginalized.**

In our brief look at the person and ministry of Jesus, already we can discern certain important things about the church's ministry. First, it is representational. Jesus is the minister when the church acts on his behalf. We represent him in the performance of our ministry. Whether it is performed by the corporate church or by an individual, whether by the ordained or by laity, whether by a parish or a diocese, it is the ministry of Christ. Ministry is fundamentally representational. At the same time it is an act that is performed. It is incarnational action. Ministry is something the baptized do. It is action by human beings toward and for other human beings. Ministry is functional. Thus we come to an awareness that ministry is a matter of both representation and function. The relation between the representational and the functional, between the church in what it is as the representative of the Christ and the church in what it does on behalf of the Christ, is being revealed even at this early point in our deliberations.

When we look even more closely we recognize a certain pattern for the ministry of the Christ. This is key. It is threefold pattern:

(1) The cosmic ministry on behalf of Jesus will be exercised in accord with the originating and sending ministry of the incarnate Lord in formation of the united and whole church.

2) The ministry of Jesus will be reconciliation and thanksgiving, healing and blessing.

3) The ministry of Jesus will be concrete and humble human service where there is need.

We may turn to an examination of the ministry of the church as we have already begun to see it shaped, and discover specific principles that further define it.

The church's mission and the ministry that is given order so that the mission may be carried out should suit the most traditional statement of the nature of the church as one, holy, catholic, and apostolic. Certain principles can be readily extrapolated simply by a brief and surface glance. When we conclude that ministry is always that of Jesus it becomes clear that any act of ministry is always that of the whole and united church, the *one* church. This is the church that is single, cosmic, global, continuing, and timeless. To be catholic is to recognize our responsibility and our loyalty to the whole church, universally and at all times and in all places through the time of the church. Even when the ministry offered on behalf of Jesus by the church is performed in particular and concrete acts of ministry, it is always the ministry of the whole church. The ministry of Jesus can never be segmented or isolated from the united whole of the Spirit-filled church, whether it is performed by a person, or by committees, or by congregations, or by particular parts and branches of the church. The ministry of Jesus is the ministry of the whole church, whether it is by someone holding an official office or an office worker. If the Spirit moves a person to exercise a certain call it is always on behalf of the whole church, for it is a call to the ministry of Jesus. **Ministry is always the ministry of the whole and united church.**

Ministry is sent. To be apostolic is to send and to know that it is Jesus, through the church, still doing the sending. Ministry is performed on behalf of Jesus and thus on behalf of the whole church. Just so there needs to be an awareness of the sending and the being sent to the ministry by the church on his behalf, and concomitantly of being accountable. Ultimately the awareness of being sent and of being accountable is in relation to the whole church. No single person is ever just working on his or her own and nor is any entire branch of the church. Therefore, ministry requires the discernment of a community that has the authority to send, providing "the minister of Christ" (corporate or individual) with the commission, each being accountable to the other. There is a continual and urgent need for discipline in the sending and in the being sent. Ministry is sent by the whole and united church.

Intentionality is a critical aspect of ministry. There are many actions that serve God's purposes, but they are not acts of ministry. When the prophet looked at the ambition of Cyrus to conquer Babylonia and establish the great Persian Empire, he discerned that Cyrus would be serving God's purposes for Israel. Isaiah never supposed that Cyrus was aware of any such thing, much less intended it. Yet releasing the Babylonian slaves so that they could reestablish themselves in the Promised Land and carry forth their role in God's causes surely served. The brothers of Joseph did not sell him into slavery on behalf of God. Yet God used this vile action for the chain of events following it, with many ups and downs, until it finally led to the Exodus experience and the long history of God's chosen people. We trust God to shape to the divine will any and all occurrences, including the mistakes that result from our best intentions, those actions attributable to our worst intentions, the actions of people who intend to serve the world and humanity without regard for the church's ministry, and even the work of those totally unaware of their role in the great events of history.

In the unity of the whole church, apostolically sent, all Christians are ministers and whatever a Christian does is ministry. The intentions as well as the results of the actions of ministry may be good or they may be bad, or any degree of value in between. Each action is an act of ministry in any case. Nevertheless, ministry is best for the individual acting and for the life of the church if it is intentional. Greater consciousness of the empowerment and the responsibility of all baptized members of the church is one of the pressing needs of the church today. Raising the level of personal intentionality in the performance of Christ's ministry would be transforming for the individual and much more effective. One may suppose the good intentions for ministry in the practice of law when a Christian relies on competence and general good will, grounded in worship and personal ethics. One may imagine the difference it would make for an attorney if she paused to pray before conferring with each client, before beginning going into negotiations, or before going to a trial, asking that Christ act through her for justice and for the good of the client and society. The hope of the church is that all baptized Christians will form habits of intentional ministry such that the performance of ministry eventually will becomes less conscious than must be necessary for most of us in this day.

Ministry is offered on behalf of the whole church to realize the radical and cosmic mission to which Christ has called the church. It is not enough to feel called by God; it is confusing to think of baptism as a "little ordination" empowering people to act on their own. Nor is it Christian ministry simply to "do good" or to act on humanitarian impulses. Ministry requires the discernment by a community or an individual of being sent as a representative of the church by Jesus himself, just as he chose and sent the apostles. The sense of being commissioned and sent by the whole church and by Jesus, the sense of being authorized and accountable to the whole church and to Jesus, the sense of being part of the fellowship of the original disciples, would enhance and will ideally be present in any ministry performed by each baptized person, each congregation, each community, each institution, each diocese, and each communion. This sensibility must regard the church as it transcends time and space, going all the way back to Jesus and those whom he personally gathered. The call to ministry and to acts of ministry must hold regard for this nature of the church, for all the saints living and dead, for all the institutions and communions and components across any and all lines, even those which might seem to separate and segment the Body of Christ. The sense of representing the whole church requires faithfulness to the tradition of the church, especially to that which has been accepted as orthodox, in order to proclaim the true gospel. This sensibility must include in its grasp the holiness that transcends human sinfulness and has its source in the holiness of the Trinitarian Spirit. The church requires a system of discipline in which this faithfulness, orthodoxy, and holiness may be guarded. **Ministry is to be intentional and habitual.**

Each baptized member of the church is called and sent by Jesus through the church to serve the Christian community in its worship and its community life, but even more immediately in the arenas of ordinary and daily life where the member lives, works, plays, and engages in citizenship on behalf of the whole society. Individuals are called into the church for the transformation of their lives and their personal growth in order to become fully human, as Christ was fully human. However, just as Christ came not simply to fulfill his personal humanity, but for the mission of God's causes, so the life of the baptized is transformed and made whole not merely as an end in itself but in order to serve as a minister of the gospel. Each baptized person is fully empowered to exercise and fulfill each and every aspect, feature, facet, and nuance of the ministry of Christ. The members of the church are called to minister corporately through the various institutional and communal levels of the church and to minister individually in their day-to-day lives. Ministry occurs anytime something is done with the intention of serving God's cause on behalf of the church, that is, in the name of Christ.

One of the charisms of baptism is the gift of the Spirit for the building of the community and the performance of the mission of the church. What should the baptized person do to fulfill this intention? How should the person or persons being ministered to know that it is ministry on behalf of the church and thus in the name of Christ? How does the church commission and send each baptized Christian to minister armed with the right marching orders? The church expects each action to conform to the consistently threefold nature of the church's ministry: (1) concrete service where human need and the need for the stewardship of creation is identified; (2) service to which Christ continues to send the whole and universal church in the global mission, particularly in the daily life of the regions, cities, towns, and villages where people live together in communities, and especially through making the life of Christ present in altar-centered communities; (3) service which is performed out of gratitude for blessings received, especially forgiveness.

Baptism sends each of its initiates to serve as a minister, or missionary, in their local area. The ministry of the church is not limited to church activities. Because it is cosmic, most ministry is performed by Christians through their individual roles in society. If one is a janitor, the cleaning of space is to be offered on behalf of God's creation and even for the broader contributions to be made by that space. The work of a business person is to be prayerfully offered to serve the economy, as well as for direct benefits to workers and consumers. Whatever one's occupation is, the church assumes it is to be exercised as a vocation for Christian ministry. The same is true for the ministry of serving those with whom one lives, in the home or dorm, in the neighborhood, and the larger community. Marriage and parenting are terribly important vocations of Christian ministry. Being a roommate and a friend is Christian ministry. Every Christian has the obligation to serve society in good citizenship, in voting intelligently, and participating in civic activities, perhaps even in public service. Recreation provides all sorts of opportunities for ministry, in the joy, relaxation, and engagements of play and leisure.

Where people ordinarily spend their time and energy is where most ministry should occur. One of the most shocking and debilitating realities of Christianity is how few of the things the individual baptized person does—outside of activities performed in the institutional or cultic life of the church—are considered acts of ministry, either by the person or by the world. Even when members are trying to "live Christian lives" they usually do so without a specific intentionality to perform ministry, and when they do, few people recognize it as such. Most Christians think of ministry strictly in terms of the ministry of their ordained church leaders, or of actions that help ordained ministry, or of actions performed as an extension of ordained ministry.

Christian ministry is most readily seen in the life of the Christian community of the congregation or parish. All Christians are called to this first line of mission, and indeed there is hardly anything a Christian can do that is more important for creation and kingdom. We are to offer ourselves in the creation of a Christian parish community that manifests the reign of God. The ministry of the community is worship and celebration, offering and sacrifice, prayer and thanksgiving. The community is to make the divine love, healing, and blessing available to one another and to the disbelieving world, so that it and the members of the parish may be reconciled to God and to one another. The community is to offer concrete human service in individual contacts and for global purposes, in religious activities, and in vocational, social, political, and civic activities. In the community that celebrates the resurrection, the members are free to embrace creation in gratitude and to find comfort in a world of suffering; in the community the members are free to take up the cross in the struggle for justice, and they are to be supported in doing so. To be a community expressing freedom from sin and oppression is to be the ambassador of grace and love to others, to be the servant of freedom and justice. The world is to look upon a community that is immersed in service to the world for the sake of God's kingdom, and that gives itself to the kingdom of God by serving the world. The full and urgent ministry of the congregation is finally about history, for it is the community of history's covenanted agents. Christian ministry, however, is not limited to the church at all. **Ministry is performed corporately or individually in all areas of life at all times and places where the church exists.**

In the holiness of the church, the world can see its values, its causes, and that for which it stands, especially on behalf of those who are in need. The great twentieth-century theologian Reinhold Niebuhr said that the first task of the church is to act as a pioneer in justice. By this he meant that the church is to begin its service by establishing justice within its structures and organization, especially in the governance of its own internal institutional life. In doing so, it issues the most genuine call for society to follow it and to do so in the great cause of justice.

As times change, society tends to look back in history to question the congruency between the image it has of Jesus and the behavior of the church. For the life and expression of an incarnational faith is subject to the limitations of its culture and its times at every point along the way of its history. One prominent example is the way our generation views the the "holy" crusades, as opposed to the way the medieval church viewed them. Twenty-first century people regard the call to arms as a contradiction of all the church should stand for, as an embarrassment to the founder of the church. The people of feudal Europe heard the call in the most highly moral and even religiously heroic terms. The person who preached the first crusade was Bernard of Clairvaux, a Cistercian monk who was known best for his sermons and treatises on love. In this we see profound irony; the medieval masses saw simple logic.

Obviously, from the perspective of any age, the church does not always act in such a manner that shows it moving history toward the kingdom. It does not always do what Jesus would have done, or what the reigning Lord would have it do. It makes human mistakes; its people sin. Somehow God takes what has been done into the divine life of the Trinity and shapes it so that even its mistakes and most awful sins are turned to the good of those who love God, toward the mission of the church. The early church was sufficiently reflective of its Lord that it gained acceptance as his representative and since then, while the public impression of the church has waxed and waned with the times, the view about whom the church represents has been consistent.

Of the intrepid examples that could be offered of the church's pioneering work for justice, two experiences in my lifetime have been major influences on me personally, as well as on millions of other human beings. Martin Luther King provided the crucial leadership for the American civil rights movement, especially in the Deep South of the United States where I grew up. Archbishop Desmond Tutu emerged as the leader against apartheid in South Africa. Both of these men acted out of their faith; their theological beliefs formed the basis for their message and the strategic map for their actions. The movements they led were manifestly ministries of the Christian church. They demonstrated the effectiveness of Christian ministry in the cause of justice, and they demonstrated the power this has to convert the human soul.

One of the primary and most effective ministries of the church has been offered in its suffering on behalf of its mission. This refers not only to the way the blood of its martyrs has seeded the growth of the church throughout its history. It is not only the faith of believers in the face of suffering and death that ministers to the human community of suffering. It is the way the suffering of the church presents a vision of God as the I Am who suffers the freedom of God's people out of the bondage of human sin and oppression. That is fundamentally what Moses heard in the name of God coming out of the burning bush. In perfectly and absolutely divine empathy with all suffering, and with certain confidence in both causes of the new creation and the liberating citizenship in the kingdom, God says: "That is who I Am." God is revealed as the Creator who suffers creation with those whose life here does not seem "providentially fair" and with those whose lives seem captured by sin, their own and that of others.

The church has served God and God's mission best when it reflects the compassion and justice of God's own life in its own institutional organization and life and when it calls society to follow it.

## SUMMARY CONCLUSIONS

With only the most cursory survey of two obvious considerations, the ministry of Jesus and the implications for ministry as the church is defined in outline form within the creed, we have uncovered what we need for our understanding of ministry. First, we may now define an act of ministry.

Ministry is any action that is (1) intentional as (2) the ministry of Jesus, (3) acted on out of a direct commission or the sense of being sent by the church, the whole church, and Jesus, accountable to each, (4) to accomplish the mission of the church. The mission of the church is God's cause of the kingdom, exercised through service to God's creation, and God's cause of the new creation in Christ, exercised through dedication and service to the kingdom. Ministry is performed in the acts of each and every baptized member, where each person or each community is and whatever is done, in every arena of life, perhaps most particularly in vocations, in the church, and in public service. The church is to be a minister simply in living the life of a community defined by mission and as a pioneer of the kingdom.

How do the ministers, corporate and individual, know what to do in the name of Christ? How does the church construct the system for the discipline so badly required? How does the world have any idea of what the church is up to and what it is truly? We take note of the three-fold pattern of ministry and we order all ministry accordingly: (1) the cosmic ministry of unity and wholeness in relation to the risen Lord and the members of the Body, (2) the ministry of thanksgiving and reconciliation, and (3) the ministry of service. These are subtle distinctions but they are key to our understanding of the church's ministry, and of the nature of the church.

When the church begins to consider ministry it tends to focus too much on the functions of ministry and on authority: what can be done, by whom, when, and where? But when it is wise the church goes back to a lesson it seemed to have learned very early on: the most important thing to keep in mind is the pattern of ministry. This pattern must be recognized, it must be clearly discernable, in order for the church to serve "like Christ" and in order to serve Christ loyally. When this pattern of ministry is manifested, in it can be discovered the profound nature of the church's ministry, and thus, with deeper penetration into the insight, the nature of the church's identity and purpose beyond its activities. The pattern seems obvious enough, and few will argue with any facet of it, yet our experience is that we can very easily lose sight of it, like the proverbial traveler who can't see the forest for the trees, and become lost in the comprehension and practice of ministry—and therefore of mission.

If one scrutinizes each and every sort, turn, and direction in examination of Christian ministry, however tediously, the threefold pattern would always be revealed. We could dissect corporate ministry and individual ministry, the ministry of the parish and the ministry of the timeless and universal church, the ministry of all the baptized and the ministry of the ordained, and so on. In each case it would be discovered that the threefold pattern is the key to each exercise of ministry. The point is that there is an inexorable logic to the three-fold pattern of ministry, such that it cannot be denied and must not be ignored.

Whether it is the church as a whole speaking through an ecumenical council with the authority of that gathered in Nicaea, or a baptized child offering a small hand in love to a parent during a time of need, or a Martin Luther King and a Desmond Tutu calling society to the kingdom's standards of justice, the ministry of the church is one of service, reconciliation and thanksgiving, unity and wholeness. The same three-fold pattern is discovered from every point of observation. A more comprehensive analysis of the corporate ministry of the church would require considerable attention on that which is offered at the diocesan, regional, national, international, and ecumenical levels. For example, the catholic family of sacramental churches view the diocese as the basic unit for church governance and ministry; in global terms the diocese is the local church in that it has the size, resources, and fullness of ministry to represent the Body of Christ in a locale. When it is, the ministry is perceived as that of Jesus, risen and living and reigning through the church.

## THE ORDAINED AS MINISTER: THE THREEFOLD ORDERING

It is clear to the reader that the same threefold pattern of ministry is discovered from every point of observation. The only minister as yet unmentioned are the ordained. They too conform to the same threefold pattern. Indeed, they are ordained explicitly in order to perform the functions expressed by the pattern, and they are ordained to model this pattern by focusing each of the particular forms composing the threefold pattern. Up to this point we have referred to each form of ministry with certain descriptive words. Instead of this awkward terminology, the church has used the vocabulary of ordained ministry to designate, describe, and define the threefold pattern of the church's ministry. When the church refers to the pattern of ministry we have been calling that of "wholeness and unity" the normally applied term is *apostolic ministry*. This is the ministry focused by bishops. When the church refers to the form of ministry we have been summarizing as "reconciliation and thanksgiving" the term is *priestly ministry*. This is the ministry focused by presbyters, more often called priests or pastors. When the church refers to the ministry of "service," the original Greek term is normative: *diaconal ministry*, the ministry focused by deacons.

Ordained ministry is not *the* ministry of the church. It is one particular ministry of the church, that which provides leadership and is a sign, or model, of the church's threefold ministry, ordering this ministry so that the whole church, especially the vast numbers of baptized members who are not ordained, will provide the ministry properly and continually with their lives. The whole *laos*, including the ordained and the unordained membership, makes up the *ordo* of ministry. The ordained membership orders it as threefold. All baptized are part of the sacrament of order. It is the ordained membership that orders the whole.

The sacrament of order tells the world what it is that the church intends to do in Christian service, while it focuses and provides leadership for the performance of each aspect of that service. Ordained leadership serves as sacramental leadership so that the church may minister effectively as the sacrament of Christ.

# THE SACRAMENTAL NATURE OF THE CHURCH'S MINISTRY

## SIGN, SYMBOL, AND FUNCTION

We have reached a point in our analysis where the whole scheme of ministry is glimpsed. It should be helpful now to pause to consider the sacramental nature of the church's ministry. We begin by returning to where we started. The church is the sign of the risen Lord's presence in this world; the church is commissioned to continue and complete the ministry of Christ. The churches that view reality as sacramental summarize and explain this in those terms: the church is the sacrament of Christ to and for the world and the kingdom.

The key to understanding this is in the concept of symbol. It is especially important to heed the way sign and symbol are dynamically connected through function. In this instance there is a consensus among Christians about the representational nature of the church, that is, about its role as a sign of the transcendent Christ and of the reign of Christ in the world. It is similarly clear that there is consensus among Christians about the functional role of the church, that is, about its character as the agent performing ministerial functions on behalf of the transcendent Christ and of the kingdom in this world. What has been lacking is a common understanding of symbol as something sufficiently real and powerful enough to be sacramental, without further need of an explanation that claims to be either scientific or metaphysical, whether or not those are available.

A symbol is, first of all, a sign. A sign is something that can be experienced by the senses and is concretely of the world. Usually it can be created or formed by human beings. A sign is some "thing," a *res*, which points to a reality beyond itself. The reality to which it points may be specific and unambiguous, like a restroom sign saying, "Women," or it may be complex and culture-bound, like the sign in the South a generation ago saying, "Colored Only." For example, a stop sign along a road points to something drivers should do. Another sign that can be seen too commonly by the driver of an automobile points beyond a billboard with painted words and images to a product that can be purchased. It points to this reality for the purpose of motivating the observer to desire it, and conjuring enough psychic energy in that motivation so that the observer will go to a market where it is available and purchase it. Signs can be far more complicated. Language utilizes a highly sophisticated and complex system of verbal signs called words. When spoken these words may be less significant in themselves than the body of "language" or signs which accompany them and, taken together, communicate some very refined meaning to which they all point. In a church one can find all sorts of art that points beyond itself to something transcendent of the senses, usually something sacred. The last thing to be said about a sign, for our purposes, is that it is "merely" a sign of that to which it is pointing: the reality to which it points is truly beyond it; the sign is not that reality and it does not partake of that reality.

A sign, however, can become a symbol. A symbol starts there; it is a sign. However, a symbol not only points to something beyond itself, it participates in the reality toward which it points. A symbol can carry an observer or participant in the symbolic representation into the reality toward which it points. Through the sign, human beings can participate in the reality toward which it is pointing. For example, a commonly recognized symbol is a national flag. A flag is simply a sign of the nation and what the nation "is," what it stands for, what it values, its land, its people, its laws, its institutions, its opportunities, its schools and businesses, its sports and religions, and so on. For the vast majority of the world the flag can be nothing more than a sign representing the nation for various utilitarian purposes. For a citizen of the nation whose flag is shown, however, it is probably imbued with the power of a symbol. Looking upon the flag takes that observer directly into the reality of that nation, of all that that nation is and signifies to that particular person.

One of the characteristics of a symbol is that it carries a simultaneously positive moment and negative moment. As one participates in the reality toward which the symbol points, the participant is aware that the mediating sign is not the reality itself, yet it is experienced as the reality. Christians know this in our experience of the sacraments, as nationalists know it in the experience of a flag.

The Jesuit scholar Roger Haight suggests the nature and importance of symbols for revelation in his fine Christological work, *Jesus, Symbol of God.* He begins by noting:

> A symbol is that through which something other than itself is known. A symbol mediates awareness of something else. Sometimes the only way this "other" can be known is through some symbolic mediation. For example, there are layers of the self that do not lie on the surface, open to our own immediate self-awareness, but must be revealed through other forms of activity such as dreaming or writing or painting or behaving....Psychology and art are completely at home with symbolic forms of knowing.[1]

Avery Dulles explains that symbolic knowledge is not an attenuated form of cognition, but an extension of the range of human awareness, what may be called engaged participatory knowledge.[2]

Symbols are very rare. A few can be learned, like the flag. None can be created. None can be chosen. All have to be discovered. Certain symbols are universal. A shared meal and a common cup are two universal symbols of incorporation. Water is a universal symbol that can express things about death and resurrection, or new life. The Christian church makes use of most of the universal symbols in its sacramental system. It makes far more use of symbols than any other religion, even animistic religions, because as an incarnational faith it is the earthiest of the religions.

When human beings see a symbol it is known; symbols are experienced cognitively. Yet we cannot explain a symbol; they are supra-rational. They have too many voices and too many meanings operating at too many levels to capture in any explanation, even with a comprehensive series of rational statements. Nevertheless, symbols are rational. They make sense in themselves and they make sense of the world. It is one of the great mysteries of the human makeup, but certain things and actions of the creation as it is given, not as we create it, can have the incredible power and meaning of a symbol. They can carry us directly into another realm and grant us experiences of the most profound and mysterious sort. Nothing in our psyche, conscious and unconscious, including our entire range of emotions and ideas and memories, gives each of our individual lives more meaning than that formed by the nexus of symbolical meanings carried in our minds and in our hearts.

A symbol that points toward and participates in the reality that is the transcendent other is called by the church a "sacrament." Bread and wine can become the risen Lord's body and blood; water can become the cleansing source of new life. The church not only offers certain sacraments as symbols through which the faithful participate in the life of the Lord, but the church itself is a symbol, and thus a sacrament. The church is the sacrament of Christ; all of the sacraments it offers flow from this foundation.

A sign, however, becomes a symbol only when the function of the sign is congruent with the reality toward which it points. If a nation is not acting in accord with the values and standards its flag is said to represent, that flag will not be capable of operating symbolically for a patriotic observer. If the gathering of a community of Christians around an altar is not part of the striving of that community to be the Body of Christ in that place, especially in the exercise of its mission, the bread and wine are soon going to be experienced with frustration and, finally, as relatively empty gestures instead of as the body and blood of Christ. If the church manifests the life of Christ in its life of companionship, ministry, and worship, it is because and to the extent that the church is experienced as a sacrament. The sign has to be capable of being a symbol. Then, the appropriate functioning of the sign triggers the symbolical, freeing the sign of whatever boundaries circumscribe it, through their function, through the actions that give truth to that which they claim to represent.

Ministry is both a matter of being and doing, function and sign. There can be no ministry of mere presence. Most Christians see reality as sacramental. This sacramental understanding of the church began very early in the life of the first-century Jesus movement, and quickly baptism and Eucharist were being offered in those sacred terms. The preceding discussion regarding symbol and sacrament is crucially important in order for Christians who are founded in a sacramental view of reality to understand ministry and to sort out various problems of clericalism and authority.

## THE RENEWED APPRECIATION OF SYMBOL

Surely one of the most important developments in the twentieth century has been the gradual re-appreciation of the power and value of symbol and of myth. For too long symbol has been misunderstood and depreciated. It has been improperly placed in opposition to that which is "real," functional, and effective. But more recently philosophy, psychology, anthropology, literary scholarship, and theology have all contributed to the growing realization that the symbolic is a profound and integral factor in that process, conscious and unconscious, in which the human being finds meaning.

It is significant that the sacramental system developed at a time in history when there was profound appreciation of the symbolic. To make a radical distinction between symbol and reality would have been foreign to those sharing the worldview in which the early church was developing her doctrine and discipline. On the one side were those in the Hellenistic tradition who saw two realms of reality, the concrete reality of this world and the ideal reality above and beyond. For them, things in this world exist only to the extent that they point to and participate in the realities of the realm above. "What things are and what they point to beyond themselves were not considered radically distinct."[3] This is Platonic in orientation, although Platonism included schools of thought in which wide distinctions were made. On the other side, we find those that are Aristotelian in tendency. These saw natural and supernatural orders of reality, not entirely remote from one another, interacting and sharing in reality. It was by participating in the supernatural that natural things had their being in reality. But rather than beyond and above, this supernatural was within and underlying natural things, thus giving them substance and existence. In each case the thing of this world was readily capable of manifesting and participating in that reality of the supernatural, of being a symbol.

The symbolic was real and effective. Let me be somewhat simplistic in illustration: for some the bread and wine of the Eucharist pointed toward and participated in the life of the risen Lord, allowing the person who takes the elements into his body to participate in that risen reality, to become a part of the risen Lord's own flesh and blood. Others might have accepted the presence of Jesus within and underlying the elements of bread and wine, giving them their full unseen reality, what Aquinas later on would call their *esse*. "The elements are Jesus because they mean Jesus; being and signification are the same."[4] Either nuance of attitude leads to the same apprehension of the "real presence" of the symbolic. No one would have questioned whether it was possible to have bread and wine become a categorically different thing. It sufficed to appreciate that, according to the promise of Jesus and in thanksgiving for it, the liturgy gathers up the meaning of the gospel in the bread and wine as the Lord's body and blood. Thus the bread and wine become symbols of transcendent reality in the most profound sense: they manifest, make present, and make effective, the body and the blood of the Lord Jesus.

Notice how both the church and Western culture gradually changed their appreciation of symbol. Between the fall of the Roman Empire and the rise of the medieval "schoolmen," Europe passed through the Dark Ages when the original Platonic and Aristotelian thought systems were lost to study. By the time the scholastics examined their universe, the natural and the supernatural were separated by a great gulf. By the end of the scholastic period nominalism had carried the day, fragmenting the world into isolated particular things. It became increasingly difficult to imagine any concrete thing or any relationship reaching so far beyond itself, or so deep within itself, as to both point to and actually participate in a reality greater than itself. It became difficult to see a wholeness and unity between and underlying all things. For example, ask ten Christians who regularly participate in it to identify the sacrament of the Eucharist and you are likely to hear all ten reply that the sacrament is the bread and wine validly transformed into the body and blood of Christ. This is of course correct insofar as it goes, but likely as not it will include little or no discussion involving the liturgy as a whole. In the surviving patristic writings, discussion of the sacrament invariably involved a description of the liturgy as a whole. Nowadays, the sacraments as particular "things" tend to be separated out artificially from the liturgy in which they are performed. The liturgy has been relegated to the category of secondary, decorative, and ritual elements having no bearing on the *esse* of the sacrament. As Alexander Schmemann points out, validity becomes the preoccupation, not fullness, meaning and joy, not the *leiturgia* of the church.[5]

In the early church there could have been no liturgies in which the individuals of the congregation engaged in saying private prayers, private confessions, or performing other acts of piety in isolation from the community until the president produced the consecrated elements as "the" sacrament, ringing a bell to bring the congregation's attention to it. The idea of worshiping alongside others who are offering their personal worship, of saying one's prayers alongside others who are saying their personal prayers, would have been foreign; the prayers and the actions were corporate.

Given the normative sacramental view of the day, it is not only difficult to see sacramental liturgy holistically, but there is an unfortunate need for precise definitions of the most literal sort. By the Middle Ages there was considerable consternation over how to explain the presence of Christ in the bread and wine as something more than a "mere" symbol. Consider the tautological statement "real presence," which became the church's attempt to resolve this concern. Perhaps it is somewhat unfair to the original intention for the meaning of *praesentia realis*, but the implications of the message have been most unfortunate. Can anything be present but not real, e.g., the unreal presence of Jesus? The doctrine of "real presence" tends to imply that a symbol is unreal.

Edward Schillebeeckx, one of the more established Roman Catholic scholars of his generation, who speaks from the philosophical school of phenomenology, opened his seminal work *Christ the Sacrament of the Encounter with God* by noting that theology has tended toward a purely mechanical approach to the study of the sacraments. In consequence, "they were considered chiefly in terms of physical categories. The inclination was to look upon the sacraments as but one more application, although in a special manner of the general laws of cause and effect." This "does not always make a careful distinction between that unique manner of existence which is peculiar to man, and the mode of being, mere objective 'being there,' which is proper to the things of nature."[6]

Schmemann, as an Eastern Orthodox scholar, laments the Western tendency to construct sacramental theology, a tendency he believes the Eastern church has frequently followed. He observes that for the fathers and the entire early tradition,

> symbolism is the essential dimension of the sacrament, the proper key to its understanding....If for the Fathers, symbol is a key to sacrament it is because sacrament is in continuity with the symbolical structure of the world in which *omnes... creaturae sensibilus sunt signa verus sacrum*. And the world is symbolical—*signus del sacrae*—in virtue of its being created by God; to be "symbolical" belongs thus to its ontology, the symbol being not only the way to perceive and understand reality, a means of cognition, but also a means of participation.[7]

Those who lived in the time of the early church had a greater awareness of symbol than modern humanity has enjoyed. It is significant that the threefold order of ministry began to disintegrate when the books and the sophisticated philosophical worldview of antiquity were lost and forgotten, at about the same time during the Dark Ages when large numbers of newly converted Teutonic Christians were demanding concrete and "scientific" answers to their questions about the sacraments, especially the Eucharist. It is equally significant that we are reviewing the meaning and impact of sacramental orders, and striving in so many quarters to restore the diaconate and recover the threefold order of ministry exemplified in the documents of the Second Vatican Council only after we have started to revalue symbol. In actual fact one can only explain sacramental orders in terms of symbol. Once again culture is becoming a context in which this can occur; the church can use the word "symbol" to explain the sacraments.

## BAPTISM VS. ORDINATION AS THE LITURGY OF TRANSFORMATION AND COMMISSION FOR MINISTRY

If we have established, for those Christians who believe that God has created a sacramental world, that the church is the sacrament of Christ and of the kingdom, we can take note of the great initiatory sacrament of the church. The symbol of baptism is the foundation and source of all ministry. One way to explain the entire reformation in which the church finds itself immersed is to touch the bottom line of baptism and recognize that we are recovering our theology of initiation—what it means to be the church, corporately and individually. We are rediscovering our understanding of baptism as divine identity.

One of the reasons we lost our way so badly that we need a complete reformation is that baptism had all but lost its effectiveness as a symbol. We can see this with its full poignancy simply by attending a private baptism, or even most of our "watered down" versions of baptismal liturgy seen on Sunday mornings in our parish churches. They are filled with warm feelings and good intentions, but only a doggedly faithful and theologically sophisticated person endowed with the most highly creative imagination could claim what the church says is taking place in the liturgy: that the heavens are opened, the angels and the host of heaven are gathered, and God's passion for humanity is breaking into history to enter as Holy Spirit into the life of a person, transforming that life and making him or her a bearer of the living and risen Christ, into the Christian community, "sealed by the Holy Spirit and marked as Christ's own forever," so that the new Christian and the newly constituted church may offer the regeneration of creation and bring history to its climax in the coming of the kingdom. When the gathered worshipers look upon the newly baptized do they see the Christ? Does the action of the liturgy suggest how Christ is reshaping and reforming and reconstituting his Body? The liturgical performance and energy level simply lacks the ritualistic pizzazz needed to carry the weight of action in which the symbolic can operate and be genuinely experienced. If action counts more than words, baptism is not the great transforming action of the church today; that occurs in the liturgy of ordination.

Thomas Ray, the retired Bishop of Northern Michigan, has been the most outstanding spokesman for "lay ministry" and the proper role of baptism in the Episcopal Church during the last decade. He hurts the feelings of audiences as he forces us to laugh at ourselves, especially in comparing the liturgy of baptism to that of ordination.

> I don't know how many of you have been parents, godparents, or sponsors of someone recently baptized. How extensive was the preparation, the catechumenate? Two or three years? In some very revolutionizing places, perhaps. Probably one, perhaps two or three sessions would be the norm if you were fortunate. I have presided at baptisms when I knew there hadn't even been a rehearsal. And the neophyte, the newly baptized—deeply reverenced, respected, embraced? Often the newly baptized, if an infant, is immediately excommunicated.
>
> Later in your pilgrimage, if you seek to re-examine your life and faith, you might return to an inquirer's class. And if in these six or seven, maybe even twelve or fifteen sessions your interest and your appetite was whetted, if you are truly intrigued, drawn into this faith of ours, if you are really excited, if you are really serious about pursuing it, what can we offer you? If you are that excited, that serious, that committed, what do we offer you almost automatically?
>
> Seminary. After at least three years of preparation you would be ordained. From that ordination you would emerge with a new name signifying a new identity: Reverend, Father, Mother, Pastor. Your picture would now be taken with The Clergy, your new family by letters dimissory.
>
> Some of us gathered at a Roman Catholic retreat center. There was a picture on the wall of the Roman Catholic bishop and all the clergy. It was a family portrait, a powerful symbol.

You would be clothed with a new white garment with stole
and clericals. And, as a newly ordained person, you would
be deeply reverenced and respected as a new, fresh icon and
image of God's continuing presence; a fresh icon and image
of God's continuing, living, forgiving, embracing presence.
Is it not clear? We have turned things upside down—ordination means everything, baptism means very little.[8]

Bishop Ray is likely to conclude his speeches by asking how many
of us have our baptismal certificate hanging proudly on our walls.
Invariably, there is a paucity of raised hands. Then he teases the clergy
by asking how many of us have our ordination certificates decorating
walls, and of course, almost all clerical hands are forced to go up. The
inevitable question puts the matter to rest. "Why ordination and not
baptism? Which is, in fact, more important to you?"

Check the size of your certificates, if any of you still have
your baptismal certificate, for the sake of comparison. Your
baptismal certificate is tiny; for many of you it is simply a
card. Most of you have lost them. The certificate of ordination to the diaconate is far larger, but not so large as that to
the priesthood. And the bishop's is the most gigantic of all,
on real vellum, hand-lettered, multi-colored, with ribbons,
signatures, and many honored seals. In our society and culture, if you show your certificate, you manifest what the
expectations are.[9]

Baptism has been reduced in its significance as a symbol, especially
in comparison with ordination. Significantly, it is no longer used as a
symbol for ministry. I dare say that if baptism still acted as a symbol for
the ministry of Christ Jesus it even now would be important, and the
liturgy itself would make far more use of its symbolic elements. For
ministry carries with it an implication of status and authority in the
community. There is action there. The ordained are going to do something about being a real Christian; they are going to try to live "that
way." There is no longer any real expectation of the function of ministry
in the act of baptism. Because it is the function of what is being signified to move a ritualistic action from being a mere sign into the realm
of the symbolical, it is not surprising that we are left with little experience
or even sense of what we claim is being signified at baptism. On the
other hand, we do experience the power of the ordination ritual as a
symbol of the ministry of Christ.

It was during the Gregorian Reformation and in the life of the medieval church that baptism was reduced largely to the status of a sacrament that operated on theory rather than experience. It was here that baptism was replaced by the Eucharist as the driving and fundamental sacrament of the church. We can see clearly that this was so in reference to the ministry. In his *Summa Theologica* Thomas Aquinas stated the official position of the church at the time that there were only two orders of the church: the diaconate and the priesthood. The episcopacy was not considered a separate and distinctive order of ministry because the person ordained to be a bishop could already celebrate the Eucharist as a priest. And in the words of Susan K. Wood, "He did not see how episcopal consecration empowered the Bishop to consecrate more extensively the body and blood of Christ."[10] Because the Eucharist was the definitive sacrament, it was allowed to circumscribe the ordered nature of the ministry. This remained the theological position of the Roman Catholic Church until the Second Vatican Council in the mid-1960s recognized again the threefold order of the ordained ministry. They did so in terms that recovered the early church's identification of baptism, rather than the Eucharist, as the defining sacrament.

The recovery of our baptismal theology demands an inclusive ministry for the *laos*, to use the ancient term for the whole people of God. I find the term "lay ministry" unfortunate, undermining the richness of the term *laos*. The *laos* includes bishops, priests, and deacons together with all other baptized members of the church. To say that the ordained are chosen and set apart does not infer their exclusion from the People of God, from the community, from the wholeness that was anciently captured in the term *laos*. The ordained are set apart in the sense that an order is to be looked upon as a sign and model for the rest. Yet, while ordination orders one crucial aspect of the church's life, its ministry, this ordering is from within the one ministry of the one Body of Christ. In baptism the many are made one. In baptism every member is ordained into the fullness of that one ministry. The term "laity" has come to carry the connotation of the sort of relationship a client has to a professional—a status of ignorance as opposed to professional competence. (For example, it is said that a doctor must speak to a patient in "lay" terms in order to be understood.) We need to find another word or phrase to refer to the ministry of the vast majority of the church, the ministry of those baptized but distinguished from those ordained into one of the three orders of the church.

## THE UNIFIED SYMBOL OF THE THREEFOLD ORDER

It is at this point that I wish to present a coherent theory of ordained ministry. It should provide the reason why the church maintains ordained ministry, what its relation is to the ministry of all the baptized members of the church, why ordained ministry is threefold, and why and how the three orders are interrelated. The theory must also address the major problems and questions the church is facing: clericalism, laicism, the sparseness of "lay" ministry—in and out of the religious life of the church—authoritarianism, authority conflict, clerical leadership versus lay leadership, conflict and competition among orders, the appropriate renewal of the diaconate, and the general confusion about any issue anyone can think up.

The sacrament of order enables the ministry of the church most particularly by revealing the very nature of the church. The sacrament of order emerged historically and needs to be reformed because it is of high value. It provides clarity of purpose and identity as the church addresses its mission. It cannot be reduced to questions concerning activities or the functions of ministry, nor is it simply a matter of leadership and authority.

The foundational statement of the theology of holy orders is offered as follows: the threefold order of sacramental ministry forms a unified symbol of the church's ministry. Orders that are sacramental function as effective symbols both of God's participation in the community's ministry and of the ministering community's life in God. Ordained ministry is sacramental precisely because it forms a unified symbol of God's participation in the community's ministry and the ministering community's sharing in God's life in its threefold dynamic. That is, ordained ministry offers the church fundamental models for ministry, for its institutions and communities and for the *laos*, while exercising leadership functions which appropriately manifest the signs or models. As a symbol, sacramental orders enjoy too many values (multi-valent) and have too many things to say (multi-vocal) in meaning and content to be capable of legitimately separating into their component offices except as effective signs for focus upon particular aspects of a unified Christian ministry. The rational dynamic between these various aspects, as well as between the offices that represent them, is dialectical. This dynamic is another instance of unity in diversity and diversity in unity.

Many observers of the considerable effort expended toward reform of the church in our time believe the most important factor to be "lay ministry," as the ministry commissioned in baptism continues to be termed. Certainly, I agree that it forms the axis on which the other two reformation issues we have identified may turn; that is, lay ministry may prove to be the key instrument for the church's response to the needs of what I am summarizing with the terms "justice" and "community."

What then is the role of ordained ministry? Is it a major problem, the cause of clericalism, elitism, and professionalism? There are many that would have ecclesiastical egalitarianism, removing all distinctions between the ordained and the unordained ministers. That is what many in the reformed tradition think the doctrine of the priesthood of all believers means and intends. Most Anglicans find this unsatisfactory, but many would deemphasize ordained ministry in order to "lift up" lay ministry. At times this leads to competition. Thus we witness a rising lay advocacy, which sometimes (certainly not of necessity) takes an adversarial posture in relation to ordained ministry. We hear comments suspicious of anyone who considers a vocational call to ordination, e.g., "Why ruin a good lay person?" "He must have a need [i.e., an unhealthy need] to wear a collar."

It occurs to some, however, that the relationship between lay ministry and ordained ministry is such that the reform of one is not possible without the reform of the other. That is to say that there is one ministry. Remedial endeavors are needed to reform the order of ministry so that what has traditionally been called holy orders may serve as an effective symbol of, and for, the whole ministering community. Sacramental orders should be reflective of the ministering community while providing it with fundamental models for ministry. Until we appreciate more fully the nature and function of sacramental orders we will fail to understand lay ministry and to develop it more fully. A suitable definition could clarify this issue.

We can approach the definition by examining the different levels of symbolic operation. First there is simple function. Second, there is sign. Finally, there is symbol.

An old argument about ordained ministry pits what a clergyperson is, a matter of being or ontology, over against function or task, a matter of doing. Sometimes extreme positions are taken in which someone will describe the priest as a "professional' and someone else will define the priest as *alter Christus*. Without presently taking up the notion of the "ontological character of ordination," I must assume that ordained ministry is a matter of being and doing, function and symbol. As there can be no ministry of mere presence, there can be no Christian ministry merely of function. Sacraments, like all other symbols, become activated through the functions appropriate to what they signify. I remember the old joke about the elderly lady who shows the new curate her book of keepsakes and proudly turns a page to reveal, pressed between the pages, "my first communion." The priest responds, "Madam, whatever that is, it is not your first communion! In order for communion to occur the blessed element of bread must be consumed." Both those who attempt a "ministry of presence" without exercising the expertise of carefully learned and well-honed skills and those who cannot appreciate or utilize the depth of symbolic value they manifest will soon become personally frustrated. Very likely they will lose much of their effectiveness as sacramental persons.

It does seem to me that ordained persons who express the character of their office in effective ministry for a significant period of time can retire or become inactive relative to ordained functions within the community and yet serve as effective symbols of ministry. It is in this specific sense, at least, in which the church can legitimately consider ordination permanent.

## THE THREE LEVELS OF SYMBOLIC OPERATION

To understand this more fully we must reexamine the three different levels of symbolic operation, but this time in the explicit terms of ordained ministry. First, there is simple function. Certain tasks are given to the ordained person. Some of these tasks are interchangeable for different orders, e.g., presidency of the Eucharist, confession, and preaching; and other tasks are interchangeable for all baptized Christians, e.g., parish leadership, ministry to the sick, and baptism. Some are limited to exercise by a particular order, e.g., ordination of presbyters and deacons. Some, though interchangeable, are designated in an order of precedence, e.g., reading the gospel in the Eucharist (a deacon if present, a priest or bishop if not), leading the prayers of the people (a deacon if present, a lay person if not). No action of ministry, particularly the explicitly sacramental action, is ever a solitary function or taken in isolation from the community. The functions belong to, are on behalf of, and represent the community. Everyone is always participating in Christian community when it is operating as desired. Surely the sense of community is heightened in direct proportion to the sense of participation.

Secondly, there is sign or model. Ordered ministry determines the identity of the ministering community. When the community orders ministry into distinctive offices, the world is given a clear sign of who the community intends to be and what the community intends to do as ministers of Christ. At the same time the People of God are better able to see and thus to act on their intentions. The bishop signifies that the community is an apostolic church, faithful to the universality of the church catholic and to its tradition as given to the apostles in their appointment by Jesus. We are obedient to the church as it is gathered and sent by Christ. The priest shows us that we are a community of Christians in specific localities gathered in Christ's name, given order and coherence by the one who presides and calls us. It is a community called to worship the Lord, as well as to represent and make him available to the world. The deacon is to focus what Hans Küng calls the fundamental notion of ministry that Jesus conceived for each and every Christian: concrete and active service of others. Individual Christians are to be agents of the church community, carrying out its sacred mission of charity and justice. The church corporate is to be the servant to the world.[11]

Finally, there is symbol. In the person of the ordained, as the symbolic person, the *laos* can see an image of the ministry of Christ, can heighten their awareness of God's presence, can sense the immanence of that power which is God. It is a projection of that graced reality which they possess by virtue of their baptism, the awareness of which can be easily lost. Thus the sacramental person as symbol points to and participates in a reality greater than the person or the office, allowing one who apprehends the symbolic function also to participate in that reality. Again, however, sacraments are not precisely like other symbols, nor is the dynamic of the projection like that of merely psychological projections. When symbols are sacraments, the greater reality to which they point, the relationship that they facilitate, is ultimate reality. This ultimate reality is both transcendent and immanent—indeed, incarnate. As incarnate, the Christ ordained the very symbols of and for the relationship thereby facilitated.

Consequently, symbols that are sacramental represent God to those participating in them and represent the participants to God. Unlike the process identified in psychology, that which is projected is not just an image or idea in the mind of, or an unconscious personality factor of, the "projector." Rather, it comes from the indwelling presence of God. Urban T. Holmes stated the matter brilliantly: "The light the priest sheds on the community is as the light of the moon."[12] But the ordained person is also as the sun since the beholder perceives something other than that which is projected. The person ordained is a baptized member of the Body of Christ in whom Christ dwells and whom the community has called and anointed for the express purpose of "outward and visible" manifestation of that shared "inward and spiritual" reality. Sacramental orders function as effective symbols both of God's participation in the community's ministry and of the ministering community's participation in God.

## THE QUESTION OF SPECIAL POWERS CONFERRED IN ORDINATION

In the act of ordination the community prays to God that the one being ordained be specially blessed with divine grace. We have always been ambiguous about the relationship between the theological concepts of grace, power, and presence. Without trying to define such matters, the following is asserted: (1) Prayer is effective. The ordained person is blessed and graced with particularity. (2) The grace of ordination is the gift of God of and for the community and cannot be exercised apart from it as an exclusively personal gift, a power to be used in isolation and indiscriminately. There is no room for alchemy in Christianity.

To approach the matter from a different angle, the ontological question of what an individual is given in ordination is thrown off course by two assumptions about the "being." For most of us, the question of being must always be restricted to a particular object and limited within a static view of reality. The question cannot go beyond singular objects because, while each being in the world including a human being, has being, a number of things taken together as a unit enjoy only a conceptual sort of being—unless they form another concrete "thing." Being is conceived as static because each thing is as it is defined to be, or it is not, and if it changes, it is no longer that thing, but another. Its "being" is what makes certain things consistently the same thing through time and circumstance, though there are changes in its characteristics and appearance, and so on, called in Aristotelian philosophy "accidents." Regarding people, it is often pictured as that which distinguishes one person from another. It is usually conceived as that essential and irreducible something deep within the individual.

This individualistic and static view of ontology is far too limited in an era of the physics of relativity and quantum mechanics. Today we need an ontological understanding that is dynamic and relational, for there is no being in isolation from the "beingness" of others. There is no being which is simply fixed and unchangeable.

Nowhere is the dynamic and relational ontological reality more certain and more clear than in trying to understand that "ontological character" conferred in the act of ordination. The grace of ordination is offered in the liturgy, but it belongs to the community; it cannot be held privately by the ordinand, for it is the Body that ordination orders by placing one of the baptized into a particular relationship with the community. Ordination creates the sacrament of order that all share as the *laos*. The emphasis in ordination is on the relationship with the community of the baptized, and the relationships within that thus-ordered community, for the sake of ministry. What happens to the individual character of the ordained person is entirely relational for it exists to serve and build up the community that makes up the church, and it does not exist apart from these purposes. (Anyone who seeks personal salvation—as in a special relationship to God—through the grace conferred in ordination is a fool.) Ultimately, ordained ministry cannot be comprehended if it is limited to what it gives the person of the ordained. Rather, it must be understood in terms of the special and defined relationship that the ordained is granted within the community. There is configuration to Christ in ordination; there is also configuration to the ecclesial community. Ordained ministry cannot be understood as a private and superior relationship with Christ. It has to do far more with the relationship ordained ministry builds between Christ and the community. The ordained ministry expresses the faith of the community and the community recognizes itself in its ordained ministry.

"The sacramental order of priesthood is sound theologically only so long as it is representative of the body of Christ, the church, formed in the way of Jesus Christ, offering itself to God, accepted, blessed, and sanctified into the people of God. Sacramental priesthood is not a priesthood making sacrifices to God for the people; rather, sacramental priesthood is a sign and sacrament of the priesthood of the people of God effected in Jesus Christ."[13] In the wake of clericalism and ecclesiastical elitism this foundational theological truth was largely lost. Rediscovering and bringing to life the fullness of its implications is not only important and just, but pivotal.

Regarding the priesthood of all believers, we begin with our first principle concerning who it is that is represented: Christ is the "great high priest." The church is the priesthood of all believers. These are one and the same priesthood. The ordained sacramental priesthood (presbyters and bishops) is the objective realization and expression within the church of this one priesthood. In this way the priest represents the people to Christ and Christ to the people. The priest is responsible for presenting and actualizing the presence of Christ in a sacramental way within the Body.

The clearest example I can provide of this can be discerned in the nuances contained in the term episcopacy. It means to "epi"–"scope," or oversee. The term in English would be overseer. When I hear this word I think of a nineteenth-century field hand, whip in hand, overseeing slaves picking cotton. Unfortunately, something too close to this same image is conjured up when considering the role of the church's overseer, the bishop. In fact, while there is some validity in the use of the term to refer to the administrative role of the office it is only within the context of what the word means for the whole Body. It is the bishop who insures, through the symbol of office and the proper function of administrative and pastoral oversight, that the church is "overlooking" its own limited time and space to see the universal and timeless nature of the church and especially of its ministry. It is the bishop who helps congregations overcome their parochialism to serve the mission of the whole church together with the other parishes of the diocese and the other dioceses of the communion around the world and the other communions ecumenical and the timeless and united church in communion with the apostles and Jesus of Nazareth now alive and living in heaven—and all of humanity living and dead and to come. That role of getting the church to "epi-scope," to look out over the total picture and see the whole and thus to act, is the job of the "epi-scoper." The office exists not for the individual's "epi-scoping," "over-seeing," but the church's.

# THREE SACRAMENTAL ORDERS: Their Unity and Interrelationship

Once the term sacramental order is understood, one may still puzzle over the relationship among the orders, or even wonder why there are three. Whatever the historical development, I would urge that we renew and establish a threefold order of ministry that expresses Christian ministry in its fullness. I hope that we do not allow ordained ministry to remain so boring, so effectively monochromatic.

The threefold order of sacramental ministry does form a unified symbol. As a symbol it speaks to us on many levels of meaning and value, such that one cannot legitimately "break it down" into separate meanings, values, signs, or components. A priest in isolation makes no sense for sacramental order, and neither does a bishop or a deacon in isolation from the other two orders. The theologian can do so artificially for the virtuous risk of analysis, but to attempt to do so in actual practice distorts the symbol decisively. Consequently, sacramental orders cannot function properly as the symbols they are unless manifested in unitive interrelationship, each office functioning as an effective sign of certain aspects of Christian ministry. The aspects of ministry they respectively focus are not opposites, but may be considered as different sides of a three-dimensional sculpture. One aspect reveals an important part of the whole, but it cannot exist with the same beauty, wholeness, and effectiveness without every aspect. It is another important instance of the principle of unity-in-diversity and diversity-in-unity so prominent in the Christian understanding of reality. To review the notion explained in an earlier section, modern logic might credit this with conforming to the dialectical principle. Modern metaphysics might identify this with the pervasive principle of bipolarity and unity. In discussing Christian discipleship and the problem of "man and society," Jürgen Moltmann acknowledges that dialectic tension is a necessary characteristic not only of the individual but of any group of individuals. In fact, tension between opposite poles is characteristic of life at all levels, biological, psychological, and social. He goes on to paraphrase G. W. F. Hegel, "A thing is alive only when it contains contradiction in itself and is indeed the power of holding the contradiction within itself and enduring it."[14]

Karl Barth recognizes that the categories of ministry found throughout the New Testament reflect certain basic forms or models of ministry and reveal in their multiplicity and essential unity the real nature of Christian ministry. "Clearly the biblical and especially the Pauline distinctions are themselves, in concrete manifestation, variations of those basic forms."[15] They highlight different aspects of Christian ministry. Barth explains, quite thoroughly, that they model certain dualities or contrarieties within Christian ministry. He stresses the tension between unity and plurality (1 Cor 12) and action and witness.[16]

There have always been certain opposing tendencies creating appropriate tensions within the church's ministry: contemplative vs. activist, horizontal vs. vertical, love of God vs. love of neighbor as oneself, transcendent vs. immanent, this world vs. other world, service in the church community vs. service outside the church community, structured ministry vs. antistructural ministry, the Apollonian way vs. the Dionysian way, serving vs. healing, and so on. Ministry is most appropriate and most fulfilled when each contrariety is allowed to operate; each opposing principle is allowed to reign simultaneously. The diaconate and the presbyterate represent such polarities of ministry, held in unity by that which is represented in the episcopal order. When the fullness of the symbol is manifested, the unity is such that each order contains that which the others represent.

It is at the levels of function and sign that the symbol is sufficiently or insufficiently manifested as unitive. The symbol serves both as a model and as an "archetype." The sign task of symbol allows it to become rational, clear, and defined. It allows the symbol to inspire action. The function activates the symbol. For example, at the functional level the priesthood must always be a position of leadership within a local community or the symbolic manifestation of that office becomes muddled. The diaconate can never be purely a liturgical function apart from acts of service, or vice versa, without destroying the proper imaging. A church that functions virtually without the diaconate is asking too much of the priesthood of the bishop and presbyter. The bishop who is not teacher or pastor in actual practice, but acts only as an administrative head, betrays the symbol of ministry.

At the level of sign it is necessary that there be those offering models for how the people of God, individually and corporately, should act with intentionality as ministers of Christ. Deacons act as agents sent from the heart of the community to the important task of representing its faith and love. Ormonde Plater, widely recognized as the leading authority on the diaconate within the Anglican Communion, summarizes the principal function of the deacon's ministry as "that proclamation, expressed through the gospel and sacramental acts of mercy and justice."[17] The sign to which the diaconate points is the basic ministry of sacrificial service, especially the service of justice for those in need. This is the service all Christians are to offer without any images of status compromising its representation of humility. Obviously, both the presbyterate and the episcopacy have responsibilities for that service and the bishop has the ultimate responsibility. But historically the bishop's responsibility toward the poor, the weak, the persecuted, and any society has left in need—those for whom we recognize Jesus had a prejudice in his self-offering—was performed through the specific office of the deacon. It is in this sense that the deacon has been seen as the special assistant to the bishop. The diaconate signals to the church that the work of charity and struggle for justice is essential to the ministry of the church, that this service is of its very nature, and provides the leadership in the actual performance of this service by the whole community. This is to be expressed in the liturgy by the specific responsibilities of the deacon for the word and table fellowship.

The actions of the deacon in the early Roman church did just that. Generally, the deacon participated in the liturgical processions, was positioned next to the bishop, took the gifts to the altar and prepared them for consecration, read the gospel, served the elements of the sacrament, and carried viaticum to the sick. The Eastern Orthodox churches have steadfastly maintained the liturgically symbolic role of the deacon since the fourth century. With the Second Vatican Council Western sacramental churches have renewed this liturgical responsibility.

The following statements describe what the deacon is to represent in the liturgy. According to the rubrics of the Episcopal Church's Book of Common Prayer, the deacon is to read the gospel, lead the intercessory prayers of the people, invite their confession, receive their offering, prepare their Holy Table, serve them in the eucharistic meal, and grant them dismissal from corporate worship into their daily lives of service. The general pattern of these functions is that the deacon forms the sacramental link between liturgy as worship and liturgy as mission, the work of the people on behalf of the world and the kingdom. In proclaiming the gospel the deacon represents our awareness that the good news is not only for edification in worship and for awareness of salvation to come, but for our daily living, a present in which Christ gives us more abundant life. One cannot help but think of the moment when our Lord, beginning his personal ministry, stood in the synagogue and proclaimed the good news by reading the prophecy of Isaiah and then dramatically confessed that in him it has come to pass that the blind will see, the captives will be set free, the oppressed will be given liberty, and the poor will hear the good news. This model provided for us by our Lord for the proclamation of the gospel in liturgy refers to functions particularly assigned to the deacon, ordained to "serve all people,

priest and the bishop as a bishop. What does happen is that the symbol of Christian ministry is unhappily confused. People tend to see the deacon as a "little" or "limited" priest. When the sacramental symbols become confused they are reduced to the "merely religious," and border on religiosity. Transvesting does not work; rather it distorts something terribly valuable, and so it is a shame. What it actually does is reinforce the feeling that there is really only one ministry, the priesthood, and that order is only an up and down play on this theme. As a final warning we should take to heart the lesson of history Susan K. Wood points out: if the liturgical role of the diaconate "becomes divorced from their extraliturgical service...the office is doomed."[18] Unless the people can see the three orders functioning and functioning together, they will have no opportunity to understand the fullness and the holistic nature of their own ministry, much less to understand what ordering ministry is about.

As another example of the price the church pays for trying to capture the full significance of Christian ministry in a single image, that of the priest, consider the results of a hypothetical survey of what functions come to mind when Episcopal "lay people" think of ministry. Surely the vast majority would respond with a limited but certain pattern: "doing something liturgical like a lay reader," "performing a function for the church, such as being on the altar guild," "managing the business of the church on the vestry and other boards," "making calls," "doing one's part in the stewardship campaign," "running parish programs such as Sunday schools and fairs." Fundamentally these are all extensions of priestly ministry, tasks the priest models and calls parishioners to perform. How many people consider their acts of ministry to be part of a global and apostolic ministry which is creating the history of the world and leading to the new age of the kingdom? If the people do not see, much less experience, bishops being real bishops in the footsteps of the apostles instead of an occasional public figure with terribly limited functions, no one can reasonably expect them to see the big picture the bishop represents. Being without the appropriate model for individual ministry (which is exercised primarily where one lives in the "daily round" with family and friends, at work, in civic services, at play and recreation) and for corporate service in social action, the *laos*, including the ordained, finds it difficult to perform the servant ministry of Christ with intentionality. Notice that the failure of the church to understand, or even see, the centrality of justice as it was discussed in Section II is due in large measure to our failure to offer the focus on that service that priests and bishops cannot, due to the press of their own proper roles. Without the diaconate the church has not taught or led its membership to serve the world in a way that makes the world sit up and give notice.

The contrarieties of and for Christian ministry should be signaled and modeled in the functions of Christian ministry. If the episcopal role is properly manifested, if the people experience the bishop working with priests and deacons, if the bishop is pastor rather than merely boss to the clergy, if she is known to the people in multidimensional roles—as teacher on issues of concern for the church, as liaison among parishes, as a sign of the covenant with the church universal and apostolic—rather than in the one-dimensional roles of "confirming machine" and administrator, then the three orders are effective signs of and for Christian ministry in that they are an effective symbol and therefore unitive. The unity is such that each order contains and acts as a sign for that which the others represent. We cannot separate them out very clearly because they are inseparable. For example, at this point the priest can be fully seen as a servant figure without having to turn the stole across the chest; the deacon at work is seen as an apostolic figure; and the bishop is pictured as a person to serve both the world and the church. The full symbol is seen in any one sacramental person. That full symbol is the primordial biblical symbol of the Christ.

This is a far better effort than the previous one to express the unity and overlapping nature of the offices, based perhaps on the cosmology of a far gone age, wherein the "higher" office included the "lower"— deacon contained laity, priest contained each, and bishop contained all three. This view and the practice that sustains it, serial ordination, began as an attack on baptismal ministry and authority, a way of drawing a definitive line between the ordained and the merely baptized. It was one of the initial and primary steps in the process of separating the clergy out from the *laos* during the Gregorian Reformation and giving the clergy control of the church over the lay landlords, barons, and monarchs. This attack on "lay ministry" can be seen clearly enough in the implications of its own imagery. Those little Polish or Russian dolls are good models: inside the biggest (which is, of course, the bishop) one finds a smaller and less significant priest, inside the priest one finds a little deacon, and inside the deacon one finally finds a tiny "lay person."

It is in the way that ministry is ordered and properly functions that the Christian community can comprehend the ongoing ministry of

Christ, and thus that the community is better able to perform that ministry as its basic mission. At the same time the world can see what it is that Christians intend to be and to do in the way ministry is ordered. Ordained ministry is sacramental in that, when it does what it is ordained to do, it models and represents the ministry of Christ and the ministry of the baptized—both the whole community and each baptized person. The failure of the baptized to recognize the nature of baptismal ministry, especially regarding their power, their authority, and their responsibility, has a lot to do with the failure of the church to offer a well-ordered ordained ministry, except in theory. When the people of God see the ordained orders working together as a single sacramental symbol of Christ's ministry they should see who they are and what they are to do as ministers. The ministry of the baptized person and of the baptized community is diaconal, for the fundamental ministry of the church is concrete human service to those in need. Baptismal ministry is priestly, for each baptized person and the entire baptized community offers the healing and blessing power of God. All baptized persons serve as bishops in a sense that all are to serve as "epi-scopers," looking beyond the local church of a given moment and place to participate in the universal and timeless nature of the church and its ministry. The whole church is apostolic because we are united in Christ and sent by Jesus himself to all the world.

## FROM THE HISTORICAL PERSPECTIVE

Perhaps it is surprising that our examination of ministry did not begin in Scripture and history, for this has been the consistent pattern of the previous analysis in this work, and it is the source of information most relied upon by commentators on the subject of ministry. Frankly, I find this to be one of those rare subjects on which history is not very helpful. Reference to Scripture and history is often counterproductive. The use of "history" to justify certain positions has been less than salutary in too many cases. For example, the claims for apostolic succession, an unbroken line of bishops who have received the laying on of hands from at least three of their predecessors since the time of the appointment of Peter by Jesus to the present date, is simply not sustainable by clear and convincing evidence. That, however, does not negate the consensus among the catholic family of churches that apostolic succession is a good and meaningful practice to be reverently guarded now and in the future, a safeguard of the actual "cash value" of what apostolic succession is really about, namely, the constitutive tradition of the catholic church since the beginning—what the Lutherans have always insisted on calling "the true gospel." The claims against the ordained ministry of women that rely on historical justification are just as spurious. The problem with looking to history to understand ordained ministry is not merely in the attempts to read the theological conclusions of certain ages and certain branches of the church back into Scripture and tradition, that is, in prejudgment and scholarly manipulation. It is the lack of data, facts, or opinions about the questions that vex us today. We simply have a void; "answers" are not there. To take an irrelevant example, if we wanted to know what Jesus felt about labor unions we simply would not be able to find out. We may feel like we know what his attitude would be, based on our personal moral perspective, but it would be speculative, and if we tried to quote him in debate we would be cheating. Too often this is the case with the church's use of history relative to ordained ministry.

Much of our employment of Scripture and patristic tradition in the search for a coherent and broadly accepted theological understanding of ministry has proved too esoteric, too "thin," for the establishment of a foundation that can carry the weight of any conclusion capable of trumping other theories. It is typical for a scholar to examine the important Greek, Hebrew, and Latin terms and, in the discovery of new nuances, especially newly spotted nuances about their usage in the social, political, and religious situation of the biblical author's day, to draw implications about what these words mean to us in our contemporary translation and employment. Our scholars have been doing a truly superb job of this for some time, but the church continues to ask the same questions without having received satisfaction from the efforts. Any reasons to be offered for why and how offices developed, why and how they became sacramental, why and how the unified ministry became ordered into three offices, are necessarily the result of speculation. We cannot pinpoint all of the forces and issues that came to bear on the development of orders with sufficient precision to establish historical certitude.

However, I believe the theory of ministry offered here is entirely consistent with the past and with the tradition, at least with the theological rationale as articulated in the tradition, if not with the actual practice. It is possible that the symbolic foundation of the theory explains what actually had developed historically and been lost by the time of the Gregorian Reformation.

## HISTORICAL DEVELOPMENT OF
## SACRAMENTAL ORDERS

Eduard Schweizer has pointed out the difficulty, if not the impossibility, of reconciling any historical form of ministry with that found in the New Testament. He begins *Church Order in the New Testament* with the conclusion, "There is no such thing as the New Testament Church Order. An objective study of the earliest synoptic tradition reveals that it contains very little indeed about the setting-up, constitution and organization of a new society."[19] The basic problem is that of reconciling *any* current form of ecclesiastical institutionalism with the eschatological message that stood at the heart of early Christian understanding and practice. For the first-century church, forms of church government and organization would have been understood as provisional. Paul, rather early on in this period, advised the Christians of Thessalonica that they should take jobs, even marry if the fires of passion burned too brightly to ignore, but at any rate live relatively ordinary lives until the Lord returned—and surely it wouldn't be long.

The very earliest members of the Jewish renewal movement that came to be called Christianity had gathered in Jerusalem and formed a leadership structure compatible with the Jewish leadership structure within which it would operate. Not surprisingly, it resembled Jewish polity, perhaps copying the Sanhedrin. We find at a very early date that James, the brother of Jesus, was accepted as the head of a body of elders. (The Greek word for "elder" is *presbyter*.)

Outside of Jerusalem, followers of Jesus would have been seen as a group or a circle within the fellowship of their synagogue. There may have been unofficial leaders, but they would have been provisional and ad hoc. Ministerial functions would have been attended to as people came forward to meet the needs of teaching, preaching, and so forth, or as people would claim special gifts such as prophesy and healing. The churches founded by Paul seem to have been very loosely structured, perhaps similar to that of Antioch, which was presided over by prophets and teachers. In his letter to the Philippians (Phil 1:1), Paul addresses overseers (in Greek, *episkopoi*, or "bishops") and servants (in Greek, *diakonoi*). It is difficult to find any essential difference between the functions of overseer and elder at that point; in each case these were the notables of the community and thus those most likely to be given certain definite functions within the fellowship. In many instances the titles seem to be synonymous. Perhaps one of the panel of elders or overseers was appointed as president of the Eucharist, sometimes within rotation or according to convenience. Nevertheless, for Paul leadership belonged to apostles, prophets, and teachers, without an official or uniform local structure of authority and governance. Elders and overseers exercised leadership functions not terribly dissimilar to those of Episcopal Church vestries, or Roman Catholic parish councils, except that the offices were perpetuating. "Fundamentally the New Testament knows no distinction between ministry and office....Thus the Pauline view, which sees 'ministry' as synonymous with 'gift of grace' and 'manifestation of power,' so that it keeps its character of an event (1 Cor 12:4–6) is essentially maintained throughout the New Testament."[20]

It is not long, however, until we find that a threefold order of ministerial offices has been established. This is in place at least by the early part of the second century. Why and how this particular order emerged has been the subject of considerable historical investigation. Historians seldom seem to take into account the symbolic or sacramental nature of the orders as one of the factors relevant to their development. Instead they dwell exclusively on the organizational, functional, and practical needs that gave rise to particular offices—that inevitable institutionalization of Christian ministry in face of the decline of early Christian foundations. Finally, the historian usually notes that by the turn of the first century certain offices appeared to have representational implications, and at some point these orders seem to be part of a sacramental system. Perhaps it would be helpful to survey some of the theories most often submitted in explanation of the development of the threefold order of sacramental ministry.

## HISTORICAL PRESSURES

By A.D. 70 three things had happened: (1) the founders and charter leaders of the Christian movement had been killed; (2) following the destruction of Jerusalem and the temple, Judaism changed radically and the great schism between Judaism and Christianity was fixed; (3) the eschatological enthusiasm of the early church faded with the reality that Jesus had not returned, and began to realize that he might not do so in the immediate future. These three matters were relatively disconnected but together they threw the churches on their own resources and started the series of controversies and conflicts that stimulated the gradual definition of a common Christian tradition.

Peter, Paul, James (the brother of Jesus), and almost all of those termed apostles had left the scene, most as martyrs, by the time of the last Jewish rebellion against Rome. They had to be replaced, not by Jesus but by the people themselves. These new leaders had to protect the way things had been understood and done in the beginning and yet they had to allow the life of the church to evolve, form, and develop.

The life of the early church operated on the premise that all was temporary, in a state of transition, and no community needed to look beyond that which was immediately before it because the Lord had promised to return. His people awaited him fervently, thinking he might come around any corner any time. When enough time passed the realization sank in that it was necessary to establish the routine and round that became institutional life.

The Jewish rebellion in which Jerusalem was destroyed in A.D. 70 spelled the end of the institutional and cultic life of Judaism as Jesus and his forebears had known it. Rabbinical Judaism began its new life, struggling for survival. Gone were the various and competing opposition parties Jesus had known so well—the Sadducees, the Sanhedrin and the religious nobility, the Zealots, the Essenes, the various sects. Gone were the temple and the ark and all their institutions, together with the ritual practices and ordo of Judaism developed through the centuries. The book, the synagogue, and the rabbis survived. These could carry Judaism forward wherever there were Jews. The Pharisees were in charge of shaping this new adaptation of the ancient faith. It was the reform movement of the Pharisees that emerged as the victorious party of rabbis from among the various opposition parties so familiar to readers of the gospel accounts. In order to do their job so that their religion could survive and flourish anywhere and under any condition, they found themselves deciding on a set canon of the Hebrew books of the Bible, beginning an interpretation of these texts and purifying their ranks. They felt it was necessary to exclude all opposition and nonconformist parties in the light of the fragility of their new situation, including the troublesome Jesus movement. An anathema was pronounced against all Christians who continued to worship in synagogues (Martyn 1979:37–62), completely excluding them from the synagogue and effectively driving a final wedge between the two communities. (That "wedge" would be taken up as a weapon to be wielded by Christians far more viciously in the centuries to come.)

Other pressures came to bear upon the church in what is called the sub-apostolic age. Following are some of the most prevalent theories of why and how the church developed a sacrament of order and one that is threefold.

## Protection Against Heresy and Internal "Enemies"

The need to combat gnosticism, the desire of leadership to offset the prestige of the charismatics, the necessity of retaining the original teachings of the apostles, and the demand resulting from these and several lesser threats to determine which of the writings about Christianity were acceptable as Scripture were pressures which led to a demand for leadership safeguards. The church needed a guarantee that in doubtful cases leaders and teachers could be trusted to pass down the tradition and the correct interpretation as applied to specific questions with accuracy.

## Reintroduction of the Cultic Apparatus of Judaism

Joseph Blenkinsopp writes, "The need for some form of institutionalization reasserted itself and predictably, the forms this process took were to a great extent dictated by the Scripture, which provided the terms of reference for the early church."[21]

J. A. T. Robinson states that "all the other offices—bishop, presbyter and deacon—were evidently adapted from Jewish models."[22]

Clement is noted for his use of Old Testament parallels. He claims that Scripture provides the foundation for holy orders. For example, Isaiah 60:17 refers to overseer and taskmaster: "I will appoint Peace as your overseer and Righteousness as your taskmaster." Clement interprets this as a reference to bishops and deacons (Clement. 1 Cor 42).

## A Process of Sacralization Requiring Sacred Persons

A disjuncture "came about as the sacred and secular became more and more separated out from one another....We can say that with the increasing emphasis on the Eucharist as a sacral and sacrificial cult-action the president or celebrant was increasingly thought of as a specifically sacred person in the model of pagan and Jewish cultic leaders."[23] Hans Küng is among the proponents of this theory.

## The Cosmological Order

During the patristic era, hierarchical orders were a sign of the cosmological order. Ignatius refers to the ordered hierarchy of the angels and principalities in making a point about the earthly hierarchy in the

Christian churches, and Clement tends to insert church "orders" into the unchanging order of the cosmos.

## The Roman Political Order as a Model

Early in the process of developing an organizational structure the church began to reflect the rather rigid hierarchy of the dominant Roman culture. Several other ordained ministries emerged "under" the threefold order of bishop, presbyter, and deacon. Eventually these ministries came to serve no other purpose than to punctuate the process of the clerical student toward the priesthood. Subsequently, the diaconate was generally subjected to the same fate, in practice if not in theory.

## The Growing Complexity of the Organizational Life of Local Christian Communities

The life of the community required ordering at a variety of levels, from that of the common liturgy and the instruction of the faithful to that of the administration of discipline and of the relief-system. There arose, therefore, a distinction between people who held visible office in the community and those who did not. The former were said, like the Levites of the Old Testament, to have a "portion" or "sphere" (in Greek, *kleros*) in the church and came to be called "clergy." In practice, it wasn't clear (even during the medieval era, when almost anyone who could write was considered a cleric and thus was eligible for the benefits reserved to clergy, such as trial by ecclesiastical court) who was excluded in this category. Cornelius was the Bishop of Rome in the mid-third century. His was a very large church for those of the time. He listed "forty-six presbyters, seven deacons, seven sub-deacons, forty-two acolytes, fifty-two exorcists, readers and door-keepers, above fifteen hundred widows and persons in distress, all of whom are supported by the grace and loving kindness of the Master."[24] Other lists omit some of these offices or add others such as catechists or virgins. Such lists of "clergy" seem to indicate the classes of people supported, to one degree or another, by church funds, those having "a portion" in the church.

The Christian bishop of antiquity, that is, of the Roman classical era, should probably be viewed as the central person in what we could call a "team ministry" and a teaching focus for what that team ministry was about. In all his work he was associated with a group of presbyters and deacons. These were his staff, the bishop's *familia*, his household. They were not "professionals" in the way our clergy of today are sometimes referred to, someone earning their living from ministry and making a "career" of it. Their special training was received in the household and as catechumen. They were members of the local church, selected or brought along because of their talents. Church law discouraged them from transferring to other churches because they were understood to belong to, as they were lifelong officers of, their particular local church. They were supported partially or wholly out of the bishop's —that is, the church's—funds. Closest to the bishop were probably the deacons, who gradually began to make up a sort of college with a head called the "archdeacon." Since it was the deacons who assisted the bishop in all administrative matters, including the church's relief activities, they were prominent and powerful figures in the church. Frequently it would be a deacon who would succeed the bishop upon his death.

As the church began to revitalize the diaconate it was assumed as an article of faith that the designating term was taken from the Hellenic culture to express the sort of caring and loving service we today associate with social work or charitable service to the sick, the lonely, the poor, the elderly, and others with special needs not met by themselves or society. This has recently been challenged by scholarship, led by the work of John N. Collins, who lectures on the theology of ministry within the Melbourne College of Divinity.[25] He engaged in an analysis of the actual use of the various terms prefixed by *diakon* in the eight hundred years of the classical and Hellenistic eras and then compared these findings with the term as employed in Scripture and in the Greek texts we have available from the early church. His linguistic and semantic investigations are gaining broad acceptance and forcing an adjustment in our understanding. For example, it is worth noting that the god Hermes of popular Greek mythology was called the *diakonos* of Zeus, being sent on missions to make arrangements for love affairs on earth (not the sort of loving service Christians envision for deacons). It now appears that the office of the diaconate emerged from the way a community of the early church selected an agent, one in a special relationship to one or more bishops, and sent her or him to perform some important task reflecting the church's holiness and love.

I am appreciative of this insight for two reasons. First, it emphasizes the nature of the diaconate as an office of leadership. Too often the renewal of the diaconate has been challenged because any baptized member can perform the particular functions of service, liturgically and interactively, for which the deacon is ordained. With this fresh understanding of the origins of the term, it is even more obvious that the ordained deacon is to provide leadership, to be the agent of the community for the fullest possible expression of its heart and soul: holy service to those in need. In large measure, this ministry is to be performed by motivating and facilitating the ministry of the baptized. Secondly, the insight clarifies the diaconal role as one expressing the work of the whole church in the grand struggle on behalf of justice. The purpose of the diaconal ministry of the church is just as much to change the structures of society to suit the values of the kingdom of God as it is to care for individuals in need. This should serve as a correction in discernment for ordination that is very much needed at this point in the renewal of the office, for too many of our new deacons are relegated to assisting priests, substituting for priests, serving as liturgical janitors, and performing personal ministries on their own.

Though deacons evidently had a special relationship with the bishop and were often closer to the bishop than presbyters, they lacked the level of collegiality shared between bishops and presbyters. Presbyters often served as a sort of council or cabinet for the bishop, even in small churches. They were seen in a role similar to that of the bishop in ways that came to be called "priestly." They are described in one source as *sacerdotes secundi ordinis*. In the process of development it seems that the presbyter was seen as sharing in the priesthood of the bishop. As one who shared in the priesthood of the bishop, the presbyter would share with the bishop in the exercise of certain positions. In the East (though not in the West) they seem to have had the privilege of preaching in the principal liturgical assembly under the presidency of the bishop. Presbyters could act as the bishop's delegates, celebrating the Eucharist, teaching, and even baptizing on occasion. When the congregations multiplied in a city, or as the church expanded to include village-dwellers in the countryside, the bishop sent presbyters to be leaders of the new communities. They always acted on behalf of the bishop, as the bishop's vicar, if you will. The bishop was the pastor of the whole congregation, wherever and whenever it assembled.

## THE DISCOVERY OF THE SYMBOL OF MINISTRY

All of these factors seem relevant as far as they go, but why are the factors relative to symbolizing so largely ignored? When sacramental theology is mentioned it is usually by those who feel Jesus intentionally created the three orders, empowering the apostles to so empower their successors and their clerical colleagues in a line of succession extending to the present day. According to this view, the life of the church depends on the way ordained ministry conveys the authority of Jesus in regard to doctrine and discipline, as well as his own divine power, down through history by the laying on of hands—kind of a "heavenly electrical current" of "grace-power" conveyed through "holy touching." This became the popular notion of apostolic succession and the means for acquiring those sacramental graces given by Jesus after his ascension. Symbol has nothing to do with the matter from this mechanistic view. As the recipient of the spiritual power, those who have felt the hands of ordination are "magically" sacramental persons, pure and simple. The ordained are thus perceived as set apart from the laity.

As common as this view is among the Christian populace, the overwhelming evidence does not permit any hypothesis that Jesus, or a committee of apostles, or any agency of intentionality, either drew up the organizational chart or created the orders as symbolical/sacramental. Nor can ordained ministry be seen as something apart from the community. The power and character of the ordained person is interpersonal, something that belongs to the community rather than to the individual. It is reflective of and focuses upon the ministry of the community.

On the other hand, many fail to consider the symbolic factor sufficiently because they believe that the only distinction between the ordained and the "laity" is functional; the ordained are set apart to perform certain exclusive tasks and responsibilities. Thus the student with this perspective looks solely for the development of those different functions and their relevant consequences. John A. T. Robinson summarizes his historical study of priesthood:

> Within the Body there are, and were from the beginning, people ordained on its behalf to exercise, in the name of both its head and its members, the functions which belong to it as a whole. But this ordained ministry, which is priestly because the whole ministry of the church is priestly, is in the strict sense representative, not vicarious....It is not doing for the rest of its members what only it can do—except insofar as by ordination the church as a whole deliberately reserves certain of its functions to certain authorized persons.[26]

Not only was the ministry of the early leadership representative instead of being founded on and exercised out of individually held power, initially the functions of ministry were not even viewed as particularly "religious." The functions of leadership were more political, a job of running a society within a society. The Christian "church" was a community of Christians who lived together in a city and its immediate hinterland. Hence one spoke of the "church of Rome" or the "church of Ephesus." Yet each church saw itself as set apart from the rest of the city and from the world around it. There was much of the business of the world in which Christians could not and would not participate, even if their lives depended on it. Social intercourse was conducted under the aegis of deities whom they saw as demons fighting God's will. The community therefore constituted itself almost as a city within a city. The church was the society that knew it lived in the new age of redemption. It existed within a society that did not know it was given a new creation in the new age of redemption, that larger society that Christians distinguished with the term they coined, "secular society."

The society of the church needed its own structures, leadership, and decision-making processes. The church instituted its own structures for settling disputes, doing justice among its members, and disciplining backsliders. It had regular meetings and made important decisions, which required political skill, resources, and methods. It had its own support system for widows (that particularly helpless and, indeed, almost hopeless group in ancient society), for the poor, for orphans, and for prisoners. It had a highly elaborate procedure for testing, instructing, and inducting prospective new members. In letters and writings of the founders, in developing creeds, and in the gospels it had developed the equivalent of constitutional documents. The early leaders formed and led this political life.

Because of this the early Christians did not see their leaders as religious pros or specialists. They did not even think of them as ministers in the way we usually apply the term today. Their officers were leaders of the people, and acted more like the governors and legislators and judges of our day. They were chosen to govern the community in accordance with its basic constitution.

The model of merging the political and the religious life of a people is more common than modern Westerners seem to understand. The ancient model of society, like so many societies today, had a firmly established and pervasive religious foundation. Every officer had responsibilities for the service of the gods as well as for civic duties. Most scholars doubt Julius Caesar could have risen to the heights of power he obtained without first having established the base for that power in the highest priestly office of Rome. It did not seem at all strange or untoward for the bishops, presbyters, and deacons—and those serving in the several variety of offices out of which these three emerged, some surviving as minor offices—to administer the community's material affairs and regulate the relations among groups or individuals within it. The leaders presided at regular meetings of the community, including its liturgies, and in particular the Eucharist. They were all charged with preserving and transmitting the true faith.

On reflection, what is odd is that these early Christians ever came to think of their pastors and leaders as sacramental officers. We do know that it is a perfectly unique view of leadership. There is no suggestion that anyone regarded Paul or any other leader mentioned in the New Testament in any such fashion. Little by little sacerdotal language begins to be applied to the next generation of leaders. As the second-century church continued to evolve and moved into the third century, the terms *hiereus* (Greek for priest) and *sacerdos* (Latin for priest) were used to denote the person primarily charged with the leadership of the church within a locale, what became the congregation. Without consciousness or any sort of thinking it through, it would seem that the political and constitutional leadership of decision-making, discipline, and administration combined with the "religious" leadership of presiding over the liturgical and educational life of the community. One obvious link between the political and religious roles of leadership could be seen in the way the leader was charged with the responsibility of holding doctrine in line with the original teachings of Jesus and the apostles. This was a matter of teaching, or pastoral leadership, and discipline, or political leadership. The bishop was the ultimate leader, but his representational role began to focus one particular and defined part of that life and that action of the community. The presbyter gradually emerged from "under" the bishop in order to focus another, especially God's healing and blessing power of reconciliation. The deacon's leadership led the people into service—especially to the world, particularly to the "secular society"—and formed that ever-fragile bridge between the ordained and the *laos*.

All theories or suggestions of reasons for why this happened are purely speculative, but from my perspective, there is one that makes better sense than any others. It is the only one that suits the theological rationale, especially the representational nature of ordained ministry.

Namely, leadership became ordered and viewed sacramentally because the church came to see it as symbolic of the three forms of ministry that expressed the nature of the church and the church's mission. Let us put it another way: the key to the shift in thinking toward a sacramental understanding of leadership, and thus of ordained ministry, was the realization that many of the leadership roles were representational of the risen Christ, of the community and the ministry of each. For example, it did not take the early church long to appreciate the difference between presiding as a judge and presiding over the Eucharist. When finally the offices were recognized as symbolical, they became part of a developing sacramental system. Of course, sacramental ministry never ceased to be the ministry of leadership.

In fact, the development was quite natural. This is so, first, because a relatively profound appreciation of symbol is one of the outstanding features of the philosophical worldview contemporary to the early church. It is also because of the way holy orders evolved in a naturally emerging process of discovery rather than by invention. We now understand that this is precisely how symbols are discovered. They cannot be invented. As a threefold order began to show itself in response to the various factors of evolution, these foci for ministry quite naturally became a model of and for the total ministry of the church, highlighting its different aspects and contrarieties. These signs, or models, gradually began to be recognized as a symbol of the community's ministry. When this was realized, orders began to sacramentalize ministry as that not only of the people individually and corporately, but also of God. In hindsight it is surprising that one of the definitive factors of holy orders, their symbolic or sacramental nature, is practically ignored in most studies concerning their development.

## THE PRIESTHOOD OF ALL BELIEVERS

Meanwhile, though it would not have occurred to them to put the matter this way, all baptized Christians saw themselves as ministers. They were all given the opportunity for very serious education, usually in preparation for baptism, and had no reason to consider their comprehension of the faith, or their ability to articulate it, as inferior to that of their leaders. Their leaders were not sent off to be given special education or training prior to ordination. They did not need to be. At the same time, faith pervaded every avenue of the Christian's life, such that with what they did in their jobs, in their homes, in their play or leisure—in everything—they were serving their Lord and acting on his behalf.

When Charles Winters and Flower Ross developed the remarkable Sewanee education program by extension, they pointedly titled it Education for Ministry. Their first point of comparison was with the catechumenate of the early church. That Greek word simply referred to the preparation for baptism expected, indeed required, of all persons. Certainly by the time the Gospels and the pastoral epistles of John were written, the catechumenate was well in place and so familiar that references alluded to it without bothering to identify it as such. Winters and Ross liked to picture the contrast in dramatic terms.

When gentile pagans or Jews were touched by the life and lifestyle of a Christian of the early church, there would probably ensue a cautious and often dangerous little dance of inquiry. Meanwhile the church would draw out of each person things about their life, their needs, their hopes, each person's unique character as a child of God waiting to be born. For those who persisted in showing interest there would be an invitation into a process of exploration and inquiry, excavating and examining their deepest and most heartfelt questions and issues. If they chose to continue they would become catechumens, enrolled in preparation for baptism. Then would follow two or three years of serious inquiry. If the inquirer had a family or a household these would normally join the process, since the church quickly discovered that a Christian home was so likely to convert all those within it that conversion became expected. No one saw any reason to wait on infants to make mature personal decisions since, being raised in a Christian home and community, the decision invariably was to claim the faith as their own. The community would provide education and training for everyone and it would financially support the household if needed. The extended period of preparation would be highly personal and intensely communal. The catechumens would explore their personal lives and pilgrimage in relationship to the testimony of Scripture. They would explore how God has and is pressing in and upon and through each of their lives, and how God has been engaged in history as related in the story of the People of God, especially in the Scriptures. They would probably give up their job to devote full time to their study. There would likely be a career change, if not because of new insights and commitments then because of the circumstances of Christian life in a pagan society. Were the catechumen a teacher, or a member of any number of other work-related groups that required an oath of loyalty to Caesar, the Christian community would support them in finding a job compatible with this new faith where there is only one ultimate and primary loyalty: to God. Were the catechumen a soldier, he would need to retrain for a more compatible career, for Christians understood that respect for the dignity of every human being precluded shedding blood and killing.

The season of Lent began as a special six-week period just before the baptisms at Easter. In this season the intensity of preparation would increase dramatically, testing the candidate's commitment and readiness. It was crucial to the community that it could rely on the absolute commitment of the baptized members, for that commitment could be tested sorely by persecution and oppression. Apostasy was the dreaded possibility, tearing the community apart and weakening everyone's resolve. On the other hand, the willingness of the members to suffer and to die for the faith created a strong and growing community. Therefore, the community wanted to be relatively confident that, if a new member was challenged, the faith would be confessed and in the death of this friend of Jesus would come the conversion of others.

At the Easter Vigil the community would have been in prayer for the full three days of Easter—Maundy Thursday, Good Friday, the Sabbath, and Easter Sunday. They would be immersed in a three-day liturgy of resurrection celebration, beginning with the foot washing and institution of the liturgy, standing in vigil at the cross, having begun the three days having stood, and now bursting into songful joy of the resurrection proclamation. The candidate would rise from water with the scent of balsam everywhere. From that baptism the reborn person would emerge with a new name signifying a new identity in a new family of origin, with new brothers and sisters in Christ. All baptized infants and children were, quite literally, adopted by the community as their own. The newly baptized would be clothed in a new garment, a white alb signifying a new life of righteousness. As a neophyte the newly baptized would be deeply reverenced and respected as kings and queens of heaven, fresh icons and images of God's continuing, loving, forgiving, embracing presence. The person would stand in white, aglow with the oil of gladness on his face and the sign of Christ on her forehead, startling and attractive, standing out, entering a dramatic new lifestyle. Then, with this kind of preparation, when the community needed ordered and ordained support it could choose any respected person from the community to ordain, and it did. It was not terribly unusual, as in the famous case of Ambrose, to select a replacement of an ordained leader while the candidate was still an unbaptized catechumen. The baptism and ordination formed one continuous process. There would be no need to send anyone away for special theological education and "priestly formation." Everyone was theologically qualified; the question was simply that of who would best provide the leadership, who should preside. Then, could the church convince the person that the call they were willing to articulate was from God, it would not have been unusual to vote and ordain straightaway. Perhaps since a new leader was needed, the newly recognized leader would be ordained in a chapel on Saturday and preside at the Eucharist on the next day, the Lord's Day.

Notice how much this catechumenate process looks like the seminary experience today. We have decided to educate and train only the ordained and make the word "lay" into a synonym for a person who is ignorant of highly complicated and specialized information or a "client" of a professional. Most seminary educators recognize that many if not most of their students are called to the catechumenate. How often this is so, when the student is not truly called to ordained ministry as well, is something most would prefer not to investigate. But perhaps the greatest loss to the church and its ministry is revealed in the comparison with the theological sophistication of the *laos* then and today.

Karl Barth articulated a new demand: "'I am a mere layman; I am no theologian' is evidence not of humility but of indolence."[27] An authentic understanding of the faith has become necessary to deal with the doubt that is a part of the air we breathe. An educated laity is a value in and of itself; so is doubt. We must foster our growing sense of every baptized Christian's responsibility and identity as a minister in the way that members of the early church understood themselves. Most of that ministry will be in and to the world, where each individual Christian lives, works, and plays. The realization of individual Christians that they are ministers, actually and fully, immeasurably increases their sense of discipleship, of being a full citizen of the kingdom, of being as much a part of the church as those who have "a portion" in the church. Being a disciple implies apprenticeship, learning to be like the master by doing his work with him. It is in service that we most profoundly experience the reality of Christ's presence, and it is in continuing service that we become his companions, his friends.

## ESTABLISHMENT AND CLERICALIZATION

The next watershed in the church's historical development occurred with Constantine's triumph in A.D. 324, leading to the Constantinian Reformation. By the end of the fourth century, Christianity had become the official religion of the Roman Empire and the effective religion of the majority of the population. With the conversion of Constantine the entire self-understanding of the church was thrown into question. I have emphasized that the Christians saw themselves not as a religious society but as a people, an *ethnos*, a *genos*, the *laos*, a nation of legal aliens sojourning through a nation finally not their own. They were to serve and save this other world within which they lived and worked as a pilgrim people. The word "parish" comes from a Greek term for a license given to foreign workers in one of the lands of antiquity. The church was to be a people free from the world for the world's sake. What happens when the world becomes the people?

Is this not what we work for evangelistically? And yet this created a problem. It was not an altogether undesirable result by any means. We can say that "success" created a "good problem," but it did become increasingly problematic as we learned to accommodate ourselves to the powers of the world. Soon the church—and especially its paid careerists, the clergy—was expected to provide the religious justification for actions of the state in the way of the pagan and tribal religions. Clericalism as a professional class began to establish itself much in the way it had been known in paganism. Eusebius went so far as to envisage the empire as God's people, and the emperor as the image and representative on earth of the divine *Logos*, the Christ. The mosaics of the time depicted the Christ in churches and cathedrals with the face of Constantine.

This state religion could hardly persist in the face of historical developments. With the collapse of the Western Roman Empire following so closely upon the establishment of Christianity, the church was soon identified with a dying institution and had to find its vigor in movements such as monasticism and in an astonishing evangelical effort to convert the conquering Germanic tribes. As the ancient world of Western culture declined into what is often, and justifiably, referred to as Dark Ages it was held together largely by the church and especially by the office of the bishop of the old capital city. For various reasons, the Western church remembered the old contrariety of church and world that had shaped the life of the early communities. Augustine gave theological rationalization of the Germanic triumph over the Christian empire in the doctrine of the "two cities," the City of God and the City of Humanity. This was to prove formative for the Christian understanding of secularism, despite the inevitable exaggerations inherent in Neo-Platonism.

With the conversion of the invading pagans, the church was once more co-extensive with society. Christendom was becoming an established reality. But the society of Christendom was very different from that of the early church and the sophisticated urban Hellenic world. It was co-extensive now with a society in which the great cities had for all practical purposes disappeared and the basic unit of society was the virtually self-sufficient rural manor or estate. Bishops found themselves in a most peculiar position. During the transition from antiquity to the feudalistic Middle Ages, as the representatives of order and civilization, including divine order, they had become great magnates in the same position. The bishop inevitably became an essential factor in the fabric of feudal society. But for the same reason bishops lost touch with other clergy and with the people of their churches. The bishop continued to have a circle of clergy and staff, but the real center of power and authority and activity was the cathedral. The direct, hands-on leadership of the parish churches where people lived together was now in the hands of the presbyters. They were as often as not appointed and maintained ("beneficed") by lay patrons for service on their estates. Presbyters became more like chaplains to lay landlords than vicars in the place of the bishop. They were likely to be given a church building or chapel for the estate's population and a salary. The bishop became at best a distant patron or administrator who had no easy time supervising or controlling his clergy, even if he had the time and inclination, especially the interest, to do so.

> One obvious result…was a circumstance which is reflected to this day in the life of the Christian churches in the West. With the Dark and Middle Ages in the history of the Western church, primary and direct pastoral activity—baptism, eucharistic celebration, discipline, and teaching—became the sphere not of the bishop but of the presbyter, who, as the parochial system gradually took shape, acquired an independent jurisdiction of his own—under the bishop to be sure, but not with the bishop. It was in this way that the title "priest" became, as it is today, the almost exclusive posses-

sion of the presbyteral order (as in the well-known phrase, "Bishops, priests, and deacons"—an expression which would have baffled Christians of the fourth century). It was the same set of developments which led to the gradual desuetude of the order of deacons and resulted in the system—which the Protestant reformers, at least in conscious theory, adopted from the Middle Ages—of a one-order ministry. With these changes, almost unnoticed, there also disappeared the pattern of collegial or "team" ministry under the leadership of a chief pastor.[28]

There was another significant result: major reform, known as the Gregorian Reformation. The external drive for reform ushered in the shift from antiquity to the feudal or medieval world. The church adapted and was an enormous influence in shaping the society that emerged from that period of transition. However, the new society depended on a system of large land ownership and the power of fealty. This was well and good for the establishment of relative order, economic stability, and peace. For the church, however, it was a profound threat. The church drew close to a point of being taken over by the barons, including monarchs and even bishops. Nevertheless, the struggle was viewed as one between the structure of church authority, all that it protected in terms of tradition and practice, and the power of lay landlords. The word "lay," when seen as a threat or a force within society, began to be used in the sense of "secular." The tradition of two separate if not entirely distinct realms represented by church and world disfavored the secularization of the church by having taken over the control of ecclesiastical offices, by royal and baronial lay, or secular, offices.

In very practical terms, let us say that a nobleman wanted to care for the people of his land and castle and would build a church or chapel to do so. He would, of course, hire a priest to provide the sacraments and pastoral service. If the bishop, remote enough anyway in many cases, were to require something of the church or its priest that the nobleman opposed, it was likely that the one paying the bills would have his will performed. The church fought back. This grew into major conflicts. Images come to mind of Henry II and Thomas Becket, or Henry at Canosa standing outside in the snow for hours, begging the Pope for reconciliation.

Gregory knew what to do, and it worked for his age. If the reform sought to liberate the church from worldly control to be true to its own distinctive calling there could be only one thing to do in a society in which church and world were co-extensive. It would be done in two steps. First, the clergy would have to be freed from lay control. Secondly, the clergy would have to be in complete charge of the church and the sacramental system that became vast and mysterious (that is, distant from the people and dangerous to approach). Mainly, it was absolutely necessary for salvation. The plan of the Gregorian reform was to make the clergy a separate caste, with special duties and responsibilities, higher standards of training and education, unique privileges, and a distinctive way of life. This caste, so separate from the people that they could not marry or enter into the same society in the same way, controlled the faucet through which heaven's grace could flow and be dispensed: the sacramental system. They could turn it on and turn it off, give or refuse. That is, the church as the clergy, not the church as the people or the community, controlled salvation, and preached of a very real hell.

The word laity had reached the new meaning of its evolution. It now defined those who were not clerics, those relatively uneducated, the "uninitiated," "clients" of ministry rather than ministers. What they were up to was "secular" except in relation to the clergy and what the clergy provided them, mostly on Sundays and feast days. The reform was effective in separating the clergy from the body of the church, from the *laos*, now merely laity, just as the "Presbyterianism" of the medieval church separated the bishop from other clergy and left future generations an officially monochromatic ministry of priesthood. (By this time the diaconate was no longer effectively a distinctive order; deacons were merely apprentice priests.) There can be little argument with the Gregorian Reformation. It was the right move to resolve their problems. Their solution has become our problem.

## LEADERSHIP AND AUTHORITY

It should be clear that ordained ministry and leadership go hand in hand. This is one matter on which history is abundantly clear and without contradiction. It is the appropriate and congruent functioning of leadership that triggers that which ordained ministry signifies, moving it forward into the powerful realm inhabited only by the symbolical. The operative terms for ordained ministry should be (1) its leadership function and (2) its representational nature. Since the functions of ordained ministry are essentially pastoral, that is, forms of community leadership, it will be necessary that most leadership and ordained ministry continue to go hand in hand.

For many of the leadership functions no one ordained is required. However, some of those functions are representational in nature, and if they are performed by someone who is not ordained, the person assuming the functions will come to be viewed in representational ways, signifying something beyond themselves and the functions they exercise. I believe this is precisely what happened to the leaders in the early church. It seems as well to be what happened to the leaders in the Protestant churches that wanted to reform the church by enhancing "lay" leadership but only created more powerful ordained leadership. This is represented in the famous observation that the Presbyterian minister became the former priest "writ large." Consequently, this is one important reason why the present wisdom of the church requires that someone ordained as an officer of the sacraments perform those functions that are explicitly sacramental. Within smaller communities most or all of the decision-making functions of leadership can be performed by lay members while someone else who is ordained "supplies" the sacrament or serves in what might be called the role of a chaplain. This will inevitably result in unhappy confusion and vocational frustration. On the one hand, I have never met anyone called to sacramental ministry who did not feel called to leadership as part and parcel of that vocation. On the other hand, because the exercise of exclusively lay leadership within a Christian community quickly will be seen in representational terms it will lack the clarity, the order, and, as I am trying to make clear, the value of the sacramental.

The leadership of the church will remain clerical because of its representational nature, but it will of necessity and for good reasons be shared both in function and in authority. It must also be "given" by the community. The relationship of sacramental ministry to the ministry of all the baptized is subtle and easily subject to abuse in each direction. The interrelationships among ministries, lay and ordained, must not be hierarchical in theory or in fact.

Leadership is suspect throughout the American church. There is continuous pressure to limit it to support, advice, and—where it is clerical—to sacramental chaplaincy. In many instances, on the other hand, leadership is experienced as overbearing, tightly defining, and protecting of areas of authority and responsibility. Ordained leaders are often condescending and controlling in relation to "lay" leadership. "Lay" ministry and leadership are too often limited to being an extension of "priestly" ministry and leadership, or a watchdog against it. A number of observers believe "lay" abuse of clergy seems to be on the rise, with members picturing the church as "theirs" and clergy as their "hirelings," blackmailing the parish with financial and political power, undermining the ministry of the clergy and sometimes driving them from office. The exercise of leadership is terribly difficult in congregations. Active church members have become suspicious of any leadership, especially ordained leadership. All of this exacerbates an authority problem, one shared by all institutions in American society at large.

Clergy are terribly threatened. Their respect in society has dropped dramatically along with that of their institution and even their religion. They have never, in our day at least, made much money. Most feel terribly guilty, despite how irrational it is, to see how much of the parish budget goes to their salary and how little of it goes to mission. Now their most ancient and lasting role of leadership is very much in question. On the one hand, contemporary political ideals of equality and participatory democracy have led to talk of a priesthood which is "of the people" in the sense of not being in any way "different" or "set apart." On the other hand, contemporary ideals of leadership have encouraged a managerial or "professional" style for ordained persons as "enablers," administrators, or as "one-on-one" counselors who "fix" the problems of lay clients. These models are taken from the way that contemporary society likes to see people who are in power. In the background of all this there still lurks the figure of the person who is "minister of Word and Sacrament," over whom the church's ordination prayers ask God for more than certain skills, ask God for more than the ability to make certain mechanical actions of ritual for the sake of validity—ask God, indeed, for some kind of mysterious and empowering grace to perform one of the most difficult and demanding, if satisfying, jobs in the world.

All baptized members of the Body of Christ are ministers of the Christ. Leadership is a form of ministry. Leadership within the Body is lay and clerical. It is important to recognize the value of lay leadership. Leadership is not hierarchical. Leadership carries authority, but not from the top down. The source of authority is the community. The leadership of the bishop, the rector, other priests, and deacons is sacramental, that is, it symbolizes the ministry of and for the Body of Christ, thereby enhancing the ministry of all baptized members. The ministry of the baptized, lay and clerical—that is, the ministry of the whole church—symbolizes the ministry of Christ.

One problem is that ordained leadership continues to be perceived incorrectly as hierarchical. One valid reason is that it, incorrectly, tends to be performed hierarchically. There is little distinction recognized between the need for ordered leadership and the desire for hierarchical leadership. By and large sacramental holy orders have been hierarchical according to theory and design, and even include the notion that the orders are cumulative. Non-sacramental Protestant leadership is at least as authoritative and hierarchical in actual practice. The problem comes in viewing the ministry of the community as being derived from the authority of the clerical hierarchy rather than from the proper understanding that the authority of the ordained emanates from the community, that it flows from the waters of baptism bubbling up from the earth.

## APOSTOLIC SUCCESSION

Some within the catholic family of churches stake the very life and validity of the church on the validity of the ordained ministry. The operative theory is that of apostolic succession. No catholic Christian can minimize the importance of apostolic succession, for what it is really about is the catholicity of the church. The fundamental catholic principle is that it is important for the church of a particular moment to interconnect loyally with the life of the church at all times and all places, especially as it was founded in the early church. It is deemed vital that the church today parallel the life of the apostolic church as much as possible. Catholic churches feel a genuine responsibility for the universal church both in terms of time and space. Catholic churches feel a real affinity for the church as it has always been; indeed, they are a part of that continuing church. They feel accountable to the saints who have lived and still live in the one communion.

Many things follow from this, aspects of the catholic church that come close to its very heart and existence. Experience has taught Catholics that if these traditions are not safeguarded diligently in terms of its ministry, specifically in terms of apostolic succession as the church's outward sign of this interior loyalty, then the church will sit too loosely in the saddle to the past, and will find it easy to forgo understandings and practices which historically have been considered quite important. Where apostolic succession has been denigrated in the church, so has the symbolic or sacramental understanding of the ordained orders, especially of that of bishops; indeed, the entire sacramental system will always suffer significant accretions, in practice if not in theory. For example, when the church of the Reformation redefined apostolic succession it did not find it difficult to remove the sense of sacrifice as Catholics understood it. There are no exceptions to the correlation of the importance of apostolic succession and the importance of the sacraments as a whole. Such memories become tenacious. Learning from experience, Catholics demand that great care be taken regarding the laying on of hands at all ordinations. It is easy to see how the validity of ministry, based on the criteria of the apostolic succession, becomes crucial. The sacramental system and catholicity itself seems to be at issue.

Nevertheless, while what is at stake is of real value and demands the drawing of lines, the actual argument for apostolic succession is a rather ludicrous caricature of catholicity. Apostolic succession, as it is most rigidly presented, supposes that all validly ordained priests and deacons received the laying on of hands by at least one bishop who received the laying on of hands from at least three other bishops validly ordained with the laying on of hands and that this process of holy touching must go back in an unbroken succession to the apostles who were personally appointed by Jesus. These touchings are seen as providing a direct line of grace, kind of like a pipeline extended down through the centuries, beginning at its source, Jesus of Nazareth.

The bishops are presented as the literal successors to the apostles: "He who hears them hears Christ while he who rejects them rejects Christ."[29]

A once-and-for-all delivered ministry suits a once-and-for-all delivered faith. The idea finally demands the absurd: that Jesus had a blueprint for the church in his mind, drew it up, and handed it to Peter for perpetuity. Accordingly, unless the ministry of the church is maintained according to that blueprint, the church is not the church; Jesus cannot perform his ministry of salvation except in that one form of church government.

By understanding apostolic succession in its relationship to ordained ministry alone, the life of the church is left dependent on its validly ordained clergy. Thus the ministry, its authority and its power to act for God-in-Christ, exists entirely apart from the community of the church. At best the community derives its authority from the hierarchy of the ordained. For example, a bishop is seen to hold in his hands (most of those who insist that the line must be drawn at this notion of apostolic succession do not yet recognize the theory that it could be a "her") the power to perform any of the sacramental actions of a bishop, such as ordination. Since he has been empowered directly and exclusively from God he may perform episcopal actions on behalf of God wherever he pleases—no matter the decisions or desires of the community that makes up the jurisdiction where the actions may be performed. The only thing stopping him from any arbitrary action as a bishop is canon law. It is well established that prophetic Christians must, from time to time, defy canon law out of conscience. Theologically, perhaps most of the church believes the bishop is endowed with the power to act on behalf of a Christian community even when that community does not want him or her to, indeed, when it believes the action the bishop is taking is directly opposed to their welfare. This is a very real problem right now.

The Vatican recognizes that members of churches lacking a valid apostolic succession are not completely disqualified as Christian, but neither are they considered fully "there." Such churches do not belong to the one true, and perfectly valid, church. Other churches in the tradition of Luther and Calvin also define the church in terms of the valid function of its ministry, but not in terms of a valid succession. They posit that the apostolic succession is counted as present where the gospel is truthfully proclaimed and the sacraments are rightly celebrated. They often insist that the right doctrine be stated in certain terms, specifically in the Protestant Reformation tradition of justification and grace.

A respected friend of mine says that apostolic succession has been used as a synonym for different denominational obsessions. For Roman Catholics apostolic succession has been a synonym for the papacy. For Anglicans it has meant a church with bishops, and one that is just as catholic as the Roman Catholic Church. For Lutherans it has stood for doctrine, right doctrine in the tradition of Luther. This will continue to be a fighting matter, with no quarter offered, until one is ready to compromise on the issue of what apostolic succession represents for them and to acknowledge the importance and validity of what it represents for others.

I confess that while I hope I would be willing to compromise where possible, especially in terms of past practice, I do not see how Catholics can give up their insistence on the laying on of hands in the manner they now require for ordination. It is a powerful sign of fidelity to catholicity and of care for the sacraments. The action can be seen as a kind of constitutional safeguard. However, it seems clear that Catholics of all sorts are going to have to give up on the "current of grace" and "blueprint of the church" theories, together with the unsupportable contention that there has been a perfect line of holy touchings which confer the mechanical power to control the grace of the sacraments. All of the churches are going to have to recognize the fullness and "validity" (read "reality") of the Christian ministry of each other through the centuries. Finally, these tired old shibboleths are only counter-productive caricatures and barriers to truth and fellowship. They are rapidly becoming as offensive to most mainline and traditional Christians as American fundamentalism.

The question regarding the extent to which authority was shared remains relatively open. We know that the early church did not practice democracy to the extent of modern Anglicanism or Luterism, among others. On the other hand, if the bishops appointed the presbyters and deacons they ordained, the bishops themselves were chosen by the people, or at least their election was ratified, and rule was not rigid. Certainly, the bishop's authority was limited, partly by the people and clergy without whose consent he could not function, and partly by the external constraints imposed by councils of his fellow bishops. The bishop not only represented the constitutive tradition of the Catholic Church to his people, he represented his people to the church at large. Woe betide the bishops who failed to do so: Eusebius of Caesarea was nervous to the point of being apologetic, if not apoplectic, when he tried to explain to his flock why he had signed the creed of Nicaea. There was an early sense of what may be called participatory authority. The leaders sought the will of the people and relied on the Holy Spirit to form consensus when important decisions were to be made. Rarely do we find their decisions and actions arbitrary or overbearing. If the exercise of leadership soon became hierarchical, it was strongly tempered by the voice of church councils.

What I want to avoid is the clericalization of the membership. Clerical elitism is so well established that, as in any other such case, those who have been made second-class citizens of the community can only imagine being equal by copying the very elitism that had been so very undesirable. Therefore I can imagine how we can make people appear to represent the new status and ministry of what continues to be called "the laity" by "clericalizing" them in clever ways. Notice the garb liturgical lay leaders don. In fact, most of the roles of ministry fostered for laypersons are clerical in nature, and almost certainly they are limited to functions needed within the church. We seldom talk about the ministry of the church by referring to people's jobs or even to their marriages or the parenting or the friendships or the politics of the members. Leadership authority has become a major issue of controversy between Episcopal clergy and people within the parishes they serve. However, the authority to minister to the world is seldom at controversy, for the "people" in question are in fact pictured, conceived, and treated as a "religious organization."

If we are going to have genuine "lay ministry" and shared authority we will have to recover the notion of the church as a "people," whether set over against, or mingled with, or co-extensive with, a larger society we are to serve and offer salvation. The only time there is a controversy concerning the authority to minister to the world, it involves the attempt to exclude religion from the political and techno-economic spheres of society, as though Christianity's only business is an individual's "spiritual" (and perhaps cultural) life. This brings us to our next issue: the need for community.

✦ ✦ ✦ ✦

# SUMMATION

The mission of the church is the renewal of creation and the coming of the kingdom, each of which is established in Christ. The church is called and empowered to serve as the earthly representative of God-in-Christ for the accomplishment of this mission. The ministry of the church is that of our Lord Jesus, risen and reigning. The minister is always the Christ. Ministry is the function of the church in its representative role. The ministry of the church is not limited to church activities; because it is cosmic most ministry is performed through the roles Christians hold in society. Ministry is any action that is (a) intentional, (b) on behalf of the church, and (c) to accomplish the mission of the church.

Ministry is always whole and united, for it is on behalf of Christ and the church. Yet it is ordered into distinctive forms. The sacrament of order is a threefold pattern: (1) The ministry on behalf of Jesus will be exercised in accord with the originating and sending ministry of the incarnate Lord in formation of the church. It is intended to represent the whole and united church, faithful to the universal church in its catholic and orthodox tradition and primarily to the mission, as given to the original apostles in their appointment by Jesus himself. (2) The ministry of Jesus will be reconciliation and thanksgiving. It is intended to represent the reconciling ministry of a genuine community of thanksgiving gathered in the name of Christ in specific localities around the world and called to worship and service, in order to make God-in-Christ available to the world, offering the saving power of God to bless and to heal. (3) The ministry of Jesus will be concrete and humble human service where there is need. It is intended to represent the church as servant of the world and of the kingdom in meeting concrete needs of human beings and of the earth. These distinctions order Christian ministry most appropriately. They signify the three distinctive functions of ministry and reflect three different aspects of the nature of the church. Taken together, the three distinctive aspects of ministry disclose the single whole.

There are several churches that share a catholic view of sacramental reality. It is legitimate to refer to them as the catholic family of churches. The largest bodies within the catholic family of churches are Eastern Orthodox, Roman Catholic, Anglican, and Lutheran. Most of the churches within these traditions understand the representational nature of the church and of its ministry in sacramental terms. When the ministry of the church is congruent with what it signifies, that is, when the function of ministry accords with the threefold nature of the church's ministry, the church is recognized as a symbol of the transcendent ministry of Christ. The church ministers effectively as the sacrament of Christ.

The baptized members of the church are all individual ministers of the church, fully empowered to exercise each and all components of the threefold pattern of ministry. As the baptized people of God they are called and empowered to do so corporately and individually, the former exercised at the various institutional and communal levels of the church and the latter exercised where each person lives, works, plays, and performs his or her role as a citizen of society.

Certain members of the *laos* are ordained to order the sacramental ministry of the church. This means that they perform leadership functions of the ministry that the threefold pattern of ministry expresses and it means that they have a representative role. They model this pattern by focusing each of the particular forms of the three-fold pattern, and by providing a unified symbol of the total ministry as they work together in interrelationship. The personal ministry of an ordained leader is narrowed to a particular focus on one of the threefold orders of ministry. The wholeness and unity of the church's ministry is focused by the apostolic ministry, that of bishops. The ministry of reconciliation and thanksgiving is focused by the priestly ministry, that of presbyters. The ministry of service is focused by the diaconal ministry, that of deacons. Taken together the threefold order is a unified symbol or sacrament of the ministry of the church, and therefore of the Christ. It provides functional leadership for the church and a model for the ministry of the *laos*, that is, it orders the whole ministry of the baptized, and it informs the world about what the church intends to do in specific terms.

## NOTES

[1] Roger Haight, *Jesus, Symbol of God* (MaryKnoll, NY: Orbis Books, 1999), 8f.

[2] Avery Dulles, "The Symbolic Structure of Revelation," *Theological Studies*, 41 (1980): 60f.

[3] Charles Winters, *Education for Ministry* (Sewanee, TN: University of the South), bk. 7, 46.

[4] Ibid.

[5] Alexander Schmemann, *For the Life of the World* (Crestwood, NY: St. Vladimir's Seminary Press, 1973), 67.

[6] Edward Schillebeeckx, *Christ the Sacrament of the Encounter with God* (Kansas City: Sheed, Andrews & McMckee, 1960), 3.

[7] Schmemann, *For the Life of the World*, 139.

[8] Speech before the 1992 Conference on the Episcopacy, sponsored by Associated Parishes for Liturgy and Mission.

[9] Ibid.

[10] Susan K. Wood, *Sacramental Orders* (Collegeville, MN: The Liturgical Press, 2000), 66.

[11] Hans Küng, *The Church* (New York: Sheed and Ward, 1973), 139.

[12] Urban T. Holmes, *Priest in Community* (New York: Seabury Press, 1978), 88.

[13] Timothy F. Sedgwick, *American Theological Review*, Vol. LXIX, no.2, 163.

[14] G. W. F. Hegel, *Werke* IV, 67. Quoted in Jürgen Moltmann, *Theology of Hope* (New York: Harper & Row, 1965).

[15] Karl Barth, *Church Dogmatics*, vol. 4, pt. 3 (Edinburgh: T. & T. Clark, 1962), 860.

[16] Ibid., 865ff.

[17] From an e-mail to the author, dated July 4, 2002.

[18] Wood, *Sacramental Orders*, Liturgy Press, 2000, 175f.

[19] Eduard Schweizer, *Church Order in the New Testament* (London: SCM Press, 1959), 13.

[20] Joseph Blenkinsopp, *Celibacy, Ministry, Church* (New York: Herder and Herder, 1968), 16.

[21] Ibid., 23.

[22] J.A.T. Robinson, *On Being the Church in the World* (London: SCM Press, 1960), 72.

[23] Blemkinsopp, 22f.

[24] Eusebius, *Ecclesiastical History*, 6.43.11.

[25] John N. Collins' books include *Diakonia: Re-interpreting the Ancient Sources, Are All Christians Ministers?*, and the forthcoming *Deacons and the Church* (September 2002).

[26] Robinson, *On Being the Church*, 2.

[27] Barth, *Church Dogmatics*, 871.

[28] Richard Norris, Retired Professor of Theology and Church History. Union Theological Seminary.

[29] *Lumen Gentium*, 1, 8 in W. Abbott and J. Gallagher, eds., *The Documents of Vatican II* (London: Chapman and America Press, 1966), 40.

# V.
# COMMUNITY

When God wanted to communicate with the people of the world a community was called into being. Jesus spent most of his ministry in the gathering of a community. The primary task of Christians is to build communities in which Christ is manifestly present and reigning. We yearn for the genuine community to which Christ calls us. Yet, we do not experience the communion of community, our genuine and actual unity in Christ, because we have lost our sense of corporate reality. We have come to the point where we live in an "object world," one in which we experience only a series of discrete and independent entities, with little or no grasp of their interconnectedness. This is personally frustrating because it means that we are each an object to all others, and even feel that way toward ourselves. It is frustrating to the church because the church cannot build community beyond that based on personal feelings and attitudes, particularly those founded on like-mindedness.

Our radical individualism is the pivotal characteristic—and perhaps even the underlying cause—of the object world. However, that is combined with other attributes of our Western culture to form the object world in which we find ourselves. The public and shared features of daily life are giving way to privatized preferences, whether referring to facilities or politics or economics or cultural matters or any other aspect, including religion. Consumerist materialism is the dominant philosophy of society, and it drives the engines of society; people identify themselves more by their consumer choices than by their social choices and opinions; religion and faith—or non-faith—identity is a private and individualistic consumer choice. In an object world there is no room for God. In an object world we can hardly imagine the shared subjectivity of all humanity that ultimately is rooted in Christ. The primary hope for overcoming our object world and having a future ability to create Christian community seems to rest in the sciences that are increasingly aware of the corporate and interconnected nature of reality. We, in the meanwhile, are to remain faithful to our vision and practice holy yearning.

# THE CHRISTIAN VISION OF COMMUNITY

## THE PHILOSOPHICAL NATURE OF THE PROBLEM

Desmond Tutu, the retired Anglican Archbishop of South Africa and the 1984 Nobel Peace Prize Laureate, has often been asked about the rapid growth of African Christianity, especially in light of the decline of the church in Western society. In a 1989 speech offered to the annual conference of Trinity Institute held at Grace Episcopal Cathedral in San Francisco, Tutu began his response to this question by reminding the audience of how much he loves the American church and how grateful he is for the crucial role the American church played in helping South Africans overcome the system of institutionalized discrimination and prejudice of which apartheid was the center. He then offered a note of congratulations for the philosophical tradition of the West, one that has been so instrumental in the remarkable development of the Western sciences and of the industrialized economies. The key to this, he surmised, is the Western style of analysis that is so ready and able for the purposes of drawing distinctions. He believes the primary reason behind our economic and technological achievements is the Western ability to distinguish, to categorize, and to recognize what makes each thing unique and different from every other thing. This ability to separate everything into different categories for analysis in order to work with precision and efficiency is one of the rich forces of the Western tradition. In addition, one of the most important values in Western culture is the high regard for what makes each thing singular, together with the desire to uphold those unique qualities and to struggle for the worth of each thing in and of itself, especially each human being. Archbishop Tutu was ready to recognize the weakness of the African philosophical tradition as a basis for science, technology, industrialized economy, and human rights. Even so, he went on to explain the advantage his tradition has for Christian community and therefore for evangelism.

According to my notes, Archbishop Tutu held up the African's cultural ability to see the way people are interconnected and united, to see the whole of which each is a part and to understand that the whole is real—not to mention that it is greater than the sum of its parts—and finally, to appreciate how each component would not exist as an individual part without the whole. He used the word "interconnectedness" in describing the understanding Christians of Africa have of community. He used the word "participation" in describing the life of the individual in the Christian community. He said, "When South Africans join the church they are not becoming a part of something abstract. They are becoming a part of a 'people,' the most concrete thing in human experience, a community. They have a place in the universe and in the long history of the world. They belong. They belong to the Christian community. In that is their salvation now and in the age to come." Each time I review his insight I find these words terribly exciting and terribly disturbing. They excite me because I believe Archbishop Tutu's insight in comparing Western culture and African culture is crucial for an understanding of the Christian enterprise within each. They excite me because I believe the process of reformation will cause the church of Western culture to rediscover the corporate nature of reality. They disturb me out of frustration over the present inability of the Western church to grasp the interconnectedness between people as a basis for genuine Christian community, in order to appreciate what may be termed "the biblical world," and in order to make room for the true God. Perhaps the most frightening thing is that Peter Lee, Archbishop Tutu's former staff member and the highly respected Bishop of the South African Diocese of Christ the King, told me in 1999 that he believes the American influence of radical individualism is beginning to successfully invade South Africa and the rest of the continent. Like Archbishop Tutu, he understands the consequences.

During the 1998 Lambeth Conference[1] of Anglican Bishops considerable interest was taken in a certain observation about international trends. On the one hand, globalization is producing cultural conformity, on a rather grand scale and the sovereignty of nation-states is becoming more relative in the face of rapidly developing international law and standards for human rights. On the other hand, nation-states are having problems with the demand for decentralization and autonomy made by ethnic and geographical groupings within the national boundaries, many of which are experiencing difficulty in living side by side. Of course the glaring examples occur where there is armed conflict and attempts at genocide, such as took place in Rwanda and throughout the Balkans. The newly engaged struggle against terrorism demands highly increased international cooperation and softer national boundaries. However, the phenomenon was best symbolized for this meeting of bishops in the validity of two different books that became extremely well known at about the same time. One was titled *The Tribalization of the World*, the other, *The McDonaldization of the World*. How, the question was asked, can we have expanding cultural conformity and escalating "tribalism"? I do not believe the conclusions drawn by the titles of the two books are paradoxical. It seems to me that the more fundamental movement toward the radical individualism being spread by American culture carries a certain logic in which the collapse of cultural diversity and the tension within, and even collapse of, broader communities composed of diverse peoples, such as nations, operate together. When "the self" becomes the overwhelmingly dominant reality, which is where our individualism has taken us, then a tribal society of cultural conformity—one reflecting me and mine and operating for me and mine—becomes the only acceptable way to organize life, even on a newly global scale.

Please understand that I am not saying that our Western failure to see the corporate nature of reality, to see the whole and the interconnection of all the varied parts of creation, is a simple matter of the will. We have engaged in a long and gradual philosophical process that has brought us the several benefits to which Archbishop Tutu alluded, but which has also brought us to the point where we cannot see other than particular objects, however they interact as independent units. Perhaps it will be helpful to offer a kind of mental exercise to help us appreciate the difficulty. To think about this in our Western terms let us picture one of the grand inventions of our industrialized technology, an automobile engine. We comprehend the fact that the whole is made up of parts and that the whole is greater than the sum of the parts. When the maker puts the parts together properly so that an engine comes into existence it cannot be said to be the simple collection of parts which make it what it is, which make it run and perform its function. If we take all of the parts of the engine and lay them out on the ground we will not have an engine. We know very well that each part of an engine is created only for the function of making up an engine by putting them all together. No one would bother to make each part as an object to exist in and of itself, for some indiscernible purpose apart from an engine. If they do not become part of a running engine they will not be what they were created to be. When we have all of the parts laid out on the ground we will not have even meaningful parts, except as they are potentially a part of a complete engine. Take, for example, the small object called a piston. By itself, it is not a piston, it is an abstract and relatively odd little contraption made of certain materials. But a mechanic knows that it is a piston because of what it can do to start and maintain the proper running of what will be an engine when all of the parts are placed together in a construction of the whole such that each realizes its potential as an individual part. Unless there exists the whole, which is greater than the sum of the parts, the parts have no particularity or individuality—other than abstractly and potentially. However, because we are so familiar with engines and because they are so common, when we see a piston we do not think of it as existing only in potentiality or abstraction; it seems perfectly concrete and particular to us even when it is lying by itself on the ground.

For whatever reason most of us fail to see the relationship between the whole and the particular in the objects God creates in the same way we can see them in the objects we study and invent. Scientists come the closest; some scientists can study and take in the makeup of whole systems within life, perhaps even sense that of the whole creation. Most of the rest of us, even highly enamored as we are with science and the scientific method, lack this ability. We do not, for example, see how human individuality is to be realized solely through being part of a magnificent whole, in the way a piston is only a piston as it is designed and created to have a role in a mechanical engine and only realizes its pistonhood as part of a running engine. We are not awake to this reality, and when we try to open our eyes it is indeed as though we see through a glass darkly. Without the whole and the role each is to play in creation, life really makes little more sense for each component, including human beings, than would the purposeless creation of a piston without any concept of an engine. It would be an object of absurdity. No wonder so many in our day and age have come to just this conclusion about human existence.

There is no one single reason for our inability to see the whole and interconnectedness of all that is. Nevertheless I personally believe our philosophical tradition has been a very significant factor in influencing our worldview today. I believe it is important to understand this process to fully appreciate the nature and the extent of the difficulty. I believe we all suffer from the limitations of our philosophical worldview. Certainly I know that I do. Today in Western culture, we are captured in what I am calling an *object world*. First, let us grasp some sense of the Christian vision of community to be found within our tradition, of the possibilities for fulfillment when human beings appreciate the corporate nature of reality together with the gift of individuality.

## THE PASTORAL AND ANTHROPOLOGICAL NATURE OF THE ISSUE

Ann McBride and I were on a train returning from a visit with a mutual friend. Dorothy Cecelski's brain tumor had matured over the last year and the time of departure was near. Ann, former president of Common Cause, is a life-long friend with whom I have shared many important experiences and ideas. We are accustomed to discussions in which we explore our deepest questions, bring to bear all our resources of mind and heart, and discover what we really think and feel. We loved and admired the lady to whom we had just said our last goodbye, and we were feeling the impact. We were feeling particularly sad and troubled because our friend's husband, Arthur, had died suddenly and unexpectedly only a few weeks before and Dorothy was suffering terrible pains of grief over his loss. It was too much for anyone. Dorothy was having to do the extreme work of reconciling herself to her own death and giving way to it, while doing the equally taxing work of grief over the death of her husband of almost 50 years. Plus, as hard as her family and friends were working for her, she couldn't help but make her habitually graceful effort to care for everyone who came to see her.

Ann asked about a particularly poignant moment during our visit when Dorothy and I had talked about her loss and the task she faced. Every pastor knows that there are two things people fear most at the time they face death. There is evidence to suppose that in the Middle Ages hell was the great fear on the mind of the dying. But there is little indication that hell remains such a significant concern for most people dying today. All current studies and experience verify two undeviating fears: physical pain and loneliness. Dorothy's sudden loss of her husband intensified and complicated the overwhelming sensation of isolation that the dying suffer. She was fortunate in having a family and many friends who were being most highly loyal and competent, offering her their loving presence and care. Yet, the natural fear of loneliness and her grief created a void too immense to be filled. A tedious and wearing psychological subtlety compounded her loneliness: Dorothy maintained a sense of Arthur's presence—one she found very comforting—and yet she understood that denial is unhealthy. She felt that she was supposed to face his death realistically. Using the delicately indirect language of insinuation so often used in pastoral situations I had opened the door to permission for her to remain in some denial because she did not have time to resolve the process of grief. Whether right or wrong, I encouraged her sense of his presence and invited her to visit with him, to argue with him, to remember with him, to let the grief of his absence wash over her without having to bring it into focus. Ann had noticed how important this moment had been; she commented on the relief that seemed to follow for Dorothy.

As Ann and I talked about this experience it reinforced how desperately important it is to every human being to avoid being alone during the process of dying and at the time of death, how badly we need to take our last journey in the company of others. Ann began to show appreciation of various implications to be drawn from this pastoral dictum. Without attempting to relate the verbatim conversation I went about making the following points.

I said that I view our insight about the fear of loneliness at the time of our death as defining of our humanity. That is, this universal characteristic of dying is strongly indicative of one of the most important factors in our anthropological and philosophical understanding of humanity. The human being can exist and experience existence only in relation to other human beings. We are not simply individuals who are social. It is just as true that a human being is a social being who enjoys individuality. In fact, we know the same truth about the corporate nature of humanity to be established even more dramatically at the other end of life, that is, at the beginning. It has been demonstrated that a newborn baby must be held and provided love by at least one human being. Otherwise it literally will not survive. Human beings cannot be without others. That is a reality that is definitive for our humanity. Even the most isolated hermits or castaway survivors cannot endure, much less prosper, without experiencing themselves in relation to others.

When the push of death comes to shove, we want to be social beings and we want this with the passion for life itself. We are no longer so focused on being individuals who are independent and on our own. When birth occurs and we are suddenly and dramatically left on our own without the help and security of the womb, we must experience ourselves as social beings or we will give up and die. I wondered plaintively, "Why can't we learn about what really counts in life from what really counts at birth and at death?"

## THE CONCRETE SELF AND THE ABSTRACT SELF

As usual Ann's intellectual curiosity was stimulated. She asked about where our individuality, our particularity, our selfhood, fit in. "I guess," she pondered, "most people imagine a self as first and primary and then see that self in relationship. Do you think that is legitimate?" I thought about that and continued my musings about the corporate nature of reality and of our humanity.

Perhaps, I suggested, it isn't a matter of what comes first, because the two realities about our selfhood are so closely related it doesn't matter. One of the most dominant and distinctive things about our age is the radical individualism that has seemed to grow increasingly more radical until it has gone over the top. By individualism I mean the belief that a human being can exist and be a self as a whole and complete person independent of others. There seems to be an attending assumption that it is the single person that is real, that an individual person has actual substance. That which is more than one person, such as a group or society or the church, is considered a mental construct that is brought together merely in the mind of an individual or as a matter of conjecture. The mental construct is considered as merely an aggregate of individuals. Intellectually, and upon reflection, it can be acknowledged that this aggregate, or congregation of persons, has a certain reality. For example, it can cause behavior individuals would not engage in without a sort of mass mentality. Nonetheless, that reality is abstract and insubstantial and finally only actual in terms granted by the individuals composing the aggregate. Our individualism is radical because we are limited to a full appreciation only of the singular and particular units of reality, without grasping the interconnection between them, or the concrete reality of the corporate.

What seems to be missed in our culture is this: the self which is engaged in relationships is the historical and concrete self, while the self which we assume is fixed and the "real me" inside is, at best, an abstraction. It is the solely internal self that is insubstantial. It is often an illusory self. So, I contend that there is the individual self each human being usually calls "myself," but in itself it is abstract and indefinable except in some vague sense of ultimate mystery. Then, there is the self of concrete experience.

Ann immediately understood. She acknowledged that this was a new idea for her, and she wanted me to elaborate. I continued to try to articulate something I consider important and misunderstood. Our primary experience of ourselves is as sentient creatures—moving, feeling, sensing, thinking, acting, and deciding. That is what we think of as being alive, and it is our basic experience of life. It is possible to consider that experience of feeling, thinking, smelling, tasting, and so forth as something that happens to an unchanging and given self that stands outside of the experience and is acted upon. This isolated self is the person; "it" is deeply inside the self; and "it" takes in experiences from the outside. But that self is an abstraction. Such a self is merely "posited." It is abstracted out from who we are in our real history, from who we are in a process of constantly becoming our self. It can't be proven even that such a self actually exists except as a concept. Of course the self of historical and concrete experience enjoys continuity throughout the personal history, but it is not an immutable or non-relational reality that goes along unaffected by what happens. Perhaps the idea of a soul is closest to what we mean when we say that there is a fundamental self beyond human experience. (Many, such as the Greeks, have assumed that a soul preexists human birth as well as survives human death. This is not a Christian concept.) What human beings really experience is...well...the experiencing self, the self that has a concrete history. Our concrete historical self is a history of relationships. I don't really know who I am unless I respond with thoughts and actions to what others tell me about myself, unless I relate to people. My actual, concrete, embodied self is constantly coming into being and being shaped by relationships and experiences of life.

We each become the particular person we are in any given moment precisely because of our relationship to the particular family, the particular friends, the particular loves, the particular conflicts, the particular struggles, the particular joys, the particular surprises, the particular events, all of the particular experiences that belong to our individual history. Each of us is who we are, with or without reflection on it, because of the ideas that have taken hold of us, the persons who have entered into our lives, the history of our special life up to a given moment. In conclusion, humans are each profoundly, fundamentally, and definitively relative, or relational, beings.

We do seem to experience an aspect of our person, a highly abstract aspect, which is not affected by other persons. There is a sense in which we simply exist. We can legitimately abstract certain characteristics from our concrete actuality to an understanding of our existence and "essence." As merely existing with certain abstract characteristics we are relatively unrelated to others. Yet, as a minimal conclusion, we cannot maintain that such characteristics are exhaustive of the personhood each of us experiences, and certainly not of the concrete people our friends know. In another aspect of our reality, our actual and concrete personhood, we are intrinsically and deeply related to others. In my abstracted self I am related to my own body; in my concrete self my body and I are one. In my abstracted self I am related to my own mind; in my concrete self my mind and I are one. In my abstracted self I am related to my spirit, in my concrete self my spirit and I are one. As I actually am, my body, mind, and spirit form a united whole, a self.

I would go so far as to say that this refers to that which is meant by the Christian concept of "bodily resurrection." This doctrinal phrase is a way of declaring that it is the real and historical and whole person who enters into eternal life, not a part that escapes from the body, "these mortal coils," as through a keyhole. Christians do not believe in the idea that our eternal soul will be some abstract and pure self without a history or concrete personality. Rather, Christians believe in the resurrection of the whole self as we emerge from our mortal life and continue to develop. Your glorified body will be a transformed spiritual body, according to Paul, but it will not be just a part of you; rather, it will be the full fruition, the completion of all you are. You will be more, not a mere part—the spiritual part—of yourself.

By "bodily resurrection" is meant the resurrection of the whole person experienced concretely as a self with an actual history, a history that is redeemed. Our history of relationships and actions defines who we are. We are most concretely, and thus most really, a self in relationship to others and our actions and our experiences. So it will be in the life to come. We will know ourselves in a community, a genuine communion in the fullness of God's glory.

## THE GIVEN NATURE OF COMMUNION

Ann concluded: "It's finally all about love, isn't it?" I laughed with delight at the way she cut through to the heart of the matter. That ended our conversation on just the right note.

God is love, life is about love, human beings become themselves and find meaning in love, and love is by definition relational. In the created order, love is the manifestation of our innate demand for relatedness to others, a demand based on the way creation is ordered, a demand for conformation to the corporate nature of reality. Love clarifies the reality that nature is both particular and corporate. Love clarifies God's nature as both particular and corporate. Love is the clearest and most experientially understood meaning of our word "God." It describes the inner life of the Trinity. It describes the authentic relationship of the God who is Trinity to human beings, to all of creation, and to self. It characterizes the gracious God fully related to all humanity that is set forth for all to see in the event of Jesus Christ. It informs us how we are in the image of God. The meaning of God's being as Love is the divine life of creative communion with the creatures of creation; not, of course, merely the sentient creatures, but we believe this is special in relation to people. God values each person in that individual's selfhood, *and* as a participant in the cosmos and in the creative history of the world.

Communion is another word for love. The experience of communion is disclosed as grace. Communion, like love, is of God, and a gift of God's own life. Christians are clear about all of this. What Christians and others in our society are confused about momentarily is how communion, like love, transcends the feelings of love one holds toward a person or persons at a given moment. Communion transcends feelings. Communion is a given. Ultimately communion cannot be denied, for it is a fact of life, and without it we could not be, just as God could not be without the communion of the Trinity. This is what is indicated in the words of an ancient prayer many of us use regularly, in which we confess that it is God in whom "we live and move and have our being" (Book of Common Prayer, 100). All creatures share in this "being" in God. Every person is a participant in the society of being. In the structure of personal relationships there is a "humanity" between us that is more than what we now are, which is between us and yet beyond us, but in which alone we can be human. There is humanity between each of us and our neighbors, and between all of us and God. This "humanity" is not an impersonal principle, but is the formal possibility of our being in communion with the whole of creation and the Creator. Thus are all human beings in what we call communion.

The great poet and Anglican preacher John Donne declared, "no man is an island." Donne was not lecturing us to take others into account or to be considerate of others. He was stating the fact that constitutes our existence, that we are bound in one bundle of life. The newly born self is thrown into an incomprehensibly vast creation, a world teeming with other creatures, and other selves. Each human self begins an incredible effort called life to find where it fits in this immense, threatening, confusing turmoil. It is the primordial need to belong in creation and in the human community that drives the self into this life to become its own self, satisfied with who it is and fulfilled in its selfhood. The primordial need to belong is both physical and psychological. It is the search for what Dante called our true home, our native land, for knowing where we are and who we are as we grow in freedom to deal with the creation, that is, for becoming a lover.

Human beings are authentic selves only in direct proportion to the ability to be affected by and related to other selves. We feel sorry for a person who cannot be reached, who cannot be affected by others. To the extent that people are closed, especially from other people, they fall short of their humanity. The only way one can be completely cut off is to be dead, but the Christian faith claims that even death cannot separate us from the love of God in Christ Jesus, so for Christians communion is ultimately the reality to which we must conform. The self is constituted by its entire history. To be a self is to belong in the great society of being, and belonging is not destroyed by death. We are created to become lovers. In this life, the human being must find love in and with others for it is the genuine fulfillment human life offers, and it is the life to come.

It is not enough to become a lover with another person, as wonderful as is the passion and intimacy of coupling love. Emil Brunner said that human beings are the creatures who can respond to the claim of the other and give oneself. He did not mean by this that we can do so only with another. There is no such thing as loving another merely for him or her self. The humanist claims to be able to do so, but Christians know better. Christians understand that we have to love the bond that makes us one with the people we love, for that bond is a fundamental dimension of our life and it is that which makes us a person. It is the love of God as God is found in each person. This awareness distinguishes Christianity from humanism. We must become lovers of creation, yearning for the fulfillment of our desire for love as is promised in the consummation of the kingdom. John Updike comes to mind as someone who helps us understand the folly of trying to put all our eggs in the one basket of a love relationship, of relying solely on marriage and the nuclear family for the satisfaction and fulfillment of love's promises—or on affairs. William Temple, the 98th Archbishop of Canterbury (1881–1944), imagined an ever-widening circle of love and moral concern, spreading gently and smoothly like waves when a rock is thrown in a pond, to finally take in the whole world as neighbor.

Thus do we finally fulfill the great commandment by loving the whole world as neighbor, and in that way loving the Creator. That is the ultimate aim of the passion and intimacy between lovers and the relationships of communion in a family. Human beings find security in giving ourselves to the service and enjoyment of God in creation, especially in other people, and in the kingdom of God. This is the ultimate context of every human love.

## THE SELF AS THE WILL TO BELONG

The fundamental human desire is to belong, to count in the community of being, to have one's freedom in and with the response of others, to enjoy God as one who makes us members of one society. The will to belong designates most precisely that psychic and organic energy that drives our lives, that shapes our ambitions and gives us an appetite for achievement, that forces us to risk meaningful relationships. The will to belong points to and explains almost everything we observe in human motives, cravings, sacrifices, satisfactions, and perversities. When we ask what really constitutes being for humanity we discover that it is belonging, or communion, which constitutes its heart. The will to belong is the core of selfhood. To be human is to search for the terms on which the self can be itself in relation to every other self.

We see this reality rather starkly in the lessons of the beginning and the end of our lives. The root anxiety is of not belonging, of not counting. Human beings are not so afraid of being dead, of not existing, nearly so much as we are afraid of not being wanted within the community of humanity. This is proved not only on the deathbed, but daily when ordinary human beings are willing to risk death, or even to seek it, for the sake of someone they love, for the sake of a loyalty they hold in their heart, for the sake of a protest they hope will improve things. People will kill themselves over social embarrassment, for they fear isolation and rejection more than death itself. It is tragic and absolutely wrongheaded to give up and prefer death to life, much less over something like embarrassment; yet it is eminently human, for without belonging there can be no selfhood.

Most societies throughout human history seem to have known the defining centrality of the will to belong. It is radical individualism that has placed Western thinkers at the wrong angle from which to observe and understand individuality. In Western tradition the individual claim for knowledge of existence is, "I think, therefore I am." In other traditions the claim is, "I belong, therefore I am."[2]

## THE HISTORICAL AND CHANGING NATURE
## OF BEING HUMAN

We are also changelings. Time is real and our history within time causes us to struggle with an evolving selfhood. This constant dynamic of becoming who we are is the source of great joy, in much the same way that we enjoy variety and range within music or art or play; it is spice in the food of life. The self as we actually experience that self is an illusion if it is not engaged in a process involving change and continuity, a process linking both internal relations with all "outside" reality and the distinct temporal modes of present, past, and future. People who do not recognize the need to change are not as interesting or as much fun as those who do enter into the risk of growth and enjoyment. Rigid or self-satisfied people diminish their own humanity. Alfred North Whitehead put it most pointedly: "Good people of narrow sympathies are apt to be unfeeling and unprogressive, enjoying their egotistical goodness. Their case, on a higher level, is analogous to that of the man completely degraded to a hog. They have reached that state of stable goodness, so far as their own interior life is concerned. This type of moral correctitude is, on a larger view, so like evil that the distinction is trivial."[3]

Change, however, requires risk, and risk is frightening and painful. People, by and large, are willing to grow; indeed, as people mature the desire to grow matures. However, people need to know that they can maintain or increase their present security in the process of growth. This neither can be comprehended nor guaranteed sufficiently enough for comfort. Consequently people seek to "save their lives" by holding on to them as they are. This is the first manifestation of the Fall.

The idea of the self as a constant, fixed, internal reality that deals with a life that moves around it and affects it with relationships and a history of experiences is a myth, and it is a false one. The myth is also a destructive one in the face of reality.

## THE BIBLICAL REVELATION OF THE CORPORATE NATURE OF REALITY

The Bible regards human life as a history in which God seeks to create a community of those who love, who gratefully celebrate God's love by embracing the creation humanity has as gift, who serve the fulfillment of creation. The human being is created for communion but loses it and loses the power to recover it. Unless communion can be recovered, love cannot be recovered. This communion is recovered in the new creation in Christ Jesus and will find its consummation for all of creation in the kingdom brought by Christ. Scripture plays out the triple theme of the gospel: Creation is good and humanity bears the image of God who is love. Humanity's love falls into disorder and creation contains evil as an experienced reality. In Christ there is a new creation, restoring humanity's integrity and the human power to enter into communion. Every Christian theology is an elaboration of this triple theme.

## GOD, ONE UNDIVIDED TRINITY

The corporate nature of things is so deeply embedded in the heart of reality that it defines the very life of God. The wholly other God revealed in Christian Scripture is Trinity. God's own inner life is perfect and absolute community. It is this life together in community, the life of pure love, which Christian tradition has recognized as the source of divine creativity, the motivation for going out from the Godhead into creation of others in accord with the nature and purposes of love itself. The concept of the Trinity is necessary to make sense of the Christ event. It evolved as an explanation of the early church's experience, and was hammered out in the conflict of heresies and newly formulated orthodoxy. The doctrine of the Trinity is valued in part perhaps because it reflects the complexity and incomprehensible mystery of God's own inner life. But its real value, with myriad implications for human life and for social justice, is the understanding that at the heart of things is community itself. Ultimate Life, and thus ultimately life itself, is communion.

## CREATION

For learning and knowledge today it is difficult to imagine a more exciting and dynamic discipline than what is termed cosmology. Our eyes are being forced open by a grand vision of all that is. It takes in religion, philosophy, physics, and all disciplines of thought and vision.

What is so amazing is how close the "new discoveries" of advanced science are to the original insights of Scripture and theology. (Fundamentalism distorts the one as much as the other.) One cartoon image I recall was that of scientists laboriously climbing the mountain of scientific discovery, obtaining heights no one "yesterday" dared dream could be conquered, and finally reaching the mountain top in a state of exhaustion, only to discover the Bible.

Creation is grand and whole and filled with an unimaginable plethora of diversity. Creation is a process with a beginning and a culmination. It is conscious, unconscious, psychic, spiritual, and physical. Part of the challenge for humanity today is to gain a new and fuller appreciation of the cosmic reality, to gain a new sense of what it is to be human within it, and to accept responsibility for our special role in it. That, surely, is a much more important and urgent mission for Christianity than most of the activities on which the church expends its energy, time, and resources. Human beings are called to go beyond our species' isolation, even beyond our planetary isolation, to enter into that far larger and far grander community of the created universe. We would not be here if any part of it were not here. Creation is held together and holds all things together precisely in one solid but ever so delicate and tender embrace. A new sense of reality and of what is valued is required, one including the interconnectedness and wholeness of all that is in creation. For example, this generation's steadily growing awareness of ecology is forcing us to recognize how the environment and all living forms of the planet establish a single system. The human at the species level needs to fulfill our role within this community life, else we will not survive, much less prevail and flourish. A primary allegiance to this larger community is required. This begins with the ability to open our eyes more widely and "see it."

The prominent environmental theologian of creation, Thomas Berry, posits a universal system based on three principles: differentiation, subjectivity, and communion.[4] The differentiation is crucial; it is what Berry calls "the primordial expression of the universe." If we take the "big bang" for the way creation began, either as scientific theory or as metaphor, we see the original energy flung throughout the vast regions of space as differentiated particles, making up galactic systems composed of highly distinctive objects in an overwhelming variety of manifestations including, evidently, anti-matter. Thomas Aquinas, in his *Summa Theologica*, speaks of the importance of this differentiated diversity, and of its essential unity. Couched in his medieval terms (e.g., by "creature" is meant any single object of creation, whether or not sentient) he deducts that because the divine goodness "could not be adequately represented by one creature alone, he produced many and diverse creatures, that what was wanting to one in the representation of the divine goodness might be supplied by another. For goodness, which in God is simple and uniform, in creatures is manifold and divided; and hence the whole universe together participates in the divine goodness more perfectly."

The second primary principle Berry defines as subjectivity. He describes this as an ever developing process, much in the tradition of a Teilhard de Chardin or an Alfred North Whitehead, from the shaping of the hydrogen atom to human consciousness and along a scale of increased unity of function through greater "complexification" of organic structures. It is a capacity for interiority, and with this interior subjectivity is associated the numinous quality that traditionally has been associated with every reality of the universe. If we but had the ability to see, in even some minor way, as God sees we would be overwhelmed by the numinous reality in every human face and within every created object, not only in the Grand Canyon and purple mountains majesty.

The third principle of the universe is the communion of each reality of the universe with every other reality. My tendency is to speak only of this universe, but newspaper reports of scientific evidence that our universe is a bubble within a greater reality, and one that remains balanced in part because it can leak energy, must cause us to pause and consider even greater reality. Finally, even God must be taken into account in comprehending the total relation of all creation to itself and thus to its creator in whom it has its being. All is in communion.

Theology finds science as its greatest ally in explanation of its fundamental insights about creation and especially about the corporate nature of all reality. If there was once friction between science and religion, that day has passed. It is science that is forcing society to review the radical and fragmented individualism that developed in the Western world. It is an individualism that developed largely due to both early scientific theories and to the church's positions. The Christian church desperately needs to get past this individualistic view of reality in order to engender genuine community, community that is based in something more profound than feelings, agreements, and similarities. The church seems to be relying heavily on the scientific community to lead the way. Contemporary physics, chemistry, and biology provide a magnificent overview of a universe that is a single, even though multiform, event. One can examine primitive creation myths around the world, review Plato's *Timaeus*, and credit Newton's theory of gravity in his *Principa* to find previous statements of the exhaustive unity of creation, but twentieth-century science presents this comprehensive genetic relatedness with fresh and compelling clarity. We may look to Einstein and his theories of relativity to appreciate something of our new awareness of how to conceive the dynamic nature of relatedness in the universe.

> It is especially important...to recognize the unity of the total process [of creation], from that first unimaginable moment of cosmic emergence through all its subsequent forms of expression until the present. This unbreakable bond of relatedness that makes of the whole a universe becomes increasingly apparent to scientific observation, although this bond ultimately escapes scientific formulation or understanding. In virtue of this relatedness, everything is intimately present to everything else in the universe. *Nothing is completely itself without everything else.* [Author's emphasis] This relatedness is both spatial and temporal. However distant in space or time, the bond of unity is functionally there. The universe is a communion and a community. We ourselves are that communion become conscious of itself.
>
> As regards the planet Earth, any adequate description must include its every aspect....We would not know the real capacities of hydrogen, carbon, oxygen, and nitrogen were it not for their later expression in cellular life and indeed in the entire world of living beings, including the remarkable world of human consciousness.[5]

## The *Imago Dei*, the "Image of God"

The *imago Dei* is the will to communion.

Irenaeus was perhaps the first systematic theologian. Under any circumstances, he is the theologian Anglicans have traditionally looked to more than any other for a patristic theological foundation. He took note of the fact that two Hebrew words are used in Genesis 1 to assert that God has created human beings in the divine image: *tselem* and *demuth*. He uses the subtle distinctions of each term to explain the difference between our uniquely human gifts and our similarities with God. Irenaeus points to the human responsibilities of reason, sovereignty of nature, and dignity; then he points to such similarities to God as summarized in Paul's three-word description of what makes human beings God-like: faith, hope, and love. In the combination of the two words *tselem* and *demuth* is found the reconciliation with creation and God that humanity seeks. One does not have to look deeply to discern that human relationships and the relation to creation offer the key to the realization of what is implied in each term. Neither the gifts nor the similarities are of much use except for relations to others and to creation, and thus to God. According to Irenaeus it is the similarity to God that is lost in the fall. The image of God in terms of gifts and responsibilities remains intact in humanity.

This distinction has formed the ground plan of all subsequent Catholic, Orthodox, and Anglican theology. Grace completing nature became accepted as the pattern of redemption. In this way Irenaeus, and the church, were able to ensure that the act of creation remains part and parcel of God's act of redemption. Theologians of the Protestant Reformation did not find this entirely adequate, but for our purposes it will suffice to establish the context for understanding the *imago Dei* without quibbling over sixteenth-century niceties that have become largely irrelevant.

Karl Barth and Dietrich Bonhoeffer are two great twentieth-century Protestant theologians who follow Irenaeus at least in speaking of the *imago Dei* as the distinctive form of existence that is human and that, they claim, is life in community. Human community indicates the meaning of the image of God in humanity. Barth reminded us that the image of God is an image of God as Trinity and that Scripture quotes God as saying, "Let us make man in our image."

St. Augustine had long before established the suggestion that in the being of humanity is found a reflection of the divine community of the holy Trinity and in this is the *imago Dei*. The image of God in humanity, he concluded, is human community, reflecting the Trinitarian community. Many theologians, ancient and modern, have followed suit, recognizing that the *imago Dei* is not merely some set of attributes or qualities possessed by a human being or by humanity. The *imago Dei* is to be conceived of in dynamic terms as the relatedness that God has established between the Trinity and humanity and humanity's response in relations with one another, the relationships for which the human being is created with the neighbor before God.

Communion or love is the core meaning of the *imago Dei*. Human life is created for communion, that is, for personal existence in community with others. In this, as Irenaeus discerned, is found the meaning underlying the special capacities of the human being for reason, moral judgment, artistic creativity, and religious awareness.

## SIN

Sin at root is the failure to realize life in love, that is, in communion. Sin is turning away from life in communion with others and with God. It is the useless but pain-producing attempt to separate one's self from the human community and the will of God in putting what is perceived as the good of one's self above the good of others and the values which further creation and welcome the kingdom. The willful violation of our created goodness is, in part, a matter of violating our place and responsibility in creation. The ultimate mystery of evil is that the human being, in becoming human, denies that which makes him and her human: freedom in communion.

We know that where we fail in our humanity is in our relationships, in our need to compare ourselves to others competitively, and in our refusal to appreciate and love others for who they are as children of God. This is largely founded in our inability to see how we share a common subjectivity that is rooted in the subjectivity of God. That is, we fail to see our very real interconnectedness and to realize that the way we treat others is the way we are treating ourselves, that as we sin against someone it is ourselves and God against whom we sin. Human evil is in some sense a rejection of life, that is, a rejection of what makes us truly human beings. To be human is to search for the terms on which the self can be itself in relation to every other self. We find that we kill what we love, that is, we kill others, because we refuse to love on the terms which life gives.

Every self is unique—and God loves every self in its own particularity, as perfectly and completely as though each was a full cosmos. Nevertheless, we can only experience and live into our uniqueness by entering into love of others together with God.

Part of the reason we understand human sin to be "original" is due to the way we all experience it in our life as a propensity within our very make-up. We can't seem to avoid it; it is in the way we show up. There is a real sense in which we do not choose sin; the given propensity is so strong that it can be deemed unavoidable. We find that sin is a state of being. Our experience is that it comes as part and parcel of the human condition. We only choose the particular sins we commit, and even those tend to conform to our personal make-up and personality traits. Each of us knows, all too well, our inability as individuals ever to operate purely out of the creative goodness we know is within our personhood, our self. We can't find our self exactly, nor can we find satisfaction in who we are as a self, abstractly out of community, in community, or concretely within history. We can never find love or a community of love that is not a troubled love, for no group and no person can provide us with the security for which we yearn. No human community can be as completely fulfilling as we wish, and moreover we have to live with threats to its existence, just as with the self, both from within and from without. This realization is extremely, overwhelmingly painful. Yet, we experience the fact that sin is "original" as a relief in a certain sense— for we can't take on the full responsibility for the sinful reality of our particular and personal human nature. We can only struggle with sin by taking responsibility for each act of sin and by truly accepting the forgiveness in Christ. We can struggle with sin throughout our lifetime by developing habits of prayer and behavior, a lifestyle of yearning for God's presence and God's will that is held so paramount in our own conscious and unconscious being that God rules even at the deepest levels of our being, what we call our spirituality. Finally, this struggle to be free of the bondage of sinfulness is a struggle to open ourselves to God's grace and receive the freedom that is already there, the freedom in communion to love. We do this in giving our lives to Christ and in serving the causes for which he was willing to give his life. To return to where we started, in the freedom of Christ's forgiveness our repentance is offered in part by accepting the reality of original sin; we accept the fact that we will always sin and fall short of God's glory. When we forget ourselves and we deny this we know we will awaken to know ourselves as fools. In fact, rather than being a put-down of human nature, the awareness of each individual that our personal sinfulness does not originate with us helps us accept our personal forgiveness without hypocrisy.

There is another side to original sin that is equally frustrating, because we certainly cannot control it, and yet awareness of it is equally freeing. Sin is not solely personal—sin is corporate. Social and legal and economic structures are more responsible for sin than perhaps any issues of individual make-up and personal choices. We have to realize that the sins of our mothers and fathers and the sins of our society are not something we can entirely avoid. In our relationships, in our circumstances, in our culture, sin comes to us. We know this, we know the way this bondage feels and is concretely experienced. The person who lives in a racist society and claims to be free of racism is that fool referred to earlier, and one blindly less capable of doing something about the sinfulness within the self as well as in society. It is like the person living in a democratic society who denies that he or she has anything to do with the execution of a criminal, but pushes responsibility off onto the abstract reality of the state. Sin is corporate, because we are all a part of the corporate nature of reality, and this carries very real burdens as well as very real joys.

Victor Hugo identified the corporate nature of sin in a heart-stopping insight quoted by Martin Luther King just before his assassination. "Whenever there is a soul in darkness, there will be sin. The guilt is not with the one who sins, but with those who create the darkness." One of my favorite novels is *Handling Sin* by Michael Malone. The antagonist is an uptight yuppie trying to live the American dream of small town suburbia by relying on a morally and socially rigid rule of life, a modern version of the age-old effort to justify one's life through law without the complications and human ambiguity, the earthy messiness, of gospel freedom and grace. This yuppie's father, a deposed Episcopal priest, manages to send his unwitting son on an adventurous and hilarious journey, an unsuspecting if heroic journey of an ordinary contemporary in search of his own soul. It is no accident that the story ends during worship on Easter. The whole point of the book is that sin is corporate, and that one learns to handle it only by coming to accept the lack of control we may wish to enjoy over it, embracing the reality of the sinfulness handed to us, and thus the forgiveness which is there for all of us, individually and together.

## REDEMPTION

Does anyone really think he or she has the personal ability to discover the gospel, decide to follow Christ, and do so faithfully alone? One of my law professors was fond of declaring that none of us has the stamina for the journey of faith that is a Christian life—alone. Redemption comes to each of us through the community of faith, in the community of faith, and as a community of faith. This follows from the reality that life is corporate as well as particular, and it is the way God has worked in history.

## ISRAEL

Faith belongs to a community. When the fullness of time arrived for the redemption of creation, God acted by raising up a community. That is, when God wanted to communicate the divine nature and the divine plan for the human family to the world, a community was called and formed as God's own.

As was rehearsed in Section II, the first chapters of Scripture lay out the story of creation, the fall, and the spread of sin in its extraordinary breadth and depth. The rest of Scripture tells the story of God acting to redeem creation, beginning with the story of Abraham. It culminates in the new creation of human society willed by God, and the kingdom proclaimed in the gospel of Jesus Christ. A new order of society and of life could not have been imposed upon the world except by the sort of force to be expected by the powers of the world, and that would have been self-defeating. Instead, God began at some place in history and in the world to create something new, first in one people. Thus the story of redemption becomes a story in which God raises up a community of redemption, a people to represent and act on behalf of God. God did not call individuals out of Egypt, nor did God make individual covenants. Israel could not have understood any notion of deliverance or salvation apart from the community.

It began as an isolated tribe in a remote corner of the globe, but in the fullness of time this community was to carry the good news of Christ into the entire world, calling forth a community of salvation. It was to do so largely out of its weaknesses and failures. Israel was not chosen for its own sake, but as a sign of universal salvation for all nations and peoples, for the reign of God in its final form in the kingdom. God identifies with this community.

That community is still gathering members and working for the causes of God: creation and kingdom. We are called into the community commissioned by God and incarnating God's life in the world. It is as a community that we are formed and shaped into the life of Christ, dying and rising. This special community is called to understand how our interconnectedness is rooted in God, and how our interconnectedness is as real as our individual autonomy. This is not to be so merely in some mystical sense removed from the concrete and ordinary experience of daily life; rather, God's gracious and loving presence is to be discovered in the concrete interrelationships and patterns of life we create together in a commitment to one another in God. Our commitment to God is to be our commitment to one another and the community, to build a community life together according to God's nature, a community life which reflects and welcomes the realm of God's reign as it is in heaven—the realm Jesus proclaimed as the kingdom of God. We are called to live as a society that connects heaven and earth as we work and pray for both the world and for the coming of the kingdom, as we bring the world to God and offer God to the world.

Our fundamental corporate attitude is to be one of gratitude for creation and for God's grace and presence with us. This faithful attitude is to be expressed in corporate celebrations of praise and thanksgiving. The fullness of our individuality is to come to fruition in this community, for in the call and redemption of the community the individual discovers God's love for all persons no matter their station or merits, no matter even their sinfulness. If life has meaning it is because God is present in the community. If life has meaning it is to be found in this community's ministry for God's justice and God's future as spelled out in the promises to Israel and the new work of God-in-Christ. God has created persons *for* community, and only within this sustaining community is God's creation of authentic humanity complete.

## JESUS

When Jesus was baptized he began his ministry by laying out the foundational message of the kingdom and gathering a community. At first, it seemed to be a terribly small community, but even then it was evident that the divine intention was to gather the whole people of God and commission them to their task on his behalf. It is significant that Jesus chose twelve to be his official disciples. For example, Mark 3:16 says, "He created the Twelve." Notice the use of *the* here. This had a representative purpose, a demonstrative purpose; for Jews of the day it was an obvious gesture, though it may not be so immediately obvious to the twenty-first century gentile reader.

The actual role of the Twelve is notoriously difficult to assess on the basis of the scriptural account. There can be little doubt that Jesus gathered many more followers beyond the number of twelve. We know by name at least three men who belonged to Jesus' group of disciples but not the pre-Easter Twelve: Cleopas, Joseph Barsabbas, and Matthias. Five women who followed Jesus and supported him with their possessions are also known by name: Mary Magdalene, Johanna the wife of Chuza, Susanna, Mary the mother of James, and Salome. Indeed, more than twelve individuals are officially named as "the Twelve disciples" in different places in the gospels. (1) Simon, called Peter, (2) Simon the Zealot, (3) Simon the Cananaean, (4) Andrew, (5) James, son of Zebedee, (6) John, son of Zebedee, (7) Matthew, also called Levi and once named as the son of Alphaeus, (8) James, son of Alphaeus, (9) Bartholomew, (10) Philip, (11) Thomas the Twin, (12) Thaddaeus, (13) Judas Iscariot, (14) Judas, son of James, (15) Nathanael of Cana in Galilee.

Tradition reconciles these discrepancies by certain speculations, such as the assumption that Bartholomew is the same person as Nathanael. Not only were there many other followers of Jesus beyond "the Twelve" and more numbered among that company than the number allows, but those named did not coincide with the actual leaders of the Christian community left by Jesus. With the likely exception of Peter, they were not missionaries, in spite of the custom begun by Luke of calling them "apostles." Nor do we have evidence that they acted as pastoral leaders. Peter and John, to be sure, were among the leaders of the church acknowledged by Paul when he visited the church in Jerusalem, but no one else is mentioned while others outside of the Twelve are explicitly named. For example, Acts clearly informs us that James, the brother of Jesus, was the head of the church in Jerusalem, though he was not one of the Twelve at all.

We should not make too much of this confusion, either way, for precision in who makes up "the Twelve" and what became their eventual role is not the point. What matters is that it is uniformly and carefully stipulated in the gospels that Jesus took the trouble to choose exactly twelve disciples, and to specify *the* Twelve. These were the official companions in his daily ministry, the representatives he officially sent out to preach his message of the kingdom and to perform the signs of its breaking into history, and the official witnesses of his resurrection. There was a purpose in designating some disciples as "the Twelve," and for being far more careful about the exact number than about who in fact made up the number. The twelve disciples represented the twelve tribes of Israel, the people God raised up for the redemption of the world in the new creation and kingdom to come. This was highly sym-bolic action and it spoke volumes.

At the time Jesus appears in Scripture there were only some two and one-half tribes left intact, Judah and Benjamin and about half of Levi. The commonly accepted expectation that had developed in the Jewish tradition and which was handed on to Jesus demanded the restoration of the Twelve Tribe People of God at the culmination of time and history, the time when salvation would be established. The end-time expected by Jews at the time of Jesus was interpreted, reenvi-sioned, and proclaimed by Jesus as the kingdom of God. Calling together the Twelve was to be recognized as a sign of the awakening of Israel and its gathering in that community which is the agent of salva-tion. The Twelve were thus explicitly sent by Jesus to proclaim his mes-sage of the kingdom to *"the whole house of Israel."*

Another very important indication of gathering the community of the whole house of Israel into the community of the kingdom was focused in what is called the Lord's Prayer. It is a prayer for gathering: "Hallowed be your Name; your kingdom come." There is a sense in which it could mean that we are called upon to sanctify God's holy name and to bring about the kingdom, or at least that we are to acknowledge the sanctity of God's name and the coming of the king-dom. Each petition prays for God's action, God's own work.

For Jesus the kingdom is not merely very near, but already arriving. He is teaching a small community to interpret his mighty works to see that the kingdom is already becoming present in him. For example, the context in which Matthew pictures Jesus teaching followers how to pray is that of the Sermon on the Mount, the great description of the kingdom with its promises and demands. The two petitions in the prayer of our Lord correspond. They offer the very present hope, in effect, that God will sanctify the divine name in powerful action, because in Jesus this powerful action is starting right now, "in your hearing." When Jesus prays "hallowed be your Name; your kingdom come," it is legitimate to hear him asking God to gather and renew the whole people of God and shape them into the true People of God, the citizens of the kingdom. Jesus was obviously convinced that this end-of-time salvation gathering of the People of God had already begun, just as the coming of the kingdom was taking place through him. This is what Jesus taught his disciples to pray for, and for which they were thus to shape their belief and ministry.

This is primarily what Jesus did; this was the focus of his ministry, articulated in the preaching and portrayed in the signs of the kingdom. Jesus went about trying to gather the People of God. He sought the restoration of *lost* and *scattered* Israel; first the Twelve, then a larger circle of disciples, and finally, in a wider circle, the whole people.

Luke takes care to use the extraordinary term *laos* in his designation of the people Jesus is gathering. This was the solemn word for the chosen people taken from the Septuagint (the Hebrew Scriptures translated into the Greek language by Jews living outside of Judea, in particular those living in Egypt). In that text of Scripture *laos* is the Greek word employed to refer to Israel in its role as the People of God, chosen and led by God.

For many people, at least since the Protestant Reformation and the responding Counter-Reformation and perhaps still dominating the popular mind today, the ministry of Jesus has been reduced largely to that of saving the souls of elected individuals. Supposedly he did this by preaching and teaching and healing. Then, there is the great sacrifice, what in doctrinal terms is called the atonement. But this definitive act for salvation seems to be thought of in terms of the salvation of individual souls. Too often the mission of Jesus and of the church is thought of in totally individualistic terms. Jesus did come to save the soul of each person. The church does take care of individuals; it is made up of congregations or groups of individuals who help each other in their spiritual life. However, it is clear that Jesus was concerned not just with the individual, with the soul and its God. In fact, Jesus spent most of his ministry in gathering a community. Jesus saw the building of a community, the gathering and restoring of the community of God's kingdom, and in this the completion and fulfillment of creation, as his mission.

When the greater part of Israel, especially the religious leaders, began to reject this call, Jesus began to concentrate his attention on his special disciples, but not as a holy remnant of Israel, and still less as a replacement of Israel. It represented the whole of the true Israel, a community in anticipation of what the Israel of the time of salvation, fully gathered, would one day be. Thus, when Israel as a whole did not accept Jesus' message, the disciples acquired a new symbolic nature: the sign of repentance and complete dedication to the gospel of the reign of God, the sign of radical conversion to the new way of life of the kingdom even now and in the age to come which has alredy begun, and the sign of a gathered and apostolically sent community of divine communion in Christ.

God's incarnate call forms the Christian church into that community of divine communion in Christ. It is not merely an aggregate of individual Christians, seeking our own spiritual growth and personal salvation as one of the elect, and offering it to other individuals out of personal concern for them. Christian faith cannot be reduced to privatized and merely personal religion. There can be no legitimate attempt to make the church private and exclusive, a free association of like-minded people, or of people who feel good about one another. Obviously, Jesus addressed individuals; just as obviously he did not insist that each individual decide in isolated freedom and constantly reevaluate her or his decision for the gospel. Isolated individuals cannot exemplify and live the social and corporate dimension of the kingdom.

The will of God in Christ was the new creation, (1) restoring the proper relationship of the human being to the created order and (2) bringing the kingdom, which begins with the gathering of the true Israel into the citizenship of that kingdom and culminates in the consummation of creation. The new Israel became the company of believers in Jesus and the gospel he offered. This was not an aggregate of individuals. It was an organic body, a communion. In Scripture it was to be referred to in the concrete terms familiar in that day as a "people" (*laos*), as an "ethnic minority" (*ethnos*), as a "race" (*genos*). This was to be a contrast-society, one not ruled by the violent structures of the powers of this world as portrayed so dramatically in the first chapters of Genesis, but rather with mutual reconciliation and communion. It was not to be an elitist community. It is for the world. It is not just an institution. The church is a corporate reality; it is an organic whole; it is the Body of Christ. It is not an ordinary body. It is a mystical body.

## THE NEW TESTAMENT COMMUNITIES

The first thing the disciples did after the resurrection appearances, and after the risen Lord had taken his leave, was to complete the circle of the Twelve. There was an election to replace Judas with the twelfth disciple. The sign of the community's mission was secure and manifest. Those who represented the whole house of Israel were now to be called apostles, the messengers sent with the good news of the gospel for the world's salvation. The mission was to summon the whole house of Israel to conversion and into the new community of communion in Christ. Soon an apostle "out of time" was called to be the special apostle to the gentiles. This convert from Pharisaical Judaism to the new Jesus movement helped the early church understand that the whole house of the true Israel is to include all, whether Jew or Greek, male or female— in a word, everyone. As a sign of this and of his new life, the former persecutor of Christians had taken the Greek name Paul.

The difficulty Paul had in preaching the gospel to gentiles was not that of convincing them of God's love for humanity and for the special community beginning to be called the church. Paul found it highly difficult to communicate to the people of his day that God loves each and every individual. This was a new and exciting and central insight he had gained in coming to know Jesus Christ as his personal Lord. The people to whom he preached could understand how the pagan gods seem to love certain chosen individuals, and they grasped how the one God of the Jews could love a "people," of which they could become a part and enjoy their share of the divine love. But they had difficulty in seeing their individuality in terms that would allow them to hear what Paul was saying in the gospel declaration of God's love for them person- ally, so much so that God had become like each of them and in this Christ had suffered death for them. What made them special that God would choose them to love, what did they have in terms of accomplish- ment, prestige, or any sort of merit? The idea of God's love for each individual born into the world required a most profound shift in their view of reality and it was very difficult to imagine. Thus is it particularly ironic that the Christian living in Western culture today has difficulty grasping the idea of God's love for humanity except in terms of each individual.

Soon, the communities of the church were baptizing infants. This was a definitive indication of the fact that the church understood the corporate nature of the decision each individual is to make for disci- pleship. If a person is raised in a Christian community, beginning perhaps but not necessarily with the family, that person will be expected to live into the faith as a part of living into their community. If the person is not raised in a Christian community, they will need to make a personal

decision as an adult, but the act of incorporation will be a radically corporate act of initiation into the community of communion in Christ.
Rarely do individuals make a decision for Christ in isolation from their
cultural community; most often communities make decisions that the
individuals grow into and affirm.

When we read about the early church we cannot help but notice
how much conflict and confusion there was. The immaturity of each
and every community written about in the New Testament and the
extraordinarily guilty actions of so many of the individuals jump off the
pages for any objective reader. Yet, throughout its history the church
has always looked to the early church as the model. The reason may
not be so readily apparent in the pastoral letters.

Our congregations are also very conflictive, perhaps more so during
this particular time as we struggle with the call to reform. I suspect that
we do not handle conflict with the same determination to stay the
course together that characterized the members of the early church.
We need to learn something they had internalized as a simple part of
their view of reality. I refer to this insight about conflict in a slogan,
"neither flight, nor fight, but communion."

People of Western culture tend to see the goal of a conflict in terms
of winning or losing. We are taught to fight until our opponent gives
in, until one of us leaves the arena, or until we are somehow declared
the winner—perhaps through a vote. Some wiser heads are trying to
teach conflict management, utilizing such skills as those of collaboration,
negotiation, compromise, and mediation. However, the foundation for
resolving a conflict is very difficult to teach because it isn't in our
worldview. Conflict is a very normal part of mutual commitment to an
important and worthy cause, if there is genuine community. That is, if
those in conflict are in communion they will naturally have conflict,
but they will just as naturally know that they have to work it out without fighting or forcing separation, or perhaps even division.

People of the early church learned to forgive, not only because
they were forgiven but also because they were in a communion of forgiveness, wrought by forgiveness. They could live with disagreement
on the most important of matters, face conflict, reconcile after working
things out, and make difficult but firm decisions about divisive issues
because they were in a communion of mission and they realized how
they had to resolve issues in order to move on. The matter can be stated
in any number of ways, but paramount was the fact that communion

was a given, not based on agreement or like-mindedness or any sort of sameness, but based simply on reality, on the reality the church had experienced in God's creative action. Paul could become so angry at opponents, such as the party of circumcision, that he could tell the Galatians how he hoped the knife of circumcision would slip, but everyone knew that he would die for those people, because they were part of one people.

Another way to put this understanding of communion concerns its unique self-understanding. They did not think of themselves as joining one religious society among others. No doubt the foundation of this Christian community was religious in the sense that its identity was with God, specifically with God-in-Christ, and no doubt the Roman Empire saw it as another religious society. But the church thought of itself in the model of early Yahwistic ideals for Israel, a "holy people" set apart to be the community of God's new creation, a people separated from the world on behalf of the world, representing God to the world and the world to God. From the very beginning the believers had felt that their faith and their community transcended religion as ordinarily conceived. They were the very Body of Christ. On the one hand, Jewish believers in Jesus considered themselves a renewal movement within Judaism, yet more than a renewal of a religion, for in the Messiah was the fruition of that religion. They were a movement so eschatologically focused that they assumed the religions of this world were at an end. The veil had been torn. The one perfect and sufficient sacrifice was accomplished. At the same time, the Christian communities Paul and his colleagues founded were separatist groups, conscious of having an identity apart from, and even over against, both the local Jewish community and the pagan society of their birth.

The ultimate reality is that these communities made Christ manifest to the world, took on the powers of the secular world—even the powers of the empire—when necessary, and eventually converted the people of the ancient world to the gospel. They did this by creating communities that lived together as though the new age is the reality, as though God reigns in the here-and-now, and as though it is the love of God which holds Christians together. This vision and their actions proved to be very attractive.

What are we to make of all this for our own day and age? First we must recover our sense of being a people and of being in communion in the way that the early church understood itself. In order to do so we must understand our relation to the world with far greater clarity. Again, the early church should prove to be an adequate model for a contemporary theology of the church. The central problem in learning from the early church in our day has to do with the creation of genuine community. There are serious barriers deeply ingrained in our culture, in our worldview. In order to create community of the sort Christianity demands we must create a certain kind of culture that is distinctive from the culture of our society, a genuine community.

Perhaps it would be helpful to apply the insights of one of the great evangelical minds of the twentieth century, Lesslie Newbigin. The following lengthy quotation from his seminal work, *Signs of the Kingdom*, speaks to many of the central issues we have discussed throughout *The Songs of the Mothers*, from the role of the church in seeking justice and the way this role has been pushed to the periphery of church life, to the cosmic mission of the church and the way this has been reduced to the election and salvation of individual members. His model for reform is the early church.

> When the Christian church was first launched into the life of the Eastern Roman Empire it found itself surrounded by many religious societies which claimed to offer personal salvation to their members through a variety of teaching and disciplines. Several Greek words were in use to describe such societies (*thiasos*, *heranos*, etc.). As private religious societies they enjoyed the protection of the state. If the Christian church had seen itself in this way it would have been content to use these names and could have availed itself of this protection. But, although (for example) critics like Celsus described the church in this way, these words were never used by the church to describe itself. Of the two words used in the Septuagint to translate the Hebrew names for the whole congregation of Israel, the word *synagogos*, already used by the Jewish Diaspora, was avoided and the word *ecclesia* was almost universally adopted—the word which in normal secular use referred to the public assembly of all the citizens gathered to discuss and settle the public affairs of the city. In other words, the early church did not see itself as a private religious society competing with others to offer personal salvation to its members; it saw itself as a movement launched into the public life of the world, challenging the

*cultus publicus* of the Empire, claiming the allegiance of all without exception.

This universal claim was being made by communities which were—from the point of view of *realpolitik*—insignificant. When one remembers what these communities were in relation to the society of the time, there is something staggering about the words that Paul uses. In the Letter to the Colossians, after speaking of Christ as the cosmic head of all creation, he continues without any break to speak of him as the "head of the body, the church." In the very similar passage of Ephesians we read that God has put all things under the feet of Christ "and made him the head over all things for the church which is his body" (Col 1:18; Eph 1:22f). The claim for universal sovereignty is made in the face of the overwhelming powers that rule the world and the church is identified as the body whose head is this cosmic sovereign. The church was on a collision course with the established powers, and for three centuries paid the price for this stupendous claim.

Then came the event which the Seer of Patmos could not have anticipated—the conversion and baptism of the Emperor. It is fashionable to the present time to speak of this as a disaster for the church. In our present historical situation, when we struggle to free ourselves from the clinging remnants of the Constantinian era, this is understandable. We are painfully aware of the consequences of that conversion; for centuries the church was allied with the established power, sanctioned and even wielded the sword, lost its critical relation to the ruling authorities. But what should the church of the fourth century have done? Should it have refused to baptize the Emperor on the ground that it is better for the spiritual health of the church to be persecuted than to be in the seats of power? The discussion is unrealistic and futile. We have to accept that as a matter of fact the first great attempt to translate the universal claim of Christ into political terms was the Constantinian settlement. Christ as Pantocrator took on the lineaments of the Roman Emperor. We cannot go behind that; we have to live with its consequences and learn from them. These consequences are familiar to us. When the whole of society (except the Jews) is baptized and the church is the spiritual arm of the establishment, the critical role of the church devolves upon separate bodies: the monks, the radical sectarian groups, the millenarian movements on the fringes of the church.

But in the last three centuries Western Christendom has moved into a new situation. A new ideology has replaced the Christian vision as the *cultus publicus* of Western Christendom. It is the vision which dawned in that remarkable experience which those who shared it called "the enlightenment." It was a new vision of the world as totally explicable by means of the new tools for rational analysis which were being developed, and of man as the bearer of the meaning of his own history, and of the future as an ever-expanding mastery of man's reason over nature leading to a golden age of total rationality and total mastery over all the powers that threaten man. The word "enlightenment" (reminiscent of the experience of the Buddha) expresses the quality of this vision. Light had dawned and darkness was being banished. The previous centuries during which Europe had been christianized were darkness. The rest of the world (with the possible exception of China) was darkness. Now the light had dawned; Western man had only to walk in that light, spread that light, and all the nations would have fellowship one with another. The "blood of Jesus" (1 Jn 1:7) was not required.

At the risk of extreme over-simplification one would have to say that the church failed to challenge this new *cultus publicus* effectively and took the road which the early church had refused; it retreated into the private sector. The new vision was allowed to control public life. The "enlightened" world carried its message, its science and technology, and its masterful relation to the world, into every part of the globe. The Christian vision was allowed to illuminate personal and domestic life, but not to challenge the vision that controlled the public sector. The church took on more and more the shape which the early church had refused; it became a group of societies which were seen as offering spiritual consolation and the hope of personal salvation to those who chose to belong.[6]

We now need to understand this contemporary worldview and the effects of it on our society and the church.

# THE OBJECT WORLD

The culture in which we live presents us with a worldview. One may say that it gives us certain filters through which we see reality. The common filters of Western culture demand that we see things only in their separate, individual, discrete existence. We look out from our "self" and view a range of objects, connected only as they act on one another. Thus, I say that we live in an "object world." It is very difficult for us to see the interconnection between things or to see the whole. We have trouble seeing and believing in the actual and concrete existence of higher organic social units, units of reality such as "the collective," or "Christendom," or the Body of Christ. Understanding the limitations of our commonly held worldview can help to free us from the twentieth-century existential anxieties it seems to have fostered. It also points a way toward addressing the key theological issues we have identified.

Other cultures in history, including Western culture, have enjoyed a profound sense of the interconnectedness between people in a community. This is true today for some cultures outside of the industrialized West. The statement by Archbishop Tutu is a case in point. Our view of the dominating reality of the individual over the abstractness of corporate reality is not the only view. Indeed, our view is sadly limited. The gospel demands both that we discern and value the fullness of human individuality, and that we discern and value the fullness of community.

Americans and millions of others influenced by the American Age are disconnecting from one another in every way. There is ample proof of this available from many kinds of sources. Robert D. Putnam of Harvard created a major stir by publishing his exhaustive study of what he calls "social capital." In his work, *Bowling Alone*, Putnam overwhelms the reader with facts and statistics that bear out the reality that community in America is collapsing. The very fabric of the connections Americans have with each other is disappearing, impoverishing American life. Americans vote less, are far more meager in the exercise of citizenship, and participate in fewer civic functions than ever. Americans belong to fewer organizations, meet with friends less, know neighbors less, and socialize less within families. We have designated a category of existence as "private life" and that is to be struggled for, protected, and nurtured as an individual's most valued possession. Dr. Putnam takes the metaphor of bowling as a sign of the pervasive and rapidly increasing pattern of alienation in American life: more Americans are bowling than ever before but not in leagues. "People watch *Friends* on TV and they don't have them."[7] He points out that there are obvious and measurable benefits to community. "Social capital" is highly valuable and the more a person possesses the more likely he or she is to be healthy, happy, and productive—fulfilled as an individual. For example, the person who participates in a single club cuts in half the odds of dying in the next year, and people of faith who regularly attend church are significantly healthier than those who do not—physically, emotionally, mentally, and spiritually. Nevertheless, the trends of disengagement are startlingly clear. For example, over the last twenty-five years the age-old social practice of having friends over has dropped by 45 percent in American homes. Over the same period of time having family dinner is down 33 percent in American homes and attending meetings is down by 58 percent. Every ten minutes a person adds to the commute to her or his job means that they will be less involved in community, that is, possess less "social capital," by 10 percent.[8]

Americans do not really need to see statistics to know all of this—it is experienced.

I suggest that this is not merely the result of television, various distractions, uniquely modern anxieties, or any other range of social factors. It is first and primarily the result of the way we see the world; it conforms to reality as we have come to assume it is. Human values follow from the common belief in what life is about. Individualism has become dominant of our worldview and in each of our lives because we have come to believe that our individuality is the fundamental reality of our personal existence.

The belief that individuals are real and that community is an abstract—something less than real—is experienced as a presupposition about what to do and where to place our time and energy. This is a given, and it is the foundation for other assumptions and beliefs and behaviors, for it comes to be held culturally. Our individualism is radical in that it has become such a precious value that it has begun to exclude the value of community. We see individuality. We have tremendous difficulty with seeing the interconnectedness between things. Then we posit interconnectedness. We may even agree upon some mystical connection between things, but we can't really "see" it. At times, those with such a proclivity may be able to make something of a mystical leap to grasp the interconnectedness, which is finally rooted in God and the corporate reality of creation, but it is almost always a temporary leap and made by those with extraordinary imagination and counter-cultural motivation.

The fact is that we who are of Western culture cannot help ourselves. We cannot understand the corporate nature of reality; we cannot see the interconnectedness between things. We are limited in our reality perspective in that we can see only separate, individual, discrete objects as units of reality. We have no choice in the way we take reality in and understand it. In fact, our language says it: we can see only some "thing" or no "thing." I personally believe that it is largely because of the way our philosophical worldview filters our ability to see only "things" that our imagination is limited.

The reader may take the opportunity to pause and imagine God as Trinity, One and Undivided. This may prove to be a task, and a more difficult one than that of imagining only God's nature as One and Undivided. I suspect that there is no more crucial test of how difficult it is for the Western person to discern the wholeness, unity, and interconnectedness of reality than in the effort to appreciatively conceive of ultimate reality and actually pray to our God, to cognitively open oneself to relationship with the Trinity. I suspect that most of us can manage to pray to one person of the Trinity at a time, but we offer our relationship with the Trinity to "mystery." Jürgen Moltmann came to a dramatic and telling conclusion about the power of belief in the Trinity: had Christian Germany understood the Trinity and internalized the human values and actualities it reveals, World War II would not have occurred. Has anything improved in our belief in the Trinity and in the significance of that belief since then?

I fear that Christians acknowledge the Trinity more as an act of piety than as a statement of faith or in the process of relating to God. In the actual life of the church, the Trinity is an abstract concept, with too little consequence in belief and activity. Even as a concept it does not compute within the popular mind. Nor does the concept seem to matter to most of us. The Trinity is simply accepted without question, just as it is unfailingly saluted. This is because, first, tradition has raised it to such status that it as far above question as it is as far above comprehension; second, because few are interested enough to bother questioning something which seems to make no difference. The Trinity has been placed on the altar, so to speak, and there it is to be adored and honored. Introduced into liturgical formulae and hymns, portrayed by strange artistic designs and iconography, it lives on. However, as a concept it seems to have lost power to interpret the meaning of the living God except for the most strenuously educated.

The community of a Christian congregation doesn't exist except as we manage to approximate a picture of all of the individuals in mass. Perhaps this is why Protestant churches have insisted on calling them congregations instead of parishes. The corporate reality that we term community is, for Western folk, taken as a mental construct. Because of this the kind of community which the gospel calls for is extremely difficult, almost impossible, to build. In turn, because the formation of genuine Christian community is so extremely difficult, we despair over our ability to address the radical nature of the gospel's mission.

Radical individualism is the pivotal characteristic, and perhaps even the underlying cause, of the object world. However, that is combined with other attributes of Western culture to form the object world in which we find ourselves. The object world dominates both society and church. Sometimes the way in which the inability to see the corporate nature of reality, and the consequent radical individualism found at the base of so many of the difficulties and problematic realities of society and of church, is quite subtle and rather complex. The bottom line forms with the sense that only the private subjectivity of the individual counts, for the purposes of prediction, control, possession, and management of the environment—including the self.

The public and shared features of daily life are giving way to privatized preferences, whether referring to facilities or politics or economics or cultural matters or any other aspect, including religion. Consumerist materialism is the dominant philosophy of society, and it drives the engines of society. People identify themselves more by their consumer choices than by their social choices and opinions. Religion and faith—or non-faith—identity has become a private and individualistic consumer choice. Values have less and less importance or application. Radical individualism is proving to be amoral.

## THE ESTABLISHMENT OF A CONSUMERIST PHILOSOPHY

Following the line of thought in David Tracy's work, *The Anological Imagination* we may picture society in three distinctive spheres of activity, however much they may overlap and interrelate: that of the cultural, of the polis, and of the technological-economic-bureaucratic. The cultural realm of society is that which examines the tradition that has been handed down, offers values, fosters ideas, contributes its own creativity, and so passes on the cumulative tradition to the next generation. The polis is concerned with governance and decision-making within society. The technological-economic-bureaucratic sphere is composed of those structures and stratification systems designed to determine the most effective and efficient means to carry out all the economic and technical development of society.[9]

This is not the beginning of another humanistic or religious diatribe against modern technology, or a religious put-down of business and enterprise. There will be no pining for another era when human beings had more time and seemed to be kinder and gentler toward one another, nor will there be any negative comparison of religious ideals with pragmatic purposes. There is nothing essentially flawed or inherently wrong in technology, or in business, or in bureaucracy. There has always been technology. The plow developed by the Greek farmer was high tech in his day, and it made a great deal of difference in the development of that great culture.

The technological-economic-bureaucratic sector of endeavor is appropriate, high minded, and interesting. It is necessary for the common good. It is right that its leaders should be rewarded financially as well as honored with prizes and accolades. I personally have little patience with a romantic naiveté in which either the business community or technology is designated as the enemy of humane values. I am glad I live in the age of every technological advance we make, from medical care to children's toys. To appreciate the wealth the free market and its industrialized business community is capable of creating one need only observe the efforts of previously communistic nations to enter the global economy at the turn of the millennium. To grant today's economic structures their due respect, one only need contemplate a comparison of the free market society with the feudalism and absolutist monarchies capitalism pushed aside. The technological-economic-bureaucratic model of free market capitalism has proved that it can adapt reasonably well to the demands of democracy and there is no absolute reason to suppose that it cannot, in principle, adapt sufficiently to foster the more equitable distribution of the world's resources the future demands—the companion idea to democracy which has also become an inexorable force and which must be satisfied. Indeed, I believe much criticism of technology and business turns into a denial of the

Judeo-Christian theology of creation, particularly of the partnership into which God has called us. I hope the reader understands my appreciation for the technological-economic-bureaucratic realm of society as I proceed to offer a critique of the way our entire society is pervasively and sometimes improperly embracing all aspects of that defined sphere and imposing them on the other spheres of society.

One approach to understanding Western society is to identify the predominant *goals*, *methodology*, *criteria for evaluation*, and *motivations* used within and for life within society. The *goals* we choose to live for are *prediction*, *control*, *possession*, and *management of the environment*. From our earliest years each of us is taught these goals, and they have come to seem natural and appropriate. This is so much the case that we have developed a philosophy of consumerist materialism.

We push mystery to the side, and view it only in the way we see a mystery novel; it is something hidden but to be discovered in order to manage it. One of the realities about Christian mystery is that God has revealed it, always and in every case. Of course, even though Christian mystery always has been revealed it always is too deep to plummet, too complex to grasp, too grand to see. It is not so much *a* mystery as *part of* mystery itself. In secularized Western society, mystery in the profound Christian sense of revelation simply isn't considered.

We set the goals of our lives in terms of creating a pleasurable and satisfying environment, one in which we can enjoy the good things of the earth that please us, while offering our talents and intelligence in ways that stretch and utilize them to the fullest. This is what we think of as self-fulfillment. The goal of creating a pleasurable, fulfilling, and satisfying environment includes the primary need of creating the interior environment of the self, such that it is realized and fulfilled—what many people have come to call self-actualization or individuation. For many people the development of this part of the environment, the interior life, is what religion is about. This is considered "spirituality." If there is God, this is where to engage; church can be an important aid, but its purpose is to help create the sort of environment that will be productive for the interior spiritual life of the individual. If truth be known we assume individual spirituality and organized religion is a matter of prediction, control, even possession, and management—in other words, a matter of "spiritual" technology. Religion is one matter to deal with and use among many other matters in life.

In order to create and maintain the environment that will make us happy and allow us to be fulfilled it is necessary to be able to predict everything we can, control everything we can, possess everything we can, and manage everything we can. When the environment is not conducive one is to fix it, whether it is the inner life of the self or the people around us, or our jobs and our income and our art and whatever else surrounds us and makes up our environment.

The *methodology* we choose to employ for purposes of prediction, control, possession, and management of our environment is what, together with others, I call "instrumental rationality." This method seeks to select the best and most efficient means to achieve predetermined goals, goals that will offer prediction, control, possession, and management of something. What is best and most efficient is usually determined in terms of an objective cost-benefit analysis. Instrumental rationality accepts the idea that thinking is something disconnected from emotions and other features of the human make-up that can be considered improperly influential to rationality; it is "purely rational thinking," not unlike what we expect of computers. The possibility of motionless thought flows from such modern notions as that identified by Antonio R. Damasio in *Descartes' Error*, "the idea, for instance, that mind and brain are related, but only in the sense that the mind is the software program run in a piece of computer hardware called brain; or that brain and mind and body are related, but only in the sense that the former cannot survive without the life support of the latter."[10]

Instrumental rationality begins with goals that previously have been determined or assumed or intuited. The methodology does not necessarily include the goal-setting process, nor does it provide a process whereby values are considered. In general, the methodology employed so successfully in Western society has become a thinking process that is not about values, except cost-benefit efficiency, and it is without reference to criteria for evaluating the goals other than the question of feasibility. The only questions regarding whether or not to begin the methodological thinking process are: Can it be done? Will it work?

Notice how American use of the word "good" has become deprived of any moral content. The sports announcer asks a professional, "How did you play tonight?" The answer: "Good." When friends meet and one inquires how the other is "doing," the answer will likely be, "I'm good." Good now refers to one's ability to function, to get one's goals accomplished. Behind this is the equivalent of a cost-benefit analysis. Again, instrumental rationality is used almost entirely for selecting the best and most efficient means to achieve predetermined goals. Again, it is not unlike what we expect of computers, but who is the programmer? Again, what values are at stake?

The *criteria for evaluation* of our actions are largely limited to the questions of *feasibility* or to *intuitive urges, opinions,* and *prejudices.* The *motivation,* emanating from the sense of emptiness that existentialism has called alienation, is to *fix* what is wrong with the *environment—* including the interior environment of the self.

The methodology, goals, criteria, and motivations used within and for all of life within society are those dominated by the technological-economic-bureaucratic realm of society, and especially for the consumption of goods and services. Since the technological-economic-bureaucratic realm of the social order is concerned with the organization and allocation of goods and services it responds to the demands of consumerism. When the methodology of this realm is used for its proper purposes, when attention is paid to the values normally shaped by the agents of culture and of the polis, it is an excellent and pragmatically effective methodology. It is not, however, supposed to be the dominant or only methodology to be employed within the spheres of culture and the polis.

The problem, the difference today, lies in what we bring to the glittering successes and attractive simplifications offered by modern technology and a business-driven economy. The Greek farmer embraced the plow, but brought a worldview to that and the other technological advances of his day which took them in contemplatively. The Greek took technology like all of life and absorbed its fascinating betterment for productivity and lifestyle into the harmony of the created order, into the *logos* (the driving rational principle) of the universe. The worldview we have inherited, unlike that of ancient Greece, leads us to use the methodology, the goals, the criteria for technological-economic-bureaucratic success as values in and of themselves, to employ the motivating urges of the technological-economic-bureaucratic sector pervasively throughout society, far beyond the proper boundaries. The consumerist understanding of human nature, which dominates the worldview in our culture today, is more fundamentally at fault than technology itself, though this anthropology and the popular accessibility to high technology seem to elicit tendencies from each other which builds onto the problem.

We do not see the interconnectedness between things very well, if at all. We see a fragmented and compartmentalized world of discrete things. Yet as we look at the world of the technological-economic-bureaucratic realm we understand that everything is, in fact, amazingly interconnected in ways that we cannot grasp or manage. This is increasingly so on the international scene. Because of the nature of the world, we turn to the technological-economic-bureaucratic sphere as a model to determine how to manage all of this mysterious chaos, much of it weirdly beautiful, how to deal with every sphere of our life. This is the problem, as it comes to meet the radical individualism and forges an unholy alliance: instrumental rationality together with the consumerist goals, methodology, criteria, and motivation are overriding for all society. We have indeed all been raised, and many of us have been highly educated, to learn to predict, gain control, possess, and manipulate our "environment."

Most scientists understand the limitations of instrumental rationality and would not make the mistake of employing it in an all-embracing way. Certainly, most creative scientific thinking occurs through use of the full range of rationality, including speculation, and transcends narrow instrumental rationality. The problem more often is with those who are overly enamored of science, technology, or business affairs, without genuinely understanding them—in other words, with most of us.

Instrumental rationality has been raised to an unwarranted position in the public mind because this is the perceived way of objective science—in an era when science is rather romantically admired. But this popular perception is added to the strong model presented by a business community almost entirely concentrated on what is often called the bottom line. Business is so concerned with the immediate ends in exclusively financial terms that the means are, too often, only secondarily appreciated—from environmental factors to issues of social justice. All of this builds the attitude that if you are to be a realist, someone who "gets the job done," you must employ the exclusively goal-oriented method of instrumental thinking.

## THE PRIVATIZATION OF CULTURE AND THE POLIS

The Christian faith has a very difficult time in the sort of society and cultural reality just described. Many of the goals of most of the people within Western culture fly directly into the face of the gospel imperatives. No matter how right and appropriate it is for a business to control the various components of production in order to better the whole economy with its offering of goods, the gospel informs us that we are not to control other people and warns that our control throughout human life is very limited; the sooner we embrace this reality, the sooner we are able to embrace the gift of life as we receive it. No matter how right and appropriate it is to predict the weather, the stock market, or the political signs of the times, there is little in a very fragile life that can be predicted, certainly not anything of real and ultimate value. It is fine to try to possess the property, goods, and services to enhance your life and that of others, as long as you realize that you really don't possess anything, you only exercise the responsibility and the joy of stewardship of things during a span of life too short to use a term like ownership with its connotations of permanence and perpetuation. Management of an institution or of an undertaking is desirable and highly valued, but it is foolish to try to manage others, God, or the environment we call creation. It is just as foolish to try to manage our own life, except in a certain and limited sense. Objectivity is a great virtue, especially in analysis, but we must not fall into the old and discredited conceit that the mind is ever free from the rest of the human being. Our guts are connected to our brain and they are a legitimate and unavoidable part of our mind. If we were really individuals, merely alive to our own selves, perhaps these limited goals and methodology would work. Because people want to live as though this is the case, they want them to work. They do not.

The bottom line for the gospel understanding of the goals and methodology appropriate to, but limited to, the technological-economic-bureaucratic sector of society is that no one can make life happen for us the way we want it to be; rather, we are to cooperate with God in receiving the grace to become as fully human as each of us has potential. This will not happen because of our ability to predict, control, possess anything, or manage our environment. We find our humanity in living according to the gospel, in community with one another and God. It is well to predict, control, possess, and manage in the development of technology and business for the high virtue of contributing to human life. To try to bring those goals and the methodology of instrumental thinking into the areas of religion, art, science, politics, and so forth is wrongheaded.

Two beautiful and prophetic statements of truth come to mind as the difference is contemplated between the gospel and the all-embracing understanding of life as captured in the goals of prediction, control, possession, and management. The first is by Chief Sealth (Seattle). His truth-telling was no academic or artistic meditation and it soars above any romantic Native American lore. This leader was replying seriously to President Franklin Pierce in December of 1854, upon the government's offer to make peace and buy the land of his people in the Pacific Northwest in exchange for reservation territory. He is expressing the loss of land and culture, a way of life, as well as deep personal confusion and disappointment.

> How can you buy or sell the sky, the warmth of the land? The idea is strange to us. If we do not own the freshness of the air and the sparkle of the water, how can you buy them?
>
> Every part of this earth is sacred to my people. Every shinning pine needle, every sandy shore, every mist in the dark woods, every clearing, and every humming insect is holy in the memory and experience of my people. The sap which courses through the trees carries the memories of the red man. So, when the Great Chief in Washington sends word that he wishes to buy our land, he asks much of us.
>
> This we know: All things are connected. Whatever befalls the earth befalls the children of the earth. Human beings did not weave the web of life; each is merely a strand in it. Whatever is done to the web, is done to the human being.
>
> One thing we know, which the white man may one day discover—our God is the same God. You may think now that you own God as you wish to own our land; but you cannot.
>
> God is the God of all humanity; the divine compassion is equal for the red man and the white. This earth is precious to God and to harm the earth is to heap contempt on its Creator. The whites too shall pass; perhaps sooner than other tribes. Continue to contaminate your bed, and you will one night suffocate in your own waste.
>
> One thing we know. Our God is the same God. This earth is precious to God. Even the white man cannot be exempt from the common destiny. We may be brothers after all. We shall see....[11]

Perhaps the best single piece of literature written on American soil is William Faulkner's "The Bear." As complex and opaque as it is, the story brilliantly tackles some of the most vexing issues in human life and especially in the American experience. The primary focus is on a young woodsman's gradual grasp of the evil of slavery and prejudice, and the price he chooses to pay for living in his Mississippi community with integrity. The character portrayed becomes one of the noblest figures in literature. This young man sees with searing clarity that no human being can own another. However, this wisdom is founded on a more basic insight, the central insight regarding control: no human being actually owns anything. Possession in this short life is a matter of stewardship on behalf of God. That is the way we are to treat one another and all of creation, with the care of God's personal agent.

The central insight is offered immediately, on the first page of Faulkner's story. The young man arrives in the wilderness to learn to hunt and recognizes the inviolable majesty of the land. He realizes how illusory it was for anyone to make claims of ownership and right to conveyance, as he sees the tragedy of destroying the wilderness for the whim of thoughtless domination.

> ...the wilderness, the big woods, bigger and older than any recorded document:—of white men fatuous enough to believe he had bought any fragment of it, of Indians ruthless enough to pretend that any fragment of it had been his to convey; bigger than Major de Spain and the scrap he pretended to, knowing better; older than old Thomas Sutpen of whom Major de Spain had had it and who knew better; older than old Ikkemotubbe, the Chickasaw chief, of whom old Sutpen had had it and who knew better in his turn.[12]

There is an old joke, usually shared among young people learning to drink alcohol, about the speed with which beer goes through the body, especially when consumed rapidly and in quantity: "Beer cannot be purchased, only rented." That is an insight that should be recognized about all possessions.

## PRIVATIZED RELIGION, BELIEF, AND ART

Our analysis of the effect of closed individualism, when combined with the goals and methodology of one limited realm of society that is carried into and becomes dominant within the other realms, begins with the privatization of religion. This is not an assault on the Constitutional separation of church and state. Although many early colonial settlements in North America freely mixed the religious and political spheres, and some even practiced a rigid religious exclusivity, this nation has never experienced an official religion. The American Revolution was in part a reaction against perceived British attempts to establish an official church in the colonies, and the First Amendment to our Constitution prohibits both the establishment of religion and the limitations of the free exercise of religion. Americans believe that religious expression flourishes best if there are institutional boundaries between personal and collective religious belief and the arena of formal political and social engagement. These principles have served to sustain important liberties and rights. My arguments should not in any way be construed as an attempt to attack or undermine these principles of the institutional separation of church and state.

As the uniquely Western religion, the Christian faith has been reduced to a matter of private, personal concern. Concomitantly, it is the victim of the extreme individualism that has characterized American values. Religion, and therefore Christianity, seems to be strictly something between God and the individual, something very personal and private. Moreover, the entire realm of what we ordinarily think of as "the cultural" has been pushed into a corner of society which is reserved exclusively for individual and private consumption.

For example, art and scholarship, as well as religion, are regularly reduced to a matter of individual taste and proclivity. There was a time when people thought that art had something to do with expressions of truth, beauty, and the good. Now most people would limit this to truth as the individual observer appreciates it. Beauty is in the eye of the beholder, solely. Only philosophers, professional critics, and other participants in the narrow realm of culture are interested in what art has to do with anything one might call "the good." "One person's garbage is another person's art" expresses the attitude of society about the matter. Perception, taken largely as the feelings it produces, feelings that often are rational but not always, presents the only usable and worthwhile truth, beauty, and good.

Tom Stoppard's plays invariably deal with themes that reveal how abstract and artificial ("staged") existence is when the mystery of human life is negated in the cause of rationalism, control, and individualistic positivism.[13] Stoppard is a skeptic, admitting our inability to under-stand or to manage the mystery of life and playfully portraying the chaos and flux in it. Yet, in the mystery is found the real world, and in the skepticism is discovered a healthy struggle manifesting the joy in life. In *Jumpers*, Stoppard introduces one of his most important and most empty characters, Archie.

In this play, the Radical Liberal Party has just come to power, ded-icated to scientism. Their plan includes the rationalization of the church and to that end the Rad Lib spokesman for The Department of Agriculture has been made Archbishop of Canterbury. Dedicated to rational inquiry, Sir Archibald Jumper, M.D., D. Phil, D. Litt, L.D., D.P.M., D.P.T. (*Gym*) epitomizes the Rad Lib Party spirit in his expres-sion of positivism:

> Things do not *seem*, on the one hand, they *are* and on the other hand, bad is not what they can *be*. They can be green, or square, or Japanese, loud, fatal, waterproof or vanilla-flavored; and the same for actions, which can be *disapproved of*, or comical, unexpected, saddening or good television, variously, depending on who frowns, laughs, jumps, weeps or wouldn't have missed it for the world. Things and actions, you understand, can have any number of real and verifiable properties. But good and bad, better and worse, these are not real properties of things, they are just expressions of our feelings about them.[14]

In contrast to Archie's attitude of scientism is George's full-blooded sensuality, leading him to insist, "there is more to me than meets the microscope." He argues that Archie's attitude makes "one man's idea of good...no more meaningful than another man's, whether he be St. Francis or..."—then Archie completes the statement—"Hitler or Stal-in or Nero." George goes on to offer three sound effects: Mozartian trumpets, the trumpeting of an elephant, and the sound of a trumpet falling down a flight of stone stairs. This is to refute the positivistic contention that "it could not be said that...any one set of noises was in any way superior to either of the other two."[15]

George can't prove the existence of God, though he tries, or the fact that "good and evil are metaphysical absolutes," so he doesn't try to prove that the ideas of people like Archie are all wrong. He admits that, "the word 'good' has...meant different things to different people at different times." Thus he is able to maintain an authentic Stoppard voice in a climactic speech: "What is surely…surprising is that notions such as honor should manifest themselves at all. For what is honor? What are pride, shame, fellow-feeling, generosity and love?…Whence comes this sense of some actions being better than others?—not more useful, or more convenient, or more popular, but simply pointlessly *better*? What, in short, is so good about *good*?"[16]

Stoppard's art makes a statement that art is more than what it is in itself, that art for art's sake is valueless. That is, art reduced to a matter of private taste for private consumption is not art. He is taking the trouble to make the statement because the trend, the way our society views art, needs to be resisted. What is true about art is so for culture generally, that is, it is true about most of the aspects of society that have to do with the passing on of ideas, values, and tradition. The attitude is quite seductive: "You like certain ideas and things, so claim them as your own. It is my privilege to dismiss them without thorough examination because they simply do not appeal to me or because they do not speak to my personal experience. That's all I need to say. Thank you for sharing your personal thoughts." It is all very polite, tolerant, and easy to live with when life lacks depth—and especially in a society dominated by consumerism, when what sells is what really counts.

Is something true? That has become no more important a question than, do you perceive it to be true? If one dares to draw the distinction between perception and reality one is soon chided with the wisdom of the age: "Perception is real." This is, of course, another way of saying that perception is true for the individual beholder, or it is a mass response of subjectivity, and is not to be shared as truth except coincidentally. This subjective experience is what "sells" or doesn't—though we remain immeasurably influenced by how others view things, despite ourselves. Though conformity still rules, truth has become a matter of what is accepted by the individual observer. This isn't a form of pragmatism, or existentialist epistemology, or something genuinely philosophical and penetrating. This is puerile. There is a serious insight in the statement that "perception is real," but today's acceptance of the implications flowing from this insight is logically extended to the point of fallacy and even absurdity. Are we to live in accord with anything that can be taken as real as though it shares in truth, much less in good and in beauty? Are we to hold no one responsible for creating false perceptions? Finally it comes down to this: the farther out of touch we are from ultimate reality, the more we claim for that which is false or facile. However, I believe we have come to the point here discovered because we accept the notion that it is perception that sells, and selling is so central to what drives our society that we must conform to this great consumerist motivator.

## SECULARISM

What had been in the ancient church a separation of church and world (the original meaning of the word "secular") has become a separation of religion and all of the rest of life (the present meaning of the word "secular"). In the modern world this would take the further step of separating religion from most of public life, pushing it into the private sphere of individual taste, a part of culture out of place in the polis or the technological-economic realms of society.

Secularism cannot be exaggerated. At one time everyone in society recognized the reality, presence, and activity of God. This was a matter of the utmost import for human living. Most people within Western culture assumed that human life, and everything seen and unseen, worked the way Christianity explained it. In the same way, today, the secular worldview filters every picture of human life we look upon. The secular assumptions are those that are "given," even for the most faithful Christian. Christian precepts must be placed directly before the believer's eyes and held there for focus if they are to have a prominent part in that person's way of seeing the world; they must be sincerely prayed for, diligently sought, and practiced with discipline in order to be truly believed. We are a society with a strong Christian memory, a memory that remains highly influential, but hardly formative. Indeed, the influence of a partial and selective memory can be as harmful to a cause as enmity.

When we look to the context outside the church, we must begin by recognizing that we exist within a troubled society. Our economy may or may not be in good shape at a given time, but our culture, as well as our church, seems to be in steady decline. Again, this creates remarkable pressures which daily and pervasively affect the church's life. The church finds it difficult to provide answers, to offer directions, and even to establish appropriate values for our society. The plethora of issues, problems, and opportunities that overwhelm American society, the weight of pressures placed upon our members by the confusions and difficulties that flood the workplace, schools and all components of society have a cumulative and largely adverse effect on the church. However, for our purposes, we may focus on two fronts where the church seems to be facing the most profound defeat: secular society and other religions. Two undeniable facts have plagued Christianity in the modern era: the failure of Christianity to withstand the domination of secularism and the failure of Christianity to eclipse other religions.

## CONSUMERISM

Consumerism is a word that perhaps is too easily and too lightly bandied about when talking about American society. Fully compre-hended, consumerism is one of the most comprehensively descriptive terms to be employed concerning our society, and especially for describing the trouble it is in, down to our rationalization about truth itself. We know that we betray the human destiny in living out our lives as though we can be reduced to the simplistic target categories Madison Avenue is able to identify accurately enough for commercial or political purposes: as a sexual partner, as an ambitious businessman, as a macho blue collar worker, as a sports fan, as whatever projection will motivate us to purchase whatever is being sold. We avoid the anxiety and the boredom of the genuine search for our personal authenticity through consumption, sitting out our lives reading tons of print and watching years of television, chasing our lives in gerbil-like exercise and miles of travel.

Since his work was published in 1962, C. B. Macpherson has shown in *The Political Theory of Possessive Individualism* how freedom has increasingly been made "a function of possession."[17] People are defined through their relationship to possession rather than through their relationship to others and within society. The freedom of the individual comes from being the owner of one's own person, one's own time, one's working capacity, and/or one's property. Society becomes a market of bartering relationships between owners. Freedom makes a person a person, but freedom has come to mean merely ownership of the self—especially in that refuge of undoubted self-ownership, private life. No wonder married people tend to be increasingly confused about the desire to be in a committed relationship with its obligations over the personal freedom to act as they wish. The latter is more highly val-ued in Western society. No wonder Christian readers tend to gloss over those passages in which Paul waxes eloquent about the joys of being enslaved to Christ. Consumer society is confused about freedom because it understands freedom almost exclusively in terms of posses-sion—of things, but also of self.

By consumerism I mean much more than a crass materialistic desire to possess objects for their own sake. Our concern is focused on the way society is moving toward a consumerist society, that is, one in which the technological-economic-bureaucratic sphere is becoming all embracing for purposes of selling. In this context, Christianity is being pushed into a corner reserved for privatized, individualistic religion—a corner shared with other cultural and political areas of activity. The church is increasingly accepting of this exile into purely personal spirituality, robbing itself of its communal identity and trivializing its cosmic purpose. Christianity is endangered, threatened with being transformed into a religion of consumerism.

## THE PRIVATIZATION OF POLITICS

The privatization of politics is an increasingly apparent fact of social life in present day America. Affluent individuals and gentrified neighborhoods are rapidly coming to the point where they rely more on their own resources than on public services for protection, recreation, transportation, education, communication, and so forth. Others are stuck with the declining public leftovers. In our cities the wealthy ride helicopters and limousines while the populace goes underground or fights traffic. Those who prosper pay tuition to send their children to private schools instead of supporting the public system with equivalent tax dollars. As the public system deteriorates, the wealthy build their own infrastructure system for their neighborhoods. Those with the means install alarm systems and hire private law enforcement officers for their homes, neighborhoods, and offices while public alarm over crime periodically reaches panic proportions. The middle and upper classes communicate through fax machines, e-mail, and private express postal services, while the government postal service grows less reliable and more expensive. The affluent travel extensively and go to private parks and pools and beaches, to second homes or rented cottages, to exclusive establishments for food and entertainment. The populace crowd into disappearing public parks and pools. They can no longer afford to regularly attend the popular, crowd-pleasing sports events, which used to be one of the wonderful opportunities for all families and all citizens lucky enough to live in the cities where the games were played. Now they must watch on television while corporations, those with significant entertainment funds, and tourists who have saved up for the special expense take the seats and luxury boxes. (As Yogi Berra is supposed to have put it, "those places are so popular nobody goes anymore.") A tax-obsessed middle class has been taught to covet every possible dollar for private consumption, and to spend it straightaway, even against its own broader self-interest, and despite the fact that they are actually living off of their children's future funds for public spending. Those who can afford it are rapidly privatizing politics in ways both subtle and crass. This movement manifests an economic segregation of unparalleled proportions in process, separating those reliant on the private and on the public sectors for crucial social services much as what we have seen in the stratification and segregation of Third World countries.

"Special interests" is another way of talking about the same phenomena of the privatization of politics. Concern for the community is secondary, personal interest is paramount. The money it takes to make special interest a system, the dominant system of political influence, has become the most important factor in politics. Elder conservative politicians who retired from the fray, such as Barry Goldwater of Arizona and John Stennis of Mississippi, gave public testimony to this as an overwhelmingly obvious and dangerous fact. They stated unequivocally that the very system of representative government is under siege, that it is our very democracy that is at threat. Those without the money to contribute substantially to campaign treasure chests are proportionately less represented than those who can. The Supreme Court has declared that money is speech, in defense of "free" speech. Political office is treated as a product for the market. Issues and ideas are not as important for political election as is the marketing and control of information, primarily through manipulation of the media. The sign that was placed over the White House office desk of Larry Speaks, the public spokesman for President Reagan, the president who was called "the great communicator" read, "Don't tell us how to manage the news, and we won't tell you how to write it." The Chief of Staff of the same President, Donald Regan, bragged publicly that his staff, which he called the "shovel brigade," was capable of cleaning up statements of the President and even of turning his mistakes to political advantage by putting the right spin on them. President Clinton would not choose a vacation site without polling popular opinion. The teams of political campaign managers form a new profession, making their living from campaigns rather than from governing, and are really nothing other than public relations experts trained to sell any product.

It is hardly an exaggeration to assert that the Western political systems of democracy are succumbing to a sophisticated system of self-deception, a political and social situation wherein systematically distorted communication on a mass scale is accepted as normal and even preferable to facing the truth. We don't find ourselves having to sort out controlled information, as in totalitarian systems, but we do have to sort out managed or manipulated information. What has developed is not a more vigilant public, seeking the truth through it all; rather, the public has decided to believe what it wants to believe, to hear what it wants to hear. Who are the politicians we admire? Americans admire most those who are capable of manipulating the facts and communicating them in such a way that we can believe what they tell us, for they have learned through statistical polling what it is that we would like to hear and they have no compunction in feeding it to us with all their skill of salesmanship. It is as though we go to the theater and suspend our disbelief, except that this isn't an escapist movie, it is life, and much is at stake. Charles Dickens said that we prefer the prisons of our wishful lies to the freedom that comes of the truth. Our society is hardly free of such imprisonment, and it seems to be enjoying its bondage to privatized consumerist politics more and more.

## THE POWERS THAT BE

Today as seldom before people have to catch sight of what Scripture calls "principalities and powers." The reference today points us toward the powers of the dominating technological-economic-bureaucratic structures. They make up the wild and beautiful, frightening and exciting picture of the increasingly global world. People everywhere, from the industrialized nations to the Third World, sense that they live under the domination of large scale systems within the social order that no one seems capable of controlling or even of influencing at will. These systems sometimes are subject to the demonic. They are reminiscent of the ancient worldview of the demonic because they ignore outside input and construct self-contained "worlds." We know that we are up against huge and unwieldy international institutions and associations, which seem to have a life of their own, with purposes and effects beyond anyone's real needs or possible desires. We doubt that anyone—any groups of powerful leaders or movers and shakers—really is in charge or can be. We doubt that there is any earthly control to be taken of the motion in which these monsters have been set. It certainly doesn't seem that we can do much about "things."

Dedicated Christians and humanitarians belong to economic systems keeping millions of people unemployed, sending vast numbers of people to bed hungry each night, leaving minorities to poverty and oppression, and refusing clean water every day to countless numbers of children who will consequently die. What can any of us, from the leaders of nations to concerned citizens, do about any of society's long list of unacceptable ills? "Principalities," "powers," "rulers on high"—in our era of multinational corporations, megatrends and macroeconomics we are enmeshed in massive systems which hold us captive. As good captives, we allow them to shape our perspective as we internalize the various slogans, signals, advertisements, attitudes, curses, images and values produced for the benefit of these "powers that be."[18]

One of the vexing international problems created by such demonic forces is the devastating debt owed by Third World nations to the industrialized West. The rationale for these loans had the purpose of helping underdeveloped countries modernize, increase educational opportunities, and create industry. Did anyone anticipate how hopelessly indebted these countries would become? With no bankruptcy laws to protect nation-states, some of them have sunk far below the ability even to pay the interest on the loans and still function in accordance with their governmental purposes. Some of the leaders of these nations have declared that it is necessary to choose between debts and children, that is, between paying the debt and feeding and educating the nation's children. That is no exaggeration. The global economic community is not clear about the best course of action, though there seems to be a significant desire to solve the problem.

The antidote to "the powers that be" is not to do less with technology and economics. We must bring to them the values, the traditions, and the methodologies of those structures of society concerned with the legitimate use of power, the meanings of justice, the meanings of individual, group, and communal existence, and, finally, the full nature of reality, including the transcendental. For technological-economic goals must come from somewhere other than from personal assumptions, blind intuition, or (perfectly standing rationality on its head) from the creation of the sheer ability to accomplish something. Without that which culture has to offer we are in grave danger. Standing by, we find ourselves losing our character, and we worry about losing our lives—and the life of the world.

In preparation for the 1998 Conference of Anglican Bishops a meeting was held with a highly respected United Nations economist.

A bishop asked him for help. He explained that whenever the church debates social and political issues, especially highly complicated ones, it can be anticipated that someone will object that the church does not have the right to make decisions on such matters, not only because we are supposed to be limited to the strictly "religious," but because we are not competent to consider them. "How," he asked, "should we respond to this objection on the subject of international debt?" The officer looked at him and at the room full of bishops and religious leaders like we were all a bit daffy and replied, "One: tell us what Christian values expect or demand; two: give us our marching orders; three: tell us as the experts to get it right!"

## PRIVATIZATION AND SEPARATION OF THE RELIGIOUS, THE CULTURAL, AND THE POLITICAL

The cultural and political spheres of activity are being pushed into a corner where values and ideas—where truth, beauty, and the good— are suppressed by technical questions of feasibility and short term cost/benefit analysis. If we have the technical and economic means to do something, we will most likely do it, and without sound regard to the ultimate results. We are left to rely on our intuition to inform us as to a project's value and validity. Rational policymaking is dominated by technical or instrumental logic that rules out a more comprehensive rationality as frivolous, and even as impossible. The realm of culture has been shunted into the margins of society and set aside as matters for individual and private consideration. Simultaneously, the governmental sector is becoming increasingly subject to the reign of technocracy and bureaucracy.

In turn, these two theaters of social interaction, of culture and of polity, are separated. For example, Christians are told that religion is not supposed to have anything to do with politics or social policy. Sermons which address such matters are strictly forbidden, not only in some parishes but in entire denominations and certainly in large portions of the church. In truth, every preacher learns to be very careful in addressing politics as a subject area, no matter how biblically based and theologically oriented the material. The public arena is simply not considered the proper business of religion.

A recent diocesan convention of the Episcopal Church heard a familiar speech voicing the majority opinion. (No church gathering that addresses social issues will fail to hear the same basic speech, with little variation.) A well-groomed young man, with a voice shaking in righteous consternation, rose to address the debate before the house, saying: "I have come to a religious gathering and I am offended to be forced into debate about matters outside of and irrelevant to religion."

Religious faith is viewed as a purely private and highly personal matter of the spiritual dimension and it is not to enter the public arena, much less the political. Religious opinions depend, after all, on an individual person's taste and proclivities. They should not be imposed upon or placed before others except in the unlikely case they are asked for. It isn't even very polite to ask someone about their religious attitudes, unless there is already established a sufficiently close relationship that intimate confidences are sought.

Even though the Western world has a kind of Christian memory, religious ideas and values rarely become part of the public world. Smart Christians these days know how to work their political and social agenda without having it publicly recognized as a Christian agenda, without reference to religious motivation.

## Summary of the Object World of Society

For our purposes, the point to be focused upon is a certain general context for religion and, specifically, for Christianity. In the context of our world, in the context of our technocratic society, religious belief, as well as everything within the social order that we think of as culture, only the private subjectivity of the individual consumer counts. That is, when it comes to art, religion, or ideas, each is treated as though it is on the market. They are subjected to those criteria and methodologies for judgment emanating solely from the technological-economic realm and come down to a question of feasibility and marketability. Anything religious is treated, as is everything else, solely as an item for private consumption. This is the present context for religious belief in America and, to a lesser extent perhaps, in the Western world.

Developing technocracy fits the privatization of religion with chilling appropriateness and effect, an iron fist and a velvet glove. We are taught from the earliest age, by every sort of lesson and message, to deal with everything in our environment technocratically, as something to be manipulated. That is, we are taught to know it, so that we may predict and control it for our own purposes—if possible to possess it. We view everything in our environment as objects, even when our environment is other people. We each hate this, for we recognize that this means each of us is an object to everyone else. We truly live in an object world, one that glitters with disturbing beauty. Religion either conforms to this fundamental perspective or it is seen as something of an anomaly, pointing to a kind of reality different from a materialistic object world. In fact, Christianity has come to be viewed in both ways: civilizing conformity and spiritualizing escape.

# THE OBJECT WORLD
# OF THE CHURCH

The gospel doesn't always compute in terms of the values best understood in technological-economic-bureaucratic activities. In the technological-economic realm of business, the determined "end," the accomplishment of which demands the most efficient and rational means, is ordinarily some form of clearly definable and measurable success. That which the gospel offers can hardly be evaluated in terms of efficiency or feasibility. The "ends" which define the identity and purpose of a church are rooted in values that only the church can determine as it prayerfully seeks the mind of Christ.

Consequently, when the church uses such expertise it automatically limits technology and economic acumen to the service of values that instrumental thinking does not create or intuitively assume, and that are out of its ordinary context of concern. The technological-economic realm is being used inappropriately when it is allowed to dictate the values, and thus the terms of success and failure, for churches or for other institutions within the realms of culture and polity.

## THE GOSPEL VS. THE CONSUMER CHURCH

This is the main point for understanding the relationship of the church to the technological-economic sector, and this is where push comes to shove: the needs of people are defined by the gospel. The gospel is that which churches finally have to offer people. The gospel is not to be defined by what will "sell"; the gospel is not to be subject to the felt or imagined needs of people. Rather, the gospel exposes and defines the real needs of people. Therefore the success of the mission to which the gospel calls the church is not to be measured in terms which the technological-economic-bureaucratic realm seems inevitably to assume, namely in getting, keeping, and utilizing customers for the growth and wealth of the institution.

This must be emphasized. It doesn't matter whether the church is in dialogue with advocates of Latin American liberation or with middle class business consultants, the church does not begin by asking what the needs of the people are. Nor does the church then proceed to adjust to what people may respond to out of their needs, desires, and proclivities. In the church's experience, this inevitably leads to the problematic and usually to the disastrous—eventually if not immediately.

There is a story circulating among preachers, which is supposed to be true, illustrating my point. The parish picnic was in full gear when the rector noticed that none of the younger children were about, and so he went looking for them. When he found them, several of them were balanced on their bellies around the edge of an old abandoned well, reaching down toward some object. When he approached and looked down into the bottom of the well, his heart froze. There was a copperhead viper, its body fully stretched upward, its tongue probing and its fangs at the grasp. The children were fully extended downward, doing everything they could to grab hold of the copperhead. Every one of them wanted that snake with a desire that bordered on the desperate.

Later the priest was to conclude: "Never have I had a more pointed example of the difference between what human beings may want and what they should have."

It is the task of the church to proclaim the gospel as an "incarnational community." In doing so it identifies the concrete needs of particular people. Whether it was Nicodemus, the woman at the well, the rich young man, or Pilate, whoever asked Jesus for help heard him respond to their real needs in the face of their stated requests and of the assumptions they brought to the conversation. This continues to be a fundamental task of the church: to discern in the surface requests of people their genuine gospel needs. If the primary needs are to feed people, to combat institutions of poverty and oppression, of any sort, the gospel will define them. If the needs are to heal the psychological wounds of the abused or to nourish the affluent in the throes of emotional impoverishment, the gospel will define these needs—and may well demand that they be addressed differently than perceived and requested. The church will respond in each and any instance if it is itself listening to the gospel.

The church may, and often has, missed the gospel's understanding of the concrete situation and of the people's needs within it. The church often begins programs by assessing its resources rather than assessing the real and legitimate needs to be served. (I hope no one misconstrues what is being said as implying that congregations are to select programs of service without a proper needs assessment, one which asks the people to be served what they want and need rather than offering them what it is assumed they should have. It is usually assumed that the people need just what the church has to offer from its immediate resources.) The truth is that the church ignores its mission for justice and peace more often than not. The truth is that the church is constantly in need of leadership that has the courage to proclaim the gospel to the structures and systems that oppress, destroy, and defeat the real needs of human beings as the gospel demands they be recognized. The truth is that the church more often than not, in an effort to co-opt and use the affluent, fails to transform the emotional dysfunction so prevalent among them. However, we cannot capitulate in the face of our failures. We cannot panic and forego the gospel because of the sinful nature and failures of the church. The gospel—that is, the risen Lord—defines the needs of people the church would serve.

Peter Drucker is a Christian of brilliance, extraordinary experience, and good will. He is one of the consulting gurus the church has turned to in the technological-economic arena. Unfortunately, he was too ready to apply the consumerist standards to the church. He has been quoted as saying, "To put it bluntly, people are bored with theology. They are turning to 'pastoral' churches, a church that asks 'what do these people need that we can give?' rather than 'How can we preserve our distinctive doctrines?'"[19]

It is going to take more than a simple accusation to make any worthwhile pastor feel guilty about offering too much theology in this period of anti-intellectualism and biblical illiteracy. In fact, what Drucker is saying directly contravenes my fundamental assertion that the gospel defines human need and responds in the unique way of Jesus Christ. He claims that it is pastoral to allow people to identify their own deepest needs and it is pastoral to try to service those needs. (I submit the word "pastoral" as my candidate for the most abused word in daily church life.) He claims that those who look to the gospel to illuminate human nature and the deepest human needs are too reliant upon theology.

I believe it would be fair to read what Drucker actually says as, "People do not want to take the trouble to face the truth and complexity of the gospel; they grow weary before the mystery of daily reality. Yet, people have a spiritual hunger and they know at some deep level that they are in need. Thus people start to shop for a church. The churches they will choose are those that pander to immediate satisfaction and spiritual comforts, especially the elimination of ambiguity, that promise to soothe a tough life." This assumes that the goal of a church is simplistically consumerist, in conformity with society in general, seeking the measurements of institutional success recognized within the larger society: numbers of consumers and the money they invest. To reach the goal such churches rely upon prediction, control, possession, manipulation and management of external factors. Drucker's analysis is seriously flawed because it improperly computes the mission of the church. He is correct regarding the best means to achieve the end he has in mind, but I cannot believe such a consumerist end conforms to the reason Jesus gave his life on a cross.

## THE CHURCH TODAY: LIFE AND PRACTICE

Having described the contemporary situation and the social setting of the church, and having taken note of the exceptions, we can now examine certain of the prevalent practices and theological beliefs of the church. We begin with the practices. They will manifest many of the characteristics of the societal context within which the church finds itself. This is inevitable.

### PLURALISM, INDIVIDUALISM, AND PRIVATIZED RELIGION

Christianity is primarily responsible for the profound appreciation of the individual and for the high priority given to individual rights in Western culture. But the society has become so extremely individualistic that its very life is threatened. The church cannot go unaffected. It is just as individualistic, perhaps more so, due to the general privatization of religion.

At the same time most of us appreciate the pluralistic nature of society. We find that it enriches our lives immeasurably. We want a highly prolific society. When, however, this is combined with the factors of rank individualism and an exclusively private understanding of religion, pluralism engenders the church's adaptation to technological-economic-bureaucratic concerns, management techniques, functional or instrumental logic, and obsession with institutional perpetuation.

The range of choices with which we are constantly confronted is mind-boggling. There are precious few "givens," there is less and less which tradition passes on without question and without tests against the range of choices. The more choices one faces, the more the self becomes conscious of its discrete unit reality as an individual. One has to decide for one's self: "What will my world be? What will my loyalties be? What will I do about this, that and the other?" The alternatives lined up before us concern every facet of our life. We each have to come to "own" our life in terms of our decisions, necessitating that we dare to choose from alternatives on the basis of personal particularity.

## CONSUMER EVANGELISM AND THE CORPORATION

I feel that, once again, I need to pause and offer an important caveat. Because I am describing a situation in the process of reform we must recognize our weaknesses in order to guide the reform. It may appear that I do not want people to have a sense of personal ownership in the congregation, that I am suspicious of those who are committing their time, energy, and money, that all leadership has corrupted motives at best, and that those I will refer to as the "good people" of Christian society are all in church for the wrong reason. In fact, as I previously said, I stand in awe of the many devout Christians who are heroically living Christian lives throughout our parishes. As an institutional leader it has been difficult for me to express the extent of my appreciation for their efforts and their faithfulness. Yet, the fact is that the church has become so confused in its purpose and identity that even many of our most committed and most active members have expressed similar confusion.

We have a rich tradition of language, of words coined for Christian usage, of words like ministry, mission, and evangelism. But we have to watch them closely because they are being translated into words that are more meaningful in the technological-economic-bureaucratic sphere than in the religious. The language operates in ways the church does not intend.

The church realizes that it is one among many of the alternatives about which and from which individuals must choose. The parish is an organization with a certain "product" to commend for private consumption. That product usually is assumed to be a religious article: faith. There are various versions of this article on the market. There are Presbyterian versions, there are Lutheran versions, there are Catholic versions, there are Quaker, Buddhist, and sectarian versions, new age versions, and the list goes on and on. These present a variety of flavors, types, and packages. They are grouped in several different categories that must be studied and comprehended in themselves.

It is very much like going to the market for breakfast cereal. On the shelf are brand names: Kellogg's, Nabisco, Post, and General Mills. There are flavors: Post Toasties, Cheerios, Wheaties, Raisin Bran, as well as groupings: bran, flakes, corn, oats, or grain. Is one shopping primarily for a fiber supplement, for the sweet taste, for protein, for the identification a box of cereal may provide with star athletes?

It is difficult to choose which version of church suits one best. Is one even so much as interested in shopping? Might they be interested in some other way to meet the needs they associate with spirituality, perhaps therapy, or classes, or a twelve-step group, or self-help books? Some observers look at the plethora of new opportunities to deal with the spiritual needs natural to humanity and see a new interest in spirituality and freedom from religious experts—a sort of "lay spirituality movement." Others see the failure of the church to meet these needs. One thing seems certain to me, books and television and any other "method" for spiritual development is going to fail unless used as a supplement to corporate engagement, for they make the fundamental mistake of reducing spirituality to individuality. Usually it turns out to be a search to "fix" the self when this self has been found lacking.

If one is searching for a church it is difficult to choose which version suits one best. This is the way many potential shoppers see the church and we may be certain that the institution understands the situation and is spinning its wheels trying to meet the needs of the market. It goes about the task of packaging and presenting the product of religious faith that it has for sale.

In national denominations, there is a particular tendency for congregations to understand their church in the typical corporate business pattern. For example, the Episcopal Church has a national headquarters with a complicated organizational chart: the Presiding Bishop is the chairman of the board; the bishops are vice-presidents, with their regional home offices, staffs, and programs; rectors are assistant vice-presidents in charge of a branch, with a staff, perhaps some aspiring assistants, and an active watchdog board, which, of course, any administration can be expected to try to hold at bay with various forms of damage control. Regional meetings are held annually; national meetings are held tri-annually. In other denominations, regional ministers and local ministers fit the same organizational pattern in the typical member's mind.

A person familiar with church life can visit a parish worship service and before leaving the coffee hour, she or he will be able to identify which persons are stockholders, which are the workers, and which are customers or clients. When a church member attends a meeting on evangelism or mission she or he will find that the questions being discussed are, inevitably: "Is the product good enough? Are we meeting the needs of the customer? How can we improve our marketing strategy?"

Of course, it is likely that the language and terminology used would probably be the language of religious organization instead of market language. More and more, however, the language of the church is becoming exactly that of the boardroom. (It is interesting to see a new, respectable, and profitable growth industry developing, that of consultants for "entrepreneurial" churches.) Whatever the language, the questions are the same as one can find in the boardrooms of corporate America. Consider what is in common for the mission of an insurance company and for a parish: First, market the product for private consumption according to private needs, tastes, and proclivities. Second, maintain satisfied customers or clients. Third, where possible, turn them into stockholders and workers. Finally, grow as much as possible, become the largest and most successful of all insurance companies and parishes. Diversify as much as possible and influence the entire industry and church. Become comfortable and unworried about the upkeep of facilities and the offering of funds for altruistic purposes. Make the leadership famous. Impress any onlooker, especially those who know the industry and the church from the inside; become the envy of all.

Why? The reason seems to be deceptively simple: the successful operation and perpetuation of the corporation or institution. One works hard, helps to get customers, maintains them, and develops them into stockholders and workers for...the good of the company with which one is identified. Increasingly, the individual can only identify with the local branch and it is only the success of that branch that counts enough to motivate the workers. Finally, and this is what is so startling but so true, the product most churches commend to private consumption isn't even religious faith. The gospel is not the bottom line, but something closer to what is represented by money or stocks. Notice the extent to which those who invest in the stocks assume the right to control the operation of the organization.

The corruption of the congregation's identity and sense of purpose due to the way money operates within the organization cannot be exaggerated. One man who was stewardship chairman of a parish I served concluded his three-year term dangerously close to despair for the life of the church, saying, "I have finally come to understand the church, and it comes down to the power needs of those who control the money."

Usually the congregation's stockholders contain a smaller inner group, the aristocracy of the company, who see themselves as those who, ultimately, are in charge. Their core is the church's version of the "good ol' boys" network. It seems that there will always be a few who are well heeled, properly educated, respected in society, and significant contributors, who are expected to run things. The general aristocracy can call on them when need be. Don't dream that a good ol' boys network and aristocracy (in small congregations it can be a family) is not in charge in most places most of the time. The group does not expect to be seriously challenged. Usually it is benevolent enough, often even relatively selfless, sometimes heroic, and it is a system that, by and large, has worked for the Western institutional life up to now. The minister is viewed as having a special relationship to the good ol' boys network and their sponsoring aristocracy, something like that of a chaplain. If push comes to shove it is more than likely to become clear that the minister is considered the hireling of the aristocracy.

There are several built-in difficulties with this structure, not the least of which has to do with growth. Changes which are made within the congregation in order to meet the perceived needs of the market might, and often do, conflict with the perceived personal needs of the stockholders, and especially of the aristocracy. In a social situation within which there is such radical generational disjunction this can be exacerbated dramatically. One is very likely to hear right away from the individual members of that group that the new ways of doing things "do not meet my spiritual needs." Most of the time, of course, the needs going unfulfilled have precious little to do with spiritual needs, and the statement is usually a possessive claim that it is "my" church. But where the statement is genuinely felt we see privatized religion in its most contradictory moment. It pits the different spiritual needs of different individuals against one another, making community life a competition, and it admits that even the most important members may have to yield on the issue of some of their personal spiritual needs in order to meet the needs of the market, for otherwise the congregation may not succeed. Since the primary satisfaction in being part of an inner group of a congregation is found in the success of the organization, this places a great strain on the inner membership and on the ordained leadership. Suddenly privatized religion is hoisted on its own petard. How many well-intentioned pastors have come to realize that the congregation is not growing because the incumbent members do not really want to if it means change has to occur and leadership has to be shared.

The recommended religious language of the day seems to claim that the purpose of the church is to "save souls." This purpose, it is claimed, is far more definitive and clear than the vague goals of those who refuse to recognize the need for slogans, usually those who refuse to reduce the faith to "the spiritual needs of the individual." But in actual fact, the various slogans for "saving souls" become ever so difficult to pin down in concrete terms. There certainly is a lot of activity; something is going on. But when one objectively pushes the purpose to the bottom, when one finally arrives at what is meant by saving souls, a startling discovery is made: the goal of evangelism, often enough, is... evangelism.

Kierkegaard is still right. He claimed that the church's mission functions like a laundry that advertises with a sign in the front window: "Pants pressed—$1.00." Then when a person enters with pants that need pressing the customer discovers that it is the sign which is for sale.

We must remember that the church is not the kingdom, that the church is an instrument of the gospel instead of its goal. We found during the age of faith that European Christendom did not resemble the kingdom any more than did other periods of history since Christ, that all baptized people remained sinners, that the church could not contain the Holy Spirit. It is the kingdom we seek to establish, not the church. We will not accomplish our mission for creation and kingdom without the church, but we must not confuse the means and the goals, we must not fall into false idolatry of even that which we find most useful and valued.

Lest the reader feel that the concerns being addressed are exaggerated, the point is made by an article in *Fortune* magazine. Entitled "Turning Around the Lord's Business," the article identified what it took to succeed in congregations and how much the formula for success in businesses and in churches complement one another. Allow me simply to quote various phrases and sentences from the article:

Whatever else it is, religion is big business.

The "market" for religion hasn't shrunk....but market share has changed drastically.

Words familiar from board rooms—market research, customer satisfaction, asset management—resound in pastoral and diocesan offices.

Like successful enterprises of any kind, healthy churches know why they're in business...its core business [is] "saving souls."

If a church is to deepen spiritual lives, it has to know its members. "Churches sometimes forget who the customers are."

[The] "secret" [for success in one parish] was to find a need the competition wasn't meeting.

[C]hurches are moving away bit by bit from product-driven marketing ("This is what we have to sell. Take it or leave it.") toward a balanced approach that listens to the customers.

Sunday school teachers, choirs, workers in food pantries and soup kitchens—these "employees" are also the "customers", the members of the congregation.

THE HOTTEST PRODUCT IS BRAND X: For big churches, the traditional denominations have outlived their usefulness. They're like labor unions....Large interdenominational churches are the fastest-growing type in the U.S.... [The Leadership Network team doesn't] see theology or doctrine as the primary forces behind...growth....These churches grow because they have identified their business differently. They see themselves as delivery systems rather than as accumulators of human capital.[20]

Finally, the following quotes were offered concerning an example of a successful church:

The paradigm of customer orientation is Willow Creek Community Church, an inter-denominational Protestant church in South Barrington, Illinois. Fourteen years ago, 23-year-old Bill Hybels took a door-to-door survey that has become celebrated among church-management types....He learned that "Unchurched Harry," as Hybels calls him, "...wants to be left alone. He wants to be *guaranteed* that he's not going to have to sing anything, sign anything, say anything, or give anything."

Now Willow Creek's three weekend services draw up to 13,500 people altogether. Teams of church members direct traffic, wearing headsets and instructed by a controller perched atop the building....The minute Hybels finishes preaching a sermon, tape-duplicating machines in the basement crank out 3,000 copies, which are stacked in the lobby by the time the service ends and which the departing congregation can buy for $2 apiece.[21]

Willow Creek is the epitome of success for a congregation according to the American standards of individual consumerist religion. I wonder what anything mentioned in the description of this success story has to do with the gospel, with Jesus dying on a human-made cross for the life of the church, with God's causes of creation and the kingdom. Is this really the desire for congregational life, for Christian community: 13,500 people, an audience in a massive complex of facilities, with no commitment ("*guaranteed*...not to have to sing anything, sign anything, say anything, or give anything"), caught up in a lot of busy work of the organization, offered morally and intellectually timid teaching, herded by ushers wearing headsets and taking home tapes of the sermons (separating the preaching of the gospel from the pastoral realities congregational preaching is intended to address and from any integral place in the "liturgy"), BUT raking in a weekly profit to the parish of something over $5,000 from this arm of the "business" alone. If this is the goal, it stands as a sign of the perversion of the church—transformed by a consumerist mentality, one that in turn is founded on radical individualism. The sort of perversion of the gospel represented in the example of Willow Creek Community Church does not arise out of the conscious intention of the good-willed people nor of trained leaders of the vast majority of our churches. But the pressures are great, too great.

## THE OBJECT WORLD SUMMARIZED

In our world, it is extremely difficult for any of us truly to comprehend the corporate nature of any reality, even of the Christian community. It flies in the face of the way we look at things. We see everything that is a part of reality as discrete objects. Each of us says, in effect, "I am a subject; the rest of the world is presented as a range of objects to my subjectivity." We only know that they exist and what they are by the way we perceive them in our subjectivity. We are skeptical about our perception and suppose that it does not accord precisely with what the objects really and truly are in themselves. We are skeptical about being able to know anything or anyone as they truly are.

We see no interconnectedness between the objects of the world except what we can conjure up out of our imaginations. Perhaps we can posit a mystical connection of some sort, or perhaps we can empathize with other persons by imagining ourselves in their situation. But that is as far as we can go.

Each object has the subjectivity and the value that we grant it. Intimacy is difficult, with definite limits. Imagine this other "I" that thinks and knows but has no connection with what "I" think "I" know and which therefore has no connection with what "I" operate out of. Each "I" is an isolated autonomous self. In a strictly "object world," a world in which there is an absolute gulf between subject and object, between one person and all others, there is finally no room for genuine community.

We live in a society in which we relate to each other in terms of co-operation or co-option or competition, but not participation. Genuine community requires participation. Society, on the other hand, relies on common interests for cooperation. It recognizes the situation of being separated from one another, and consequently the necessity of using selfish interests to motivate individuals to work with each other. We cannot know each other except through clever and extremely careful communication. We have knowledge of one another, not through participation, but in the limited ways of sense perception.

In a strictly "object world" there is no room for God, for God cannot be simply another individual object known to our subjectivity. The Christian doctrine of God, the doctrine of the Trinity, is beyond intelligibility. The doctrine of the Trinity speaks of participation and interconnectedness beyond our comprehension. For us, if some thing does exist then it must be a definite thing, limited and separated from all other things. The idea of three discrete persons being absolutely united, in fact being one, is beyond our ability to conceive. For us, the Trinity is not a reality, it is a doctrine, and faith in the doctrine is a matter of irrational belief.

The venerable doctrine of the *Logos*, the principle of the divine self-manifestation, is now so impossible to explain that most Christians do not know the word, much less grasp the concept. This concept is not the description of an individual being, but of a universal principle. If one cannot think in terms of universals as powers of being, and few of us can, the *Logos* is a concept that is lost to Christianity today. Blind faith or authority must guarantee this incomprehensible tradition.

I know this is so, out of personal frustration as well as observation. I know that I can't really enter into the classical orthodox theology of Christianity except as I struggle and practice, groping for enough sense to understand, to a limited degree, the way someone else thought in a different time and place. The *Logos* means a great deal to me. I use it to resolve any number of difficult questions of theology. But, for me, this usage has become a matter of theory I have learned to bring to problems of thought. How can I bring it to my living faith?

An appropriate analogy is the study of a foreign language. It is difficult to enter into the cultural mind-set of those who speak a foreign language as their native tongue. With practice and scholarly discipline one can gradually creep toward the goal, but one is still reduced to the task of translating until the speaker of the new language is so immersed in the language and its culture that she or he actually thinks in that language. Then, it has replaced the native tongue and culture, at least for the moment. Theologically, that happens for a few dedicated scholars of orthodox theology. Most of us practice enough to understand the thought processes and apply them when we find ourselves thrown into that far country, but few have abandoned our contemporary culture and entered the mind-set necessary for the distinctively Christian doctrines to apply to our everyday living faith.

Many people see the solution in the abandonment of the language of the ancient world, the language of the early church and the New Testament. They would devise entirely new concepts. To me that seems to be only a partial solution at best. While our ability to think about the transcendent is uniquely limited, we need to overcome the limitations. Our goal is not necessarily use of the anciently developed concepts, even with new language, but to overcome our limitations. Otherwise, any new language and concepts will be relatively sterile. This is all exacerbated by the fact that in this particular society we learn from the earliest age to approach everything in our environment technocratically. If the world is a range of objects, we view this as our environment. Our environment is a range of discrete objects and it is to be known to the extent that it can be predicted and controlled for our personal purposes. We may not know what the objects of our sense perceptions are in themselves, but we try to know them well enough to use them. It may be that our purposes are altruistic and that we want to control and use our environment for its best interest. Selfishness is not necessarily the problem, although, given the problem, it is a grave temptation. The problem is one of reality perspective, of knowing.

The self is autonomous over against an environment which must be dealt with, even if the environment is other people. We are all isolated, alone in an environment which has real dangers and which we must learn to use, for purposes we are left to devise.

We all hate this object world, for it means that we are each an object to everyone and everything else. We hate being objects, categorized and misunderstood and used by everyone and everything else, an object to the subjectivity of an absolutely other person or thing, which we may or may not be able to influence to this or that limited degree. We are at the mercy of each other's subjectivity.

The thing we are most afraid of, which we are most afraid of being "in," is this object world. We hate bureaucracy because it objectifies people, reduces human beings to statistics. We feel the same way about institutions. What is the worst insult? It is to say that a person treats people like an object, like something to be used. The insult hurts because it has the ring of too much truth to it. We all know what it is to treat and to be treated as an object.

Stephen Spielberg and George Lucas may or may not be creating great art in the myths and childlike stories they tell in movies, but we are happy to pay them a fortune to portray a universe in which we use technology without allowing it to use us, in which what finally makes the determinative difference—for persons, for crises of all sorts, and for the ongoing human enterprise—are forces and instincts and intuitions and even "inspirations" that are mysterious enough to describe an understanding of reality that transcends an object world.

Once the object world is accepted it is inevitable that sometimes the environment becomes one's self. Sartre was right, if we live in an object world, when we think about it, we become an object to ourselves. Our self must be dealt with. Thus we make objects of ourselves in order to, for example, change our image. If we don't go so far as to declare life absurd, and thus pretend that there is no reason to go on living, this insight produces great puzzlement. Individuals have identity crises because they decide to have a technocratic relationship to themselves, to predict and control the self, to fix that which they decide is wrong with their inner environment.

## THE "FIX IT" RELIGION OF TECHNOCRACY IN THE "OBJECT WORLD"

What does this make of religion? Because we can't get God into an object world, because God can't function in such a world, we are left with "religion," but no God. Religion becomes a kind of working on the self to change, if not the image, then the interior state. In classical asceticism, the self was never understood as image or interior state, but as personhood. By contrast, in contemporary "spirituality" ministry becomes a matter of encouraging or inhibiting certain images and interior states. Thus has the job of ministry become a profession. One can hardly be a professional at getting on with God, or at leading other people to do so, but one can be a certified professional at helping people deal with their inner lives. One can become quite skilled at managing paradigms, symbols, words, and rituals. A minister can become a real technocrat. A parish can become a beehive of empty activity centering around the manipulation of interior states. A denomination can become a bureaucratic system of busy sound and fury. All of this religion signifies less and less for the real needs of people as the gospel defines them.

There are cycles in which the emphasis is turned from fixing the interior environment to fixing that of the exterior. In the last generation we have witnessed a classic cycle. In what we call the 60s, the church and society at large focused on fixing the object world of external society. Justice and equality are always worthy goals, but we exhausted ourselves quickly. Our lack of stamina for the long haul of prophetic ministry could have been anticipated, not least because of the misplaced motivation for deciding to "fix" the environment—meaning the quick fix the technological-economic-bureaucratic realm is so famous for when it is operating where it belongs. Most people seem to view the 60s as a failure and the response was to focus on the self. The energy was turned toward fixing the inner environment. We became what is often called the "me" generation, tending to one's own individual needs over against what is extraneously imposed by our object world. Greed and prejudice became acceptable, if not always admired. Religion became an exercise in fixing the interior environment, a quest for personal spirituality.

It should go without saying, however it has been said explicitly throughout this work, that it is the job of the church to serve and transform the world. The sincere social activists of the 60s have my most profound admiration. I was blessed by coming along soon enough to share the moment and I pray that I continue to answer the call to social justice. However, I pray that my motivation is not the technocrat's egocentric need to fix the environment, but the desire to share in the ministry of Christ.

Prayer and personal piety, any and all mystical experiences of God's presence, are a formative and a rich part of life in Christ. I am awed by those who develop the personal spiritual maturity and spiritual beauty to be called to the vocation of teaching and directing spirituality, not only to teach about the literature and to hand on the Christian tradition for personal spirituality, but to be a fellow pilgrim with individuals along their personal journeys.

But the turn to spirituality too often seems to be but another dimension of the "me" fix, another search for a saving technology. The best of efforts and motivations are easily obscured and lost when living in the perspective of an object world. T. S. Eliot is right: it is a defeating temptation to set out to do the right deed for the wrong reason.[22]

## THE BIBLICAL WORLD

Our object world is all quite contrary to the biblical world, where everything has a subjectivity and a value, a given reason for being and an interconnectedness with all else, stemming ultimately from God. When we read the Bible we enter a world that is alive. It is full of the primitive, from witchcraft to magic to animism, but it is all alive. Everything, all of creation, has a numinous quality. When we read the story of creation in Genesis it is quite evident that the world embodies life as given and sustained in the very life of God. As my former professor, Richard Norris, is fond of saying: "In the Bible, if someone spits at the world, it spits back."

The world we encounter in Scripture can invoke all kinds of things in us: hatred, delight, joy, anger. Whatever the response, there is an abiding respect for everything that is. If our world is like the biblical world, if it has value in and of itself, if it spits back when you spit at it, then whatever you may be you are not an object. You may be a mess. You may be a fool. You may be a monster. But you are not an object.

At issue in the comparison of our bright shining new world with that of the Bible is a whole mode of being in the world. The biblical way of being in the world is responsive. God gives; the world responds to its own givenness and to what it is given. The Bible expects us to answer back. Instead we try to "fix things up" in our alienated environment.

There have been other important modes. Western culture is especially familiar with the Greek mode, which is contemplative, acknowledging the intrinsic value of the creation and subtly taking the gift of creation in by way of contemplation, accepting and living into the harmonious and beautiful round of life. The early church enjoyed the biblical mode of being in the world. It was not a religious society because it considered religion to be at an end and because it could not have thought of itself as a society. Instead of a society it was a corporate reality, a real community. Sociologists, as adept as they are at evaluating and judging the church's present life, would have been required to find another name for their discipline in order to interact with the early church.

Of course, when we make the sort of blanket statements about the world and the way Christians deal with it that I have been making, we all know that it isn't the whole truth. Nevertheless, we constantly operate on the basis of this kind of hypothetical world I am calling an object world: a world in which the object world shapes our mode of being in the world. To it, we respond by fixing up our environment, altering ourselves to fit in, and vice versa. Of course, we know that a great deal of what has been said about our beliefs throughout this work is not acceptable to most of us, or to our fellow Christians in parish churches, for it isn't what we profess. Most contemporary Christians would surely protest that this picture doesn't include them, perhaps with some legitimacy since they would not choose to be in it. Yet, most of those in our parishes go on operating on the basis of what has been identified, and even according to the very terms of this presentation. The fact is, our professed belief and our actions are far apart.

This point was illustrated for me in the way I was accosted one Sunday morning by one of my favorite and most faithful parishioners. We had used the contemporary language for the Lord's Prayer at the service that day for the first time and as she came through the reception line, she questioned our reason for doing so. I tried to put her off until we could have a more complete conversation about it, and referred her to the rather extensive explanation offered in the service sheet. But she insisted: "No, tell me now. These people behind me probably want to know too."

"Well," I stammered, "if I have to say just one thing I guess it would be because the new translation is closer to what Jesus actually said."

She snapped back: "I don't care what Jesus said! I want my prayer."

I knew she didn't mean that. In a matter of seconds she was laughing at herself. Yet both of us knew the sense in which it was what she did mean, exactly! And she didn't forgive the church for depriving her of "her prayer." Despite the legitimacy of any protest lodged by those who say the creed every Sunday, I am afraid the statements I have dared to make, and which some may consider extreme, concerning the worldview and the theological posture to be found in the congregation on Main Street are valid.

The need for the reformation in which we find ourselves engaged is apparent to enough Christians that the internal demand has become inexorable. Christians will lead the way in our yearning for genuine community in the Body of Christ. At the same time, it is inevitable that our society will become increasingly aware of its social poverty and yearn for the community life that alone can satisfy our fundamental need to belong.

The reformation of the church is well underway and it cannot be stopped. It can be directed and shaped. The duty of our generation is to confront the three basic issues remaining from the previous watershed movements that re-formed and reshaped the church. We must overcome the radical individualism of the age and the church's preoccupation with issues of election and salvation. In doing so we can shape the communion of the church into a holy community of God's people. We must overcome clericalism and authoritarianism, clerical and lay, to carry out the ministry to which Christ calls us in accord with the mission for which he died—the cosmic causes of God. We must overcome our unfortunate accommodations to success and worldly power as well as our lack of concern for the world in favor of the afterlife to come. We must learn how to embrace this world with the gratitude of the eucharistic people of God and work only for the kingdom to come. We must serve the kingdom of God by immersing ourselves in service to the world and serve the world by demanding the justice of that kingdom to come. We must suffer creation and kingdom in communion with God. The church must sing the songs of the mothers.

✦ ✦ ✦ ✦ ✦

# SUMMATION

The grand shift from the medieval preoccupation with the transcendent and the next life to a more anthropocentric interest in this world formed the hallmark of the Renaissance and the foundation of the Enlightenment. In particular, the new awareness of the value of the individual human being became a great gift; it is one of the most precious insights we have from our heritage and it is one we must protect, especially regarding issues of justice. Nevertheless, what can be summarized with the term "individualism" has grown increasingly radical in Western culture, finally pushing the corporate nature of reality as well as ultimate reality off the view screen. Western society is now secular with little genuine sense of the transcendent and of ultimate reality; religion has become one among many components of society, and one in decline. Christianity is increasingly reduced in the popular mind to religion, and is seen as one religion among many others without sensibility of the distinctive Christian gospel. Meanwhile, on the one hand, people in Western society know themselves as individuals; this is something they understand without having to think it through, something they seem to be able to see and lay hold of, as though with sense perception. On the other hand, people in Western society know themselves as social creatures only secondarily, as an abstract add-on to the fact of their being. Westerners cannot grasp the interconnectedness between people and things without some mystical leap of imagination. Americans, as leaders in the radicalization of individualism, are disconnecting from one another in every realm of society, from our friends, neighbors, and families, to bowling leagues, choirs, and the body politic. Americans are becoming increasingly isolated as individuals. This is in deviance of the anthropological make-up and the deepest needs of the human being, as well as of reality itself.

There are various problematic features of our culture that are founded on our radical individualism. They threaten us in terms particularly antithetical to Christianity. They are all directly related to and dependent on—in various ways, subtle and blatant—the inability to appreciate the corporate nature of reality. If we were to understand and seek the common good based on the Christian understanding of the corporate nature of reality we would not find these various features threatening to our Christian values. The characteristics of our culture which have most affected the community life of the parish include our Western philosophical worldview with its prejudice for the particular and the individual, pluralism and rapid change, a growing tendency to technocracy without sufficient reference to values, and the privatization of religion—reduced to individualistic piety. The church must see this world clearly in order to rise above it. Instead, most of the church's energy and time is taken in conforming our mission to the standards of success in the limited world of objects, what I term the object world.

## NOTES

[1] The Lambeth Conference is convened once a decade by the Archbishop of Canterbury, who invites all of the active Anglican bishops from around the world to meet for some three weeks to discuss the state of affairs in the world and the church.

[2] From a speech given at the 2001 Interim Meeting of the House of Bishops of the Episcopal Church, USA, Burlington, Vermont.

[3] Alfred North Whitehead, *Religion in the Making* (New York: Macmillan Press, 1927), 98.

[4] Thomas Berry, *The Dream of the Earth* (San Francisco: Sierra Club Books, 1988), 45ff.

[5] Ibid., 46.

[6] Lesslie Newbigin, *Signs of the Kingdom* (Grand Rapids, MI: Eerdmans, 1980), 46–49.

[7] Robert D. Putnam, *Bowling Alone: The Collapse and Revival of American Community* (New York: Simon and Schuster, 2000), 108.

[8] Ibid.

[9] David Tracy, *The Analogical Imagination* (New York: Crossroad, 1981), chapter 1.

[10] Antonio R. Damasio, *Descartes' Error* (New York: Avon, 1994) 247f.

[11] The author copied this quotation from a poster in a friend's home.

[12] William Faulkner, "The Bear," *The Portable Faulkner* (New York: Viking Press, 1946), 227.

[13] Positivism is the theory that true and certain knowledge can only be based on natural phenomena—usually the senses—and verifiable by observation or experiment.

[14] Tom Stoppard, *Jumpers* (New York: Grove Press, 1972).

[15] Ibid., 67.

[16] Ibid., 54–55.

[17] C. B. Macpherson, *The Political Theory of Possessive Individualism* (Oxford: Clarendon Press, 1962), 3.

[18] Richard R. Niebuhr, *Experiential Religion* (New York: Harper and Row, 1972), 1–50.

[19] Thomas A. Stewart, "Turning Around the Lord's Business," *Fortune*, (September 25, 1989): 116–128.

[20] Ibid.

[21] Ibid., 120.

[22] T. S. Eliot, *Murder in the Cathedral* (New York: Harcourt Inc., 1935), 44.